Building the Healing Partnership

PARENTS,

PROFESSIONALS,

& CHILDREN WITH

CHRONIC ILLNESSES

AND DISABILITIES

Patricia Taner Leff and Elaine H. Walizer

Brookline Books

Library of Congress Cataloging-in-Publication Data

Leff, Patricia Taner, 1947-   Walizer, Elaine H., 1947-
    Building the healing partnership: parents, professionals, and children with chronic illnesses and disabilities / Patricia Taner Leff, Elaine H. Walizer.
        p.   cm.
    Includes bibliographical references and index.
    ISBN 0-914797-63-8. — ISBN 0-914797-60-3 (pbk.)
    1. Chronically ill children — Medical care — Psychological aspects.
    2. Handicapped children — Medical care — Psychological aspects.
    3. Chronically ill children — Family relationships. 4. Handicapped children —
    Family relationships. 5. Physician and patient.

    RJ380.L44   1992
    618.92'0001'9 — dc20   91-44730
                                                                                      CIP
    10 9 8 7 6 5 4 3

Permission to reprint from the following ACCH publications — ACCH Network (newsletter), Physician Education Report, Fathers of Children with Special Needs, (May, J) and Children's Health Care (ACCH Journal) has been granted by the Assocation for the care of Children's Health, 7910 Woodmont Avenue, Suite 300, Bethesda, MD 20814.

To the families

and to
John and
our boys,
Michael
and Philip

PTL

and to
Donald and
Nathaniel
and especially to
Laura

EHW

Table of Contents

Acknowledgments x

Preface xii

Foreword xiv

INTRODUCTION: THE NEW CONTEXT OF CARE 1
How this Book Came to Be Written 4
Appreciating the Parents' World 4
Recognizing the Needs of Changing Families 8
Reading Parental Narratives 11

CHAPTER ONE: HEALTH CARE PROFESSIONALS AND PARENTS:
A RELATIONSHIP UNDER STRESS 19
A Context for the Relationship 20
Attitudes and Values: Where the Worlds Can Begin to Meet 36
Handling Things Better 56

CHAPTER TWO: DIAGNOSIS 69
Introduction 69
Impact of the Diagnosis 70
Meeting Critical Needs 80
Caregiver Stress as the "Bearers of Bad News" 85
Guidelines: Conveying Painful Information to Parents 87
Guiding Parents to Sources of Emotional Support 96
Parent-to-Parent Support 97
The Meaning of Hope 103
Handling Things Better 106

CHAPTER THREE: GRIEF, COPING, AND RENEWAL 119
Introduction 119
Grief Work 120
Integration: The Dawning of a Feeling of Renewal 130
Handling Things Better 133

CHAPTER FOUR: ONGOING CARE I: RESPECTING THE PARENTS 135

Introduction 135
Parental Concerns: Common Threads.....................................136
Building a Constructive Relationship with Parents:
Respect for Parents 140
Handling Things Better 170

CHAPTER FIVE: ONGOING CARE II: RESPECTING THE CHILD 185

Understanding the Child's Perspective 185
Professionals as Nurturers 191
Seeing Beyond the Diagnosis..195
Building Long-Term Bonds..197
Handling Things Better 199

CHAPTER SIX: ONGOING CARE III: RESPECTING THE FAMILY UNIT 209

The Child in the Family 209
The Life of the Family 211
Cycles of Stress and Grieving 217
Empowerment..219
Critical Role: The Special Needs of Fathers 222
Siblings 226
Sharing Victories, Bestowing Credit..229
Beyond Care 231
Handling Things Better 233

CHAPTER SEVEN: ONGOING CARE IV: SPECIAL CONCERNS 237

Evaluations 237
Medical Records..239
Medical and Diagnostic Testing 242
Paperwork...244
The Difficult Parent 245
Negotiating for Compliance with the Treatment Program.....250
When a Child Dies 253
Handling Things Better 262

CHAPTER EIGHT: VISIONS: PRESENT AND FUTURE 269

Summary: A Journey with Families 269
Parents as Resources for Student Professionals.......................270
When Families and Students Share Experiences 273
Creating a Healing Environment 275

References 279

Parent Resources 291

Suggested Readings 295

Glossary 299

About the Authors 301

Index 303

Spinning by Joyce Autrey 308

Acknowledgements

We thank you, parents. Over the years, many parents have become "friends" — sending photos of their growing children; updating us on the course of their children's development and progress; sharing poignant vignettes in the lives of their families.

The following list represents those parents and families who wish to be acknowledged by name and whom we were able to contact. Except when parents asked that their child's name appear, we have changed the names of all children in these true stories. To those who wish to remain anonymous or whom we could not "find", we, too, offer our deep, ongoing gratitude. It is the parents who have given life, vision, and depth to our narrative. Thank you: Rosemary Alexander; Marcia F. Alig; Kathy Allely; Polly Arango; John & Joyce Autrey & family; Angel Beck; Trisha Beck & Collette Juretich; Ruth Belasco, Mobile, Alabama; Jean & Bill Brown; Jane Morrison Bubar; Jo Butts; Bernard & Ann Cacho; Sherelyn D. Campbell; Mark A. Chesler; Addie Comegys; David Cornell; Marie Deatherage; Susan Wenger Duffy; Silvia Dunne; Faye Eldar; The Epidendio Family; Connie T. Fischer, parent & nurse; Ann C. Flannagan; Judith Fried; Kenneth Fussichen; Pat Gallivan; Frank & Mary Anne Graziadei; Patricia Harman; Floyd & Ada Mae Hoover; Patty Houghland; Addie Jesswein; Diana Lynn Johnson; Gretchen Kelly, Ryan's mommy; Mary Hefner Kolovitz; Judith M. Korzenko; Shirley A. Kramer; Colette Lau & Vanessa; Carla Lee Lawson; Debbie Leon; Ronnie Londner; Diana Mathews; Marijo McBride; Marlene A. McConnell, Jeffrey's mom; Barbara McElgunn; Susan Mentzer; Pat Mooney, mother and teacher; Minna Newman Nathanson; Jennifer Paczynski; Lynn Powell; Florene Stewart Poyadue; Harriet Richardson; Catherine M. Rolow; Dorothy A. Romesberg, mother; Karen Roots; Marcia Roth; The Rother Family; Susan Rump; Kathleen Rutherford; Ann L. Scherff; Beth Stanley, mother and nurse; Jeffrey L. Strully; Judi Summers; Mary Tatro; Audrey Thomas; Cathie Thomas; Janet Troy, Autumn's mother; Lois Ann Van Orden; Shannon Ward; Conni Wells; Nancy & Jack Williams; Linda Wurzbach.

Thank you Jean and Bill, little boy and now young man, for a friendship that has spanned 20 years.

We also wish to thank the following organizations and self-help networks who have graciously granted us permission to quote from their publications: ACCH Network (newsletter); Physician Education Forum Report (1990); Fathers of Children with Special Needs (May,J.); Children's

Health Care (ACCH journal); AboutFace; Association for the Care of Children's Health; The Candlelighters Childhood Cancer Foundation; Children in Hospitals, Inc.; The Compassionate Friends, Inc.; D.A.D.S., Dads and Disabilities; Heart-to-Heart, Dallas; Iowa Pilot Parents, Inc.; IVH Parents; Let's Face It — A network for people with facial disfigurement; National Center for Clinical Infant Programs; The National Down Syndrome Congress, Down Syndrome News ; National Fathers' Network; Ontario Federation for Cerebral Palsy: Participating Families Program; Parent Resources on Disabilities, The Bridge ; The Roeher Institute.

We are grateful to the students and young professionals who movingly spoke of their struggles and hopes. Through informal discussions, sensitive journals, and a desire to share of themselves, students and professionals have broadened the scope of our book and have added a crucial dimension to our discussion of "partnership." Our thanks to Susan Grobman, Bill Grobman, and Susan Loucks whose caring and concern for children and families are reflected in compelling and powerful excerpts from their child life journals.

We wish to thank "senior" health care professionals who encouraged this project or inspired by their example: Don Bloch; Joy Goldberger; Morris Green; Alan Guard; Stan Handmaker; David Inwood; Michael Jellinek; James May; Elizabeth M. Mogtader; Hisashi Nikaido; Jack Reinhart; Dominic Sabatino; Bill Schwab; Harriet Shaffer; Ann P. Turnbull; David Zlotnick.

A very special thanks to Joan M. Chan. Mentor, colleague, and friend, Joan's unwavering commitment to humanistic and compassionate care of children and families has guided her career. Joan has set a standard for the goals expressed in our book. Joan generously shared her knowledge and skills as she reviewed the many "writings and re-writings" of our book. We deeply appreciate both her enthusiasm for our project and her gentle, but firm, critique. Joan's encouragement and faith in us have helped "to see us through" this long labor of love.

For contributing insights and thoughts and for reading the manuscript, we thank you, Donald G. Walizer and John M. Leff.

For proofreading, we thank Esther K. Walizer.

For technical assistance, we thank Thomas D. Leff.

Preface

Advances in the medical care of children are many and often joyous. Premature infants who would have certainly died just a few years ago are now able not only to survive but most flourish. Half or more of children with leukemia recover and those with cystic fibrosis commonly live into their twenties or longer rather than dying as young adolescents. The future is even brighter with advances in transplantation and genetics. Despite the obvious benefits of this progress, there are many emotional issues in the process of care especially when the course is stormy and the outcome is poor. The time frame of medical care lasts months and often years. There are painful procedures, multiple victories and defeats, wishes fulfilled and hopes dashed, suffering and, for some, tragic deaths. The emotional intensity for the child, siblings, parents, and caretakers reflects the gravity of the issues - suffering, disability, life and death - as well as the closeness of the relationships - parent and child, brother or sister, family and physician.

Although there has been much written about the emotional issues in the care of critically and chronically ill children, the perspective has largely been from the outside, as an observer or evaluator of the process. Most authors apply developmental theory to a particular chronic disease or ask parents to complete a questionnaire that quantifies a child's reactions or functioning.

Building the Healing Partnership does not observe or evaluate from a distance, but from the inside, with intimacy, understanding and compassion. Patricia Leff and Elaine Walizer have listened very carefully to patients', families', and caretakers' personal experiences. Although well versed in theory, they do not try to adhere or fit parent's reactions into neat or artificial, conceptual frameworks. Instead the book weaves together brief vignette after vignette to help us experience the essence of caring, over time, for an ill child.

The authors use these vignettes and their own extensive experience to teach us the meaning of terms that are often used naively or loosely. Terms such as communication , respect and support are almost cliches until this book teaches you that respect and support are a philosophy of treatment rather than merely a tone of voice. Respect is based on a profound understanding of the parents' perspective, rights, concerns and feelings. Respect is both generic, what all parents deserve, and also highly specific to an individual family. Support is keeping the child and family company in their hopes and suffering - anticipating, tolerating and sharing the wide range of feelings inevitable to chronic or severe illness. Patricia Leff and Elaine Walizer have a wholehearted appreciation for respect and support, appropriately extending the concept to the needs ofcaretakers rather than focusing only on children and their families, and then teaching the reader through straightforward explanations that ring true.

Building the Healing Partnership also provides practical, specific approaches and recommendations for both parents and caretakers. Many vignettes are followed by a discussion of alternatives and insights as to what other options may have been available. There are relevant and detailed discussions of confusing yet common issues such as the medical hierarchy, hospital records, compliance, medical procedures, etc. There is an extensive presentation of how parents can help themselves, each other, and "senior" parents helping those less experienced (with child newly or recently diagnosed).

Patricia Leff and Elaine Walizer have been in the trenches over and over. This book is frank and thus the stories and perspectives are not homogenized or bland but sharp, focused and painful. The book is not a polemic for parents or against caretakers, but reflects quite directly what is. In frank language the authors talk of facing death, the value of hope as well as "sharing victories" and "Bestowing Credit." These are poignant, honest, moving, passionate and at times angry stories woven together by themes that are designed to empower and support all members of the healing partnership. By being so explicit and thorough, the authors tell the pediatric patient, family, and caretakers what to expect and thereby give permission to experience and then adapt to the full range of feelings possible when caring for an ill child. Building the Healing Partnership is an empathic and practical guidebook relevant to the families of chronically and severely ill children and to those who care for them.

Michael Jellinek, M.D.
Associate Professor of Psychiatry (Pediatrics)
Harvard Medical School
Chief, Child Psychiatry Service ·
Massachusetts General Hospital, Boston, MA

Foreword

At the Beach Center we always challenge ourselves and each other to take the "shoes test." The shoes test is an attempt to stand in the shoes of a person with a different perspective and to try to speculate about what the world looks like from that person's point of view.

Although it may sound simple on the surface, it is undoubtedly one of the most challenging tests of all, because it requires that we suspend our own values, culture, training, and life experience and try to take on the values, culture, training, and life experience of someone in quite different circumstances. Passing this test requires that we listen carefully to the voices of those we seek to understand.

Those voices speak clearly and powerfully in *Building The Healing Partnership: Parents, Professionals, and Children with Chronic Illness and Disabilities*. We are convinced this resource is extraordinary in preparing health professionals to take the shoes test with families and in preparing families to take the shoes test with health professionals.

WHAT WILL FAMILIES GAIN FROM READING THIS BOOK?

- Families will experience the "other side" of health care professionals— that they not only care, but often care in a painfully profound way.

- Families will realize that professionals who may seem all-knowing and all-powerful are actually incredibly vulnerable, just like every other human being in the world.

- Families will experience the bond of hearing other families in similar and different circumstances tell the same familiar story.

WHAT WILL HEALTH PROFESSIONALS GAIN FROM READING THIS BOOK?

- Health professionals will see the "other side" of the children and families whom they serve—their pain, their triumphs, their shattered hopes, and their boundless visions.

- Health professionals will be supported in their humanness with the all too rare permission to laugh and cry with families.

- Health professionals will experience the bond of hearing other health professionals share their fears and hopes, joy and pain.

Patty Leff and Elaine Walizer, combining their professional and parental experiences, have interwoven profound first-person passages in a narrative which takes readers on the journey from diagnosis, through pain and renewal, to care on a short and long-term basis. These stories, told by people who have "been there," result in vivid andstartling insights—such as distinguishing between the more limited medical "cure" model and a more functional "care" model.

We can promise you that this is a book that you may pick up casually, but you will not be able to put down. It takes you on an incredible roller coaster of emotional highs and lows. It strips away superficiality and addresses the most fundamental essence of the human reactions of families and professionals.

We urge you to take this shoes test—to come to it with an openness and willingness to experience the healing partnership from your own perspective, as well as that of others. Patty and Elaine will gently guide you through the test, making sure that you have sufficient insight and empathy at each step—not only for the challenges of the shoes test, but also for the enhancement of the healing partnership. It is only through this dual understanding by families and professionals that the reality of the heating partnership will be equal to the vision of this book.

Finally, we confess to crying a few tears-not all in sadness that these things happen to kids and families—but also with pride in the many families we have known, including our own, who have "made it."

Ann P. Turnbull, Vicki Turbiville, and llene Lee
Beach Center on Families and Disability
The University of Kansas

The New Context of Care

I have tried to create a team of professionals who care for my child. This approach works if the professionals are open to my being on the team and if the professionals are willing to work together, in spite of differing viewpoints and areas of expertise. I want to be consulted whenever there is a change in plans and given a vote in the designation of plans. Professionals must be open to the idea that I, the parent, am an expert on my child and that my agreement and input furthers the professionals' goals for my child. (Dave's mother)

* * * *

Success lies in helping the family. (mother of Katherine, a child born with Trisomy 18 who died when she was 17)

* * * *

A great disservice has been done to you. You have been stretched beyond your limits in efforts to gain knowledge about children with chronic illnesses or disabilities. But who has assisted you in gaining knowledge and strength in interacting with the parents and families, who live with, care for, and love these children daily? (Greg's mother)

Children with serious chronic illnesses and/or disabilities are increasingly surviving to be nurtured by their families within the community. This fact, along with the heightened complexity of medical, social, economic, and legal realities, has altered the face of pediatric care.

For children with chronically disabling conditions and serious illnesses who are currently growing and developing within the sustaining arms of their families, good care is contingent upon a parent-professional partnership that acknowledges both the needs and strengths of families. The loving family unit rests at the core and heart of comprehensive services for children.

This changing focus of care highlights the critical role of parent-professional communication and mutual respect. Parents are, indeed, *the* major resource contributing to the well-being of their children in need.

Parents on a very practical level administer medications; follow through with appointments; do the recommended therapies; manage complicated equipment and procedures; negotiate the maze of medical and educational bureaucracies necessary for their child's growth.

Parents, in essence, are the "constant" in their child's life and make the ultimate decisions concerning their child's care. They alone see the child in all settings and provide the consistency and stability that will help their child achieve his or her optimal quality of life. They care most deeply about the whole child and value their children with challenging needs as "children first"—loved, unique members of the family (Leff, Chan, & Walizer, 1989).

Medical and technological advances contribute to a philosophy which emphasizes the importance of family life in the development of children with special needs. Such a philosophy adds a new dimension to the work of health care professionals (Shelton, Jeppson, & Johnson, 1987). With care centering on the family, positive parent-professional relationships become a critical component of all health care encounters. From this perspective, parents become the health care professional's best "resources," "allies," "partners."

In a community-based system, the balance of care has shifted from a primary reliance on the institutional system to a *dependence* on the parents' intelligent, caring involvement. The parent-professional partnership must value parents as equals in the decision-making process, the goal of which is to create a healing milieu. The changing reality of community-based care offers both parents and professionals opportunities for enhanced collaboration, for "joint ventures" in improving the care of children in need. The mother of a child who is technology-dependent shares:

Mark and I are not trained medical professionals, but. . . the support we received from nurses, doctors, and therapists while [our daughter] was in the hospital reinforced our belief that we could care for her at home. We knew also that once out of the hospital setting, we had a network of community-based support which. . .showed how much people care, and how much of a role we all need for them to play in our lives. You are those supporters; those people who care. . .

All of [our] success stories occurred because we have worked together as a team. Speech therapists, physical therapists, respiratory therapists, public health nurses, teachers, school officials, psychologists, sociologists, and suppliers are committed to one thing—helping this child grow. (Julianne Beckett, Comprehensive Care for Medically Vulnerable Infants and Toddlers: A Parent's Perspective, *Equals in this Partnership*, NCCIP, 1985, p. 9)

As "allies" committed to the optimal care of children, parents and professionals are able to create new ways of working together, of setting mutual goals, of solving the inevitable problems that arise when caring for children with serious conditions. Parents stress the following:

> See yourself as part of a team or, at the very least, as part of a large mosaic of service providers. All professionals have their own terms and language. . .
>
> The parent-family-child unit is the most important member of the team. . .No matter how valuable you think you are, the parent and child walk out of the door and make their own decisions regarding therapies and programs. Your commitment to work *with* them will be more effective than a "Do-as-I-say, I-know-best" attitude. (Larry's mother, a pediatric social worker)
>
> * * * *
>
> . . .How do we know what families need?
>
> First ask. Some parents will be able to tell you what they need very soon after the initial crisis has occurred. For others it will take awhile. Be there for them. Be supportive—whatever their decision is. Continually reinforce [this message:] "Together we can do what needs to be done for your child." (Julianne Beckett, Comprehensive Care for Medically Vulnerable Infants and Toddlers: A Parent's Perspective, *Equals in this Partnership*, NCCIP, 1985, p.11)

In the following chapters, parents speak directly and movingly to health care professionals. In sharing their stories with both "young and old" professionals, they hope to convey in more personal ways the process and impact of life with a child in need of long-term special care. Parental observations, thoughts, and suggestions are intended to guide caregivers as they work with children and their parents; as they learn about the needs and strengths of families; as they develop the skills necessary to create an effective parent-professional dialogue and partnership.

Professionals and students speak as well. It is hoped that such an exchange of feelings and perspectives will contribute to greater mutual understanding with the goal of tapping the strengths of all involved in the care of children with chronic conditions. Parents address the fears and concerns expressed by professionals caring for their children. As "partners in care," parents offer much practical knowledge as well as a unique understanding of the needs of their children. Parents bring their hard-won wisdom to students and young professionals as they embark on their difficult, challenging careers and as they mature and develop in their helping roles.

How this Book Came to Be Written

"Building the Healing Partnership" began in 1987 when the senior author wrote personal letters to parent organizations and individuals in the United States and Canada. These letters contained five basic, straightforward questions for parents. (See end notes for the specific questions.) The intent was to incorporate parental responses into a chapter, tentatively titled "Preventing Parent Abuse: Guidelines for Listening to Parents," within a text for student health care professionals.

Parents responded to the questions with long, moving letters; impassioned phone calls; and copies of poignant, powerful narratives from newsletters, other informal parent literature, and testimony before state and federal legislative bodies. Parents were offering students access to a different, more comprehensive way of understanding the reality of family life with chronic illness and/or disability. They shared deeply personal stories and opened new vistas largely neglected by many clinical training programs.

This compelling material—the thoughts, hopes, and observations of parents—formed an all too often untapped resource. The needs and strengths of families *from the perspectives of parents of children with special needs* were rarely emphasized, rarely discussed, in the education of the senior author.

One respondent eventually became the co-author of this work. As a dialogue and partnership developed, it become apparent to both writers that "the chapter" was in reality a book. Parents were guiding and helping health care professionals; "listening" to parents was the key to this invaluable source of knowledge and experience.

As the writing gained momentum, the concept of the book enlarged to include the thoughts, fears, and hopes of professionals, both new and experienced, working with children in need. Discussion with colleagues and professionals, notes from diaries, and excerpts from the journals of child life interns added a critical "voice" to this project.

Through their own partnership, the authors worked toward balance and compassion for all those involved in the care of children with chronic conditions or disabilities.

Appreciating the Parents' World

Throughout their stories and narratives, parents encourage health professionals to step into their world, to see young patients and clients as members of the families that love and care for them. From this vantage point, gaps of experience and understanding which have so often separated health care providers from parents and families become smaller and smaller. Growing respect for and appreciation of parents' perspectives will lay the cornerstone of this vital relationship: a parent-professional partnership that begins and develops throughout the child's care.

Parents share critical events—both positive and negative—in the lives of their children in need. Their goal is to build bridges of understanding and compassion. Although many months and even years may separate parents from the situations and episodes they report, memories and images remain—vivid, fresh, powerful (Calman, 1988). Parents who participated in the creation of this book poignantly speak of the feelings they re-experienced while recalling crucial moments in the lives of their children:

> Memories. . .so many thoughts and feelings flood my mind as I think back on the time during my pregnancy and subsequent delivery. I had spent more than five months on bedrest prior to Joshua and Miriam's delivery. . .I developed symptoms of toxemia. . .and, to no avail, my twins were born two months prematurely. . .Joshua was very sick and my little fighter. . .At one point in his long course, he became so swollen and edematous that to look at him broke my heart. My remembering now causes tears to well up. . . (mother of Miriam and Joshua)
>
> * * * *
>
> I got a little weepy this afternoon while reading the excerpts and my husband asked what was going on. I explained to him, and realized that even though we've been off the medical circuit for a year and may, in fact, be off it forever (touch wood), all the feelings it engendered are still only a millimeter from the surface. (Keough's mother)

Parents see their child as unique and dear. Their roles in the child's life are diverse and multiple as they provide physical and emotional care throughout the days, months, and years of their family's life. They wish to protect their child. For most parents, each experience with professionals entrusted with the care of their child is fresh and is highly significant. The parents carry within their consciousness the subjective experiences of living with their child. They have the ongoing responsibility for their child, love their child, and intimately share both the suffering and joy which imbue their child's life.

Successful attempts to improve parent-professional communication rest upon respect: respect for the family's role as the mainstay of the child's life. Sound parent-professional communication is not synonymous with avoidance of disagreements. Differences of opinion may frequently occur and need to be worked through and valued. Open parent-professional communication, as in all relationships, is not a static reality but a shared responsibility changing over time (Leff, Chan, & Walizer, 1989). The mother of twin boys with multiple handicaps illustrates how mutual respect paves a path toward optimal care of her children:

> When our pediatrician and I have a major disagreement, we call for a care conference. He has made it clear to me that we will work together to find an answer to the problem - no matter what it is. We focus on the children. For example, I was very worried about my son's temper tantrums—despite many reassurances. I told our pediatrician that my "head" agreed with him, but that my "heart" couldn't let it go. He ordered a routine EEG which verified that my son had temporal lobe epilepsy. When the results were back, he showed me that he trusted my feelings by gently touching me and saying: "Right again. . ." (mother of Barry and Bobby)

The spirit of collaboration and mutual respect this parent describes is an attainable ideal that most parents and professionals can realize in daily practice. Parents urge health professionals, as early in their careers as possible, not only to reach for "the ideal" but also to see "the ideal" as a pragmatic necessity. Ordinary parents and professionals working together can provide "extraordinary" care for children in need.

Respect for parental involvement and concern must also be accorded to parents whose children can no longer be cared for at home. Parental advocacy and commitment have become a driving, potent force for improving the lives of children with serious illnesses and/or disabilities in *all* settings—long-term care facilities, after-care, respite care (Pizzo, 1983).

Honesty and openness set the stage for learning from parents; honesty with compassion brings a powerful dimension to the caregiver's healing role. A mother of children with special needs discusses the impact of two very different ways professionals have related to her:

> I know that there is a certain amount of fear when a person is the bringer of bad news. I have told Dr. C. several times that I am not upset with him, but with the information he must tell me. I want him to be honest with me, and I try to be honest with him about the way I am feeling and perceiving painful events. Open, direct communication from the very beginning sets a foundation for working together for the best interests of the child. With Dr. S., who "knew all the answers," I silently disagreed and did what I felt was best. With Dr. C., I discuss my reactions and the options

available. Dr. C surprised me by saying that he had learned from me.

Professionals who accord parents respect for their critical physical, emotional, and financial commitment to their children with special needs leave a legacy of hope and support that may sustain and encourage families during times of devastation and despair (Leff, Chan, & Walizer, 1989). Parents rarely forget the professional who has touched them in this way. The mother of a child who is technology-dependent emphasizes:

> Parents and children have suffered much. Parents and children have had to fight for every moment of happiness they may have. Parents have had to put aside their hopes and dreams and watch their children struggle for every bit of progress made. Like my child Joel, these children have been put through a medical nightmare. Do not be surprised if you run into hostility and bitterness. But remember—*every* act of concern and good care is greatly appreciated. I know for a fact that many times it was the hospital staff that gave me strength to go on.

Unfortunately, the opposite is also true. Professionals who fail to communicate respect leave a legacy of justifiable anger and anxiety that adds to the burdens parents carry. Professional contacts are typically fragmentary, episodic, occasional, and transitory. The parents' roles stretch into the future through childhood and beyond (Leff, Chan, & Walizer, 1989). Caregivers support parents' abilities to work for their children by building confidence, carefully listening to parents' concerns, and encouraging hope. Caregivers and parents may share a common concern which Dennis's mother describes:

> As a parent I have faced "Fear" with a capital "F." I've always felt I could handle anything I had to face concerning myself. But having a child, being responsible for that child, the unknown becomes greater, and the fear of not being able to give him what he needs or to do for him is now present.

Professionals who care for children with chronic illnesses and/or disabilities also often face "the unknown:" unknown solutions to difficult problems; unknown cures for devastating illnesses. Nevertheless, health care professionals have much to offer in addition to specific technical skills. Respect and care for parents are in themselves powerful therapeutic tools. Responsibility for helping confronts a professional mainly when the child is present in his or her office for care; parents see this responsibility before them every day, all day, in many arenas. A partnership can energize and hearten both parent and professional.

RECOGNIZING THE NEEDS OF CHANGING FAMILIES

Fathers

Traditionally health care professionals have focused their energies and scrutiny on the mother-child dyad. All too often fathers have been placed in a subsidiary role. This skewed view of the family fails to encompass the reality of family life and to encourage services that support and welcome fathers' involvement. The "conventional wisdom" is giving way to a more balanced, less restrictive view of what fathers bring to the care and nurturing of their children, including those with special needs. Fathers challenge the limited perspectives and stereotypes that have prevented the full participation of men in the lives of their children with serious conditions:

> Fathers are almost expected to run away from the problems of raising a handicapped child. . .I feel that much of this comes from the male child raised in the "macho" image. He is told he shouldn't cry or have other feelings and that women are destined to handle certain situations. Fathers need to be reached as soon as possible to be assured that they can let go of their emotions without guilt and that they are needed in the family and can provide positive assistance. (Kenneth Braker quoted in May, 1991, p. 8)
>
> * * * *
>
> Transporting my son to a special hospital unit, arranging care for the other children, notifying relatives, clearing the calendar for the next few days—immediate involvement. . . Late that evening, when things had calmed, when thoughts began to flow free, I could feel good about the things I had done. I felt that my actions were important to my son's survival. (Dale Loftis quoted in May, 1991, p. 19)

Lives are changed in many ways. Fathers describe aspects—both positive and negative—of such changes:

> Our life style has changed—and positively—it's not for the worse. . . .I am glad she is with us. . . .I wish God had given us some money along with Sabra so that we could have bought a rambler

and a van with a lift. Maybe we'll get lucky soon. (Hameed Quraishi quoted in May, 1991, p.8)

* * * *

The fact is, having Sarah makes us different. My family is closely watched by friends and neighbors. A trip to the store or a shopping mall makes us open game for stares and whispers. Life is not typical for any of us, and we are constantly reminded of the reasons why. My love for Sarah is a deep love. It has to be, because there remains a lot of hurt that must be put aside.

. . .I used to be very good at drifting through life and basically doing as I pleased. Sarah, and what she meant to me, changed that way of life in me forever. Today, 7 1/2 years later, I have become a "giving" person who finds a real need to reach out and help. . . . (Paul Egly quoted in May, 1991, pp. 3 & 34)

Two-Income Families

The care of children with serious medical and/or developmental difficulties places additional financial stress on families; two incomes may become a necessity. (At times, two incomes may be a necessity but an impossibility; one parent may have to respond to a child's extensive medical needs by remaining at home.) Parents will often choose jobs—or even remain in unsatisfactory positions—based on their need for appropriate medical insurance and the geographical availability of special services. Jacob's father explains:

I have divided my life into two phases, before Jacob and after Jacob. Nothing is the same, but most changes have been positive. My wife and I don't have choices anymore; our lives revolve around Jacob. I have changed jobs just to get the "right" medical insurance plan. We have moved twice so that we could get into the "right" school district. (Gary Sweet quoted in May, 1991, p.10)

The difficulty of juggling the demands of multiple roles—a fact of modern life in all of society— is exponentially increased in these families. A mother and master teacher describes intense daily stress as she struggles with her many identities—mother of two young children, wife, and teacher of children with special needs:

I had to go back to work. We desperately needed my income. During the day I teach children with special needs and then I come home to the demands of raising two children—one of whom is multiply handicapped. It's been rough. I deeply love my daughter with spina bifida and want to do the best for her. I also feel very torn among my many roles. I wish the professionals working with my daughter understood my position. There is so little time for me to be just a "mommy" for my children.

Divorce, Separation, and Single Parenthood

The realities of contemporary family life—divorce, separation, single parenthood, blended families—place severe strains on parents caring for children with special needs. A single parent solely responsible for her youngster with serious, chronic learning problems describes her over-whelming fatigue:

> I am mother, breadwinner, disciplinarian, homework tutor, therapist, and more for my son. I'm chronically exhausted; some nights I am so tired that I can't sleep. Then the gnawing questions come: What will happen to my child if I become sick or lose my job? Now that my son is getting older, how will I find safe recreational activities for him—the kinds of father-son type things that I can't do with him? I never expected that I would be raising my child alone, but life throws painful surprises at us.

Separated and divorced parents may struggle to work out complicated arrangements in order to share child-rearing responsibilities and provide consistency of care. The father of a child with multiple handicaps who is receiving intensive home therapies describes such a situation:

> Hank's mother and I have been separated for several years. Hank and his brother are with me Wednesday nights and weekends... Both Hank's mother and I are totally committed to his special home therapy program. We share all aspects of the program despite the logistics involved.

A veteran parent addresses the difficult, frustrating task of helping sick babies and children gripped by socio-cultural disasters—the dysfunctional "non-families" of urban and rural poverty:

> But sometimes your families aren't families at all. They're single mothers, some of them children themselves. Some parents are drug abusers or otherwise far removed from middle-class sensi-

bilities. I wish I could offer some brilliant advice on how to communicate with them. But I can't, other than to ask that you treat them with dignity and try to build their self-esteem as parents; they'll need it. If there are interested grandparents, uncles, aunts, or even friends, talk with them. And model the type of caring you'd like to see these parents display. (Ronnie Londner, IVH Parents, 1991)

Adoptive and Foster Care Families

Adoptive and foster parents bring their children for care. They turn to professionals for support and understanding concerning critical decisions in the lives of their families.

> When my son was diagnosed as having mild cerebral palsy at age one, we were in the beginning stages of adopting him. The pediatrician expressed dismay that we would continue adoption proceedings when the child was "defective" and then dismissed us. He didn't offer referral, information about the disability, or support groups. We never took our child back to that doctor again. We then had to go out and find resources for ourselves.

An adoptive mother, who meets monthly with beginning medical students, is attempting to alter such attitudes.

> The students and residents want to know that we're not crazy— that we love our children. They ask me very basic questions: How do you do your shopping? How do you get breakfast done? How do you go to the zoo?
> I want them to know that we are a family—that my children are dear to me.

READING PARENTAL NARRATIVES

In the following pages parents share both their positive and negative encounters within the health care system. The value of studying and discussing what parents have found helpful along their journey cannot be overemphasized. Stories of parents' positive experiences infuse one's work with hope and a vision of the possible despite the stress and constraints locked within professional roles. Accounts of positive parental experiences invite and enable caregivers to talk directly with the parents of their patients; to learn what parents have personally found helpful and supportive. Jennifer's father notes with compassion:

> I've learned a lot in those thirteen years, and my temptation is to outline my conclusions one, two, three, like the college professor that I am. But these conclusions, these insights, are not so easily communicated as the results of an experiment or the findings of a survey. No, I think one learns best about a handicapped child through experience, or at least by hearing stories about such experiences (Turnbull & Turnbull, 1987, p. 261).

Analysis of parents' negative experiences is crucial. Health care professionals who have not addressed the anxiety, thoughtlessness, and ignorance at the root of such experiences are doomed to repeat them. Negative accounts may shock and alarm: they are not easy to read. Many are fraught with pain and frustration and chronicle in detail how the health care system and individuals have failed to understand or respond appropriately.

Parents offer "negative" stories with a "positive" goal in mind: to educate; to invite growth and change. When parents are able to affect professional attitudes, thinking, or behavior, they wrest some comfort and value from episodes that were, before, examples only of needless suffering. The mother of a young man speaks with hope for change:

> After the birth of Ben, our mentally retarded son, the attending physician asked me if I were awake. When I answered yes, he immediately blurted out, "Well, you drew a mongoloid. What do you want me to do about it?" I was shocked, stunned, and hurt. The scar of that remark has remained over these past 21 years. I hope that I have turned that scar into a star. I have had the opportunity to speak before hundreds of young physicians, teachers, and parents. The story of how I was told of my child's disability never fails to elicit a shock reaction and usually evokes conversation and questions.

Emily's foster care mother discusses the circumstances surrounding Emily's death and her work for improved care:

> Over a three-month period following her cardiac surgery, Emily suffered from many complications. . .We had to fight for people to believe us when we told them something was wrong, and in *every* instance, I was right as they gradually found one complication after another.

I was told to take my cues from the doctors and nurses. They didn't see her as a dying child, so I shouldn't. I was asked what my "motives" were in caring for a disabled child who wasn't even mine. The night before Emily died, I was still being told to think positively and not to be so "negative" about her condition. The list goes on.

After Emily's death, . . .I [with Emily's biological father] asked to meet with hospital administrators to air our concerns and complaints; to try to resolve some of the problems we faced; to try to improve communication between parents and health care professionals.

The hospital administrators and nursing supervisors listened to us and addressed the problems with staff. A series of discussions were held in regards to increased sensitivity of staff to the issue of family involvement in patient care, in detecting changes early and helping to correct them. . .New policies were implemented. . .

I try to find comfort and peace in the fact that Emily's life and death were for the purpose of teaching us all to listen; care; communicate openly and honestly; and to learn to work together not against each other. Avoidance, judgment, and criticism act like a cancer that quickly covers up the real issues until parents and health care professionals can no longer see what is really happening. . .

There is still much work that needs to be done, but I feel as though I helped to create a sense of awareness and heightened sensitivity. This is the type of legacy Emily deserved. . .

Parents do not intend to clobber health professionals over the head with negative statements. On the contrary, parents hope that young professionals will reflect upon their stories; talk about them with colleagues; learn from them; use them as points of departure to role-play difficult parent-professional encounters; seek feedback from parents about interactions; struggle to explore and create alternative ways of managing the complex stress and anxiety inherent in their work.

It never hurts to ask the parent and child, to welcome feedback. It would have been wonderful had anyone said to me, "When we talked that first time about Laura's problems, it was tough for both of us. Looking back, were there things you wished I had done differently? Could I have helped more?" (Laura's mother)

* * * *

I believe that parents and families need to thank professionals and tell them, in very specific terms, what has been helpful to them. Hopefully, professionals will share this information with their colleagues, and a ripple effect of good, positive practices will develop. (Lyn's mother)

* * * *

Communication is a key element in the relationship between the professional and the family. Pity is to be avoided, and caring is essential. Empathy is difficult, but perhaps if the professional pulls from his or her own life experiences, he or she could share compassion along with the facts. (Jill's mother)

A mother who has organized parent seminars for third-year medical students presents several issues:

Our format is informal. We are not threatening and our "stories" seem to stick with the students. Several times I have run into students in the hospital when getting a test for my daughter, and they have remembered me and asked about my daughter. The first step to working with parents is to see them and their child as people with problems, not as problems.

Each parent is asked to give a presentation on a particular or general experience he or she has had with the medical profession to familiarize students with his or her unique situation (i.e., birth experience, diagnosis, doctor's visit, and hospital stay).

The parents are asked not to dwell on the negative but to emphasize how the situation could have been handled better for them. These students are not responsible for what has happened in the past but are looking for ways to handle things better in the future.

In summary, few crises are as devastating as learning one's child is seriously ill or disabled. Parents communicate their strengths as well as their needs: these are ordinary people under extraordinary stress, discovering within themselves resources that allow them to nurture their hurt children as well as to share their insights with caregivers. Parents seek to show health professionals how to make their aid as meaningful, comforting, and healing as possible.

Seek an understanding of how it feels.

Challenge stereotypes — both of children and of parents.

Learn, grow, and heal.

HANDLING THINGS BETTER: AN EXPLANATION

In line with the focus of this book in pointing out critical issues and showing ways in which difficult situations can be approached positively, each chapter ends with a section entitled *Handling Things Better*. This section includes instructive vignettes which provide readers with food for thought, new outlooks, and opportunities to explore the issues discussed in the chapter.

Handling Things Better is divided into three categories. In "Situations to Ponder," significant experiences of parents and/or professionals are presented with brief commentary. "Perspectives" segments introduce a parent's, child's, or professional's viewpoint and speak directly about aspects of caring. In "Contrasts," comparisons of similar crises illustrate the divergent approaches of health care professionals in like situations and the consequent impact on the caring process.

END NOTES

The following is an excerpt from the letter requesting parental responses.
Please let us know if you would be willing to talk with us or write to us concerning the following issues:

1. What have been your most helpful encounters within the health care system?

2. What have been your most destructive or painful experiences with health care professionals?

3. What would you like "to say" to young doctors, nurses, child life specialists, social workers?

4. Do you have any specific concerns about the way medical information (diagnosis, prognosis, the need for further tests or procedures) has been communicated to you?

5. Are there any other issues (i.e., rooming-in policies, preparation policies, concern for siblings, etc.) that you would like to present to students?

Of course, this discussion will be under strict rules of confidentiality and anonymity.

SOURCES OF PARENT MATERIAL

In writing this book, the senior author contacted many parents and organizations listed in the *Parent Resource Directory: For Parents and Profes-*

sionals Caring for Children with Chronic Illness or Disabilities (Bethesda: ACCH, 3rd Edition, 1989). Parents responded enthusiastically and were eager to share their thoughts with students and young professionals. The *Parent Resource Directory* served as one source of parent information and data.

There are many roads to parent organizations, self-help support networks, and "veteran" parents. Such resources provide access to local, state, and federal organizations and programs that offer a forum for parents' irreplaceable wisdom and expertise. The following list represents a basic starting point:

Beach Center on Families and Disability. The University of Kansas, c/o Institute for Life Span Studies, 3111 Haworth Hall, Lawrence, KS 66045

Healy, A. & Lewis-Beck, J. A. (1987) *The Iowa Health Care Guidelines Project: Improving Health Care for Children with Chronic Conditions.*Division of Developmental Disabilities, University Hospital School, Iowa City, Iowa 52242.

Moore, C. (1990). *A Reader's Guide: For Parents of Children with Mental, Physical, or Emotional Disabilities.* Rockville, MD: Woodbine House.

The Exceptional Parent, 1170 Commonwealth Avenue, Boston, MA. 02134

CHILD LIFE SPECIALIST: AN EXPLANATION

Child life is a profession devoted to the psychosocial care of children and families in health care settings. Child life specialists focus their skills on nurturing positive growth and development. Their clinical training includes knowledge of normal growth and development as well as the special needs of children and families coping with illness or disability.

As members of the health care team, child life specialists provide age-appropriate play and therapeutic activities for individual children and groups. These therapeutic interventions encourage mastery over difficult and painful experiences within health care settings and foster the child's and family's strength and competence. Child life specialists:

• orient children and parents to the health care setting

• prepare children and parents for medical treatment and surgery and clarify misconceptions

- provide emotional support during painful procedures (such as dialysis or bone marrow aspiration)
- offer therapeutic play following procedures to help children master traumatic events
- advocate for children and families within health care bureaucracies
- help to ensure that the physical environment is appropriate and comfortable for children and families
- nurture and promote positive coping mechanisms as children and families face the crisis of illness or disability.

The child life specialist's mission is to contribute to a healing milieu for all those involved in the care of sick children and their families. Thus, child life specialists are deeply committed to the education of student health care professionals. (Joan M. Chan, MSW, CCLS)

Many of the quotations throughout this book come from the journals of students and young professionals helping children and parents as part of their work in child life programs. These narratives poignantly illustrate the hopes, experiences, and reactions of students on the front lines of care. Joan M. Chan, MSW, CCLS, supervised and guided these students. She encouraged self-understanding, valued compassion for children, parents, and staff, and served as a model for her students.

1 Health Care Professionals and Parents: A Relationship Under Stress

I also have some tales to tell on myself from my days as a Head Start and secondary school teacher which I "share" with professionals. I, too, was an insensitive ass once, maybe still. (Sam's mother, a specialist in developmental disabilities)

Comprehensive care of children who require complex services over many months and years of their lives rests upon positive, effective parent-professional communication and cooperation. While many of these children cannot be made totally whole or well, parents and professionals achieve good care as they share knowledge about the child and his or her needs and as they create the best "healing" environment possible for the child and family. However, the parent-professional relationship is a complex, at times difficult, partnership. What factors contribute to the stress? How can the stress be lessened?

The goal of this chapter is to discuss "a relationship under stress." Parents and professionals attempt to clarify the following issues:

A context for the relationship
   Stressors for parents
   Stressors for caregivers
   Contrasts in world views: complementary areas of expertise

Attitudes and values: where the worlds can begin to meet
   Reframing a model of care
   Human values and the less-than-perfect-child
   People first language
   Expanding one's world

Sharing one's humanity
Building bridges

A CONTEXT FOR THE RELATIONSHIP

Students in the health care professions have traditionally been placed at a significant disadvantage as they leave the classroom to begin their work with parents and children. Clinical training has typically emphasized treatment of the child's problems with minimal discussion of family needs and concerns. Many institutions have only recently acknowledged the pivotal role of parents in caring for children with chronic conditions. Training programs have not emphasized the communication skills necessary to initiate and maintain an ongoing dialogue with parents (Desguin, 1986; Diehl, Moffitt, & Wade, 1991).

Interactions with families occur randomly. Few students have had the opportunity during their training years to spend time with families outside of institutional or clinical settings; to participate with families as they shop, play, go about the activities of daily life (Widrick, Whaley, DiVenere, Vecchione, Swartz, & Stiffler, 1991). Few students have been guided in the direction of parents. Few students have been introduced to parent self-help or support groups. Few students have been encouraged to speak directly with parents about both helpful and negative encounters within the health care system.

A dearth of shared experience and parent-student exchange has resulted in many misconceptions. Understanding and compassion are replaced by unexamined stereotypes—i.e., parents are either "hovering" or "distant;" "too" emotional or "too" cold; "accepting" of their children's problems or "nonaccepting."

Stereotypes cloud professional awareness and appreciation of the complex realities families face: challenges and choices; fatigue and fear. Stereotypes blind professionals to the vulnerabilities and capacities of the real families who bring their children for help. Stereotypes encourage students to see mothers and fathers as depersonalized, uni-dimensional "parents of children with special needs" rather than the complex persons they are, with multiple roles and identities. A father notes:

> Having a "special" child is no easy task or laughing matter. I lay awake at night worrying, as if that will make her normal! It does help to have a sense of humor. The hardest thing to deal with is how the public deals with us. . . . When you have a "special" child, you become a "special" father. You will never be perceived as "normal" again. (Steven Hammon, *ACCH Network*, Vol. 8, 1990)

From the perspective of both a professional counselor and father of Jennifer, George Harris observes:

> Professionals suspect parents and vice versa, and nobody is any better off. Blaming is of little help. As the parent of a handicapped child and as a professional counselor, I can say that I've had the opportunity to be irrational from both sides of the fence. I hope that others can learn from my experience. (Turnbull & Turnbull, 1987, p. 264)

Stressors for parents

Chronic childhood illnesses and disabilities catapult parents into a strange, threatening world populated by professionals upon whom they and their needy child must depend. Parents, frightened and vulnerable, face unexpected crises and feel out of control. A mother poignantly recalls the agony of her infant's hospitalization for a devastating infection:

> It was like being swallowed by a whale. When I walked through the hospital doors and followed the directions to pediatric admissions, I felt the despair and aloneness that must have been Jonah's. (Holmes, 1980, p. 42)

Parents are often fearful of staff's power over their child and uncertain of their role in a forbidding new world. This dependency itself is fraught with tribulation. A mother shares the utter sense of helplessness, vulnerability, and despair surrounding her initiation into the the universe of the neonatal ICU:

> Five and a half years ago, when my son Nicholas was born prematurely, I felt more hostage than partner to a gang of powerful professionals who sustained his life and taught me the rules of a strange new variety of motherhood. I didn't question their competence in treating any of us: my husband and I needed to believe that someone had wisdom in this situation that had spun our lives out of control and made us wonder who we were and whether we were any good.
>
> The individuals stand out who helped me begin rebuilding a sense that I was worth something; the nurse who sat and talked with me when she had time and loaned me a nursing text when I was frustrated by my ignorance; the child life teacher who asked how I was doing and then sat down to listen as I told her; the physical therapist who celebrated Nick for what he *could* do

instead of defining him by his disabilities. (Ann Oster, *Equals in this Partnership*, NCCIP, 1985, p. 27)

The sheer numbers of health care providers involved in a child's life may be staggering. The mother of a toddler with multiple needs writes: "We have lost track, but at last count Connie had seen over 70 physicians and therapists." Parents expend much energy and time in negotiating the maze of services required to help their child. They must establish a viable relationship with each caretaker.

> In order to get help for the many difficulties we face in orthopedics, physical therapy, education, family stress, financial support, and a seemingly endless list of other concerns, we must constantly research, hound, challenge and bother people about our needs. . .This constant hassle is endless and adds to the stress we must already handle. (mother of Mickey and Todd)

A mother candidly discusses the intimate, if at times troubling, bonds that link her to the professionals who care for her children:

> The very presence of the professional emphasizes our vulnerability. Also, it is easy to become overly dependent on professionals. They have specialized knowledge I need to properly care for and nurture my children and at times seem much more capable of understanding and interacting with my children than I do.
> It is also all too easy to transfer my frustrations, anger, and fears about my child's condition or disability onto the parent/professional relationship. Then, if my child fails to progress, I can explain this as a failure of the professional and thus avoid the reality of the child's condition. While such negative feelings are obviously detrimental to a good working relationship, at times they seem inescapable. (Madelyn Iris, *Participating Families*, December, 1988)

Under enormous physical, emotional, and financial strain, parents struggle to maintain the integrity of the family, set priorities, and wrest some control over their situation. Parents may view professional involvement, however necessary, however benign, as an intrusion into their family's life. They ask professionals to understand these pressing, urgent realities and tread lightly when assessing needs and offering advice:

> . . .It is not only the child who is at stake when diagnoses, treatment plans, and transportation requirements are discussed:

it is the entire family. What good is all the treatment in the world for the child if the family cracks up from financial and physical stress, and the child loses the best possible environment for progressing? (Things Some Professionals Did that Drove Us Nuts and Made Us Crazy: Parents Speak to Professionals, *Acceptance is only the first battle*, MUAP, 1984, p. 26)

* * * *

. . .When a family says they need help in getting laundry done, help them get the laundry done; don't give them counseling as to why they haven't been able to get the laundry done. (a mother writing in *The Beach Center on Families and Disability Newsletter*, Vol. 2, 1990, p. 2)

Parents may feel unfairly judged by some professionals caring for their children. Appropriate worries and concerns about their children may be deemed suspect or the results of "over-emotionalism." Mothers write of such disturbing experiences. These unhelpful encounters place additional stress on the parent-professional relationship:

> Each of us at one time or another has been treated as a hysterical or neurotic mother or both. We've all known hysteria, but have been driven to it by stress (financial, emotional, and physical), by the professional brush-off, by a lack of information (especially current information), by conflicting diagnoses and advice, and by real fear and concern about our children's well-being. (Things Some Professionals Did that Drove Us Nuts and Made Us Crazy: Parents Speak to Professionals, *Acceptance is only the first battle*, Montana University Affiliated Program, 1984, p. 25)

Professionals have chosen their roles within the health care system; parents have not. It is hoped that young caregivers will continue to derive satisfaction and self-esteem from their professional work. Parents, however, are initially shattered by the diagnosis of a serious illness and/or disability in their child. Parents may see themselves as "failures," unable to protect their child from life's pain and injustice. The mother of Joel, a child who is technology-dependent and whose first nine months of life were spent entirely in the hospital, touchingly reminds professionals of the parents' perspective in her extreme situation:

You have chosen to go into this field of helping others. Never forget it. Parents have not chosen to have sick children. Help them to love them.

Stressors for caregivers

Initial training experiences present many young professionals with their first exposure to life's most tragic and painful circumstances. First encounters with serious illness, disability, and loss bring students face to face with sadness and sorrow, grief and mourning (Werner & Korsch, 1976; Frader, 1979; Sahler, McAnarney, & Friedman, 1981; Shanfield, 1981; Sack, Krener, & Sprunger, 1984; Hardison, 1986; Bergman, 1988; Leff, Chan, & Walizer, 1991). Young professionals are vulnerable as they tentatively, with much anxiety, step into the helping role and enter the hospital or clinic world. It is a sensitive time when confusing, perhaps overwhelming, feelings arise and deeply held assumptions about life and death are challenged. Painful feelings and disturbing shocks are frequent experiences. Support from supervisors is critical: open, non-judgmental discussion of feelings is crucial.

Child life interns, young physicians, and a nurse clinician speak of intense reactions to their beginning work with children and families in need. They share and explore new paths within themselves as they begin a long professional journey; as they open themselves to caring for children with serious problems:

> On my way to the clinic this morning, I ran into Mrs. Smith, the mother of Lilly, a three-year-old with leukemia. I have not seen Lilly in two weeks because she has been in a transitional phase of treatment and her hours have been different from mine. I have often thought a great deal about Lilly since she was one of the first children with whom I worked at the clinic. Lilly particularly enjoyed glitter and all kinds of creative projects.
>
> When I entered the clinic, I looked around for Lilly but could not find her. I knew she had to be there because I had just seen her mom. The clinic was very crowded, so crowded that patients and their families were spilling out into the hall. But still I could not find her.
>
> I know this sounds as if I am leading up to a "missing child" report, but actually Lilly had been in the room the whole time. Her physical changes were so great that I *truly* did not recognize her. She had a "moon face." Her features were swollen and her face distorted. Her skin color had changed, and her hair had also thinned.
>
> Seeing Lilly like this really shocked me. I felt very uneasy within myself. It was not only that her physical appearance had changed so drastically and that she was not as "cute," but that she seemed so unfamiliar to me at first. I did not want to think of her

any differently, but at the same time I couldn't help but feel taken aback.

Luckily, despite my feelings, we were able to pick up where we left off. I have found that Lilly is really calmed by coloring and gluing. Each time I see her, she reminds me how much glue means to her. Just hearing her say "glue" in her little voice and feeling her arms around my neck was enough to bring me back two weeks. I hope it was enough for her as well. (child life intern: journal entry)

The young professionals witness the experiences of ill children and ask if they could show as much grace in the same circumstances:

I think it was the night when I was rushed to the hospital that I was most afraid; not the most afraid I've ever been in my life, more like the most scared I had been in a while. It reminded me of when I was real little, trying to fall asleep with the lights off but plagued by the images of a black and white horror film my brother forced me to watch that night.

Darkness conjured up images of uncertainty, and I hated the way that made me feel inside. It was always cold and solitary. But I still had to do it: I had to shut my eyes and accept the darkness both in my bed as a child and in the hospital before I entered the emergency room (ER) at seventeen.

I know this all must seem rather strange. It even seemed rather strange to me as these memories flooded my mind as I passed by the hematology/oncology clinic. . . . . This set of "darkness memories" accompanied me as I began the day's work in the hospital . . .

I thought about the children I will work with and how they "have to do IT." I wonder how each individually accepts his or her circumstance. I wonder if they, too, shut their eyes sometimes and think about uncertainty . . .I know I sound morbid, but intellectually it is so difficult for me to understand how these children face every day. For me, my fears of the dark were only temporary and my bout with the ER only one night. . .

I walked in the door today to the sound of a nurse's voice saying, "We are ready for you, Margie." I waited thoughtfully and a little nervously for her response. She looked at the nurse with a smile that is hard to forget. It was a loud smile, and then she laughed. She said, "You might be ready for me, but I may not be ready for you." Everyone in the room laughed with her and relaxed as Margie dealt with going to the treatment room as she knew how. (a child life intern: journal entry)

Many fears may be aroused. Professionals feel fear for the child in pain, fear of humiliation before colleagues, fear of failing patients or clients and falling short of, often, idealized expectations of themselves:

> It had been a tough day. The ward was very busy, and then one of my favorite kids was admitted on an emergency basis from the hematology/oncology clinic. Linda had been vomiting nonstop at home since her last chemotherapy treatment. She was very dehydrated and lethargic.
>
> I was the intern taking admissions and had to start the IV. I was very scared as Linda's mother, nurse, and child life specialist huddled around her and tried to comfort her. I had never seen her look so terrible.
>
> I tried three times to to get the vein. Linda was so sick that she barely moaned. Everyone was looking at me as I tried to reassure her. All the IV's I had put in so easily that day, and this one I couldn't do. I felt like a heel.
>
> I realized that I needed help and said to everyone, "Let me get the expert." I could see the relief in their eyes. My senior resident did not scream or yell at me. I was incredibly grateful that she understood. (personal communication: pediatric intern)

As caregivers develop and mature, they will continue to cope with a series of painful, emotionally wrenching experiences. How their earliest confrontations with illness and deformity are handled will set the tone for their future growth. Will young professionals "learn" to withdraw from children and parents in pain? Will young professionals "learn" to reach out to their patients and offer support and compassion?

> As I become increasingly involved with a greater number of children, I notice a personal feeling which I will have to work to overcome. I have been in doctors' offices, and I have made quick expeditions into hospitals previously, but never before have I been exposed to such wide-ranging illnesses. It has been easy for me to think of my future career in the health field and imagine how impervious I would be to sickness and its different manifestations.
>
> "Can you deal with illness?"
>
> "Oh sure, no problem," I answer without blinking an eye.
>
> It is far from easy, however. I look at A., trying to cope with prunebelly syndrome; the walls of his abdomen falling below his

waist and numerous bags leading to his previously blocked ureter. There is B., hampered by Pierre Robin syndrome; his face severely deformed and his mouth wired since he cannot swallow. J.'s mother stands mystified alongside her child who has been seriously injured in an automobile accident: she struggles to understand that it may take months, perhaps years, for her child to regain speech and gross motor movements.

I see these people and many others on the floor, and I cannot help but feel an acute and profound inner sadness. I am not sure from whence this feeling originates—whether it be from empathy, a sense of injustice, a combination of the two, or neither. All I do know is that the feeling is present and that it competes with the happiness I receive from working with these children.

I am left, in the end, with a curious mix—a "sweet sorrow," if you will. As I look back on the day, though, the sorrow seems to dominate. This is the feeling which I must work on. (child life intern currently in medical school: journal entry)

As responsibilities mount, the intensity of such experiences increases. An intern recounts her first stark experiences with a dying neonate:

Images of the dying baby—his last gasps for breath, his mottled, blue skin—are very much alive. The eerie, bumpy, 3:00 AM ambulance voyage is a nightmare come true. The Ambu bag falls and slips; the isolette bounces open—15 endless minutes. Not even two weeks into my internship and I am brutally exposed to my own helplessness. No monitor. No laryngoscope. The painful images remain—fresh, clear, bare. The guilt remains and rests at the core of a new reality. I am in a state of shock and disbelief as we tell the mother. The night and her tears envelop me. (Leff, P., excerpts from diary, 1979)

The death or deterioration of a child may send shock waves throughout one's being and poignantly affect basic beliefs and values. A resident describes such a painful experience:

I lost a child with Reye's syndrome when she was four. I was completely involved with her and the family as a first year resident. Both that child and another child of mine died the same night. I was exhausted. The child's mother was pregnant. That picture got to me. The child had so much done to her. I felt exhausted and guilty that I'd done all of that to her. . . (Sack et al., 1984, p. 679)

The pressures and demands of caring for children and families in crisis never cease. A sensitive pediatrician notes:

> Keeping a "stiff upper lip" is the credo of teaching hospitals. Last year I helped care for a drowning victim in the emergency room. While the residents participated in the unsuccessful resuscitation attempt, I listened to the mother talk about her daughter, who happened to be the same age as my own. After it was over, I spoke briefly with the residents about some technical matters and then went out to my car and wept. I later thought how much more instructive the case would have been for the residents had they witnessed my crying. (Bergman, 1988, p. 261)

Permission to grieve—to cry with parents; to attend the funeral if desired; to make follow up phone calls to parents; to express one's feelings of helplessness and despair openly with peers—begins a process of healing. Hospital memorial services for children who have become part of the "hospital family" can help bring staff members together in their mourning and affection for the child and family (Leff, Chan, & Walizer, 1991). A nurse clinician recalls:

> Several years ago a child whom I had known since I was a nursing student died. She was a little girl with a trach who had been abandoned by her teen mother. Maggie longed for a home and real mommy. For years, she was "our baby" while the various agencies fought among themselves. We, too, had major disagreements about letting her go with the trach. We dressed her, rocked her to sleep, bought her her favorite foods, played with her. But no institution could give Maggie what she cried and prayed for as she watched children go home with their families.
>
> Finally, wonderful, competent parents were found. Maggie was the happiest little girl I had ever seen. She now had her own home and special, loving mommy. For a full year, she lived a normal life and progressed beautifully. Then around Christmas time while driving home from a party, a terrible accident happened with her trach. Maggie died in the hospital lobby.
>
> Her foster mom was devastated. The whole staff grieved. A memorial service in the hospital helped all of us. Without our coming together, there would have been recrimination and nasty bitterness. We cried and remembered Maggie. We remembered her one year of happiness with her own mom and family. (personal communication: nurse clinician)

Parents offer their thoughts concerning the stress and burdens on sionals:

> My compassion goes out to "the other side" because I remember as a caseworker how hard it was to absorb the anger and fear and grief and all the other feelings of my clients, with nowhere to go with it since my supervisor refused to help me. I just couldn't take it—I felt the vise was closing every day— my supervisor pressuring me to do more work, my clients unloading their feelings. (Bill's mother)

* * * *

> Counsel young professionals about their own responses to loss and grief. It will always be part of the medical profession. Substance abuse, burn-out, marriages that fail are all symptoms of a larger problem. . . and they happen from the inside out. Physicians and nurses need emotional tools and strategies to deal with the continual barrage of pain and suffering and stress. It seems that their training is the ideal place to begin. (Sherelyn Campbell, *A Few Words to Young Health Professionals*)

Contrasts in world views: Complementary areas of expertise

Parents and professionals do see the child from widely differing perspectives (Darling, 1983). This is natural. Parents as parents are deeply involved with their child on all levels, emotional and physical. The professional's "case" is their child, beloved and unique. Keough's mother examines the emotional and physical worlds separating parents and professionals:

> There will always be conflicts between parents of handicapped children and professionals offering services to those children and their families. Perhaps the biggest reason for these conflicts, and the most insoluble problem, is that there is a vast difference between understanding a situation intellectually and understanding that same situation emotionally. This is a problem for both professionals and parents.
>
> While professionals may really know their business, unless they have actually lived with and been responsible for a handicapped child, it is probably impossible for them to fully comprehend the 24-hour-a day, 52-week-a-year implications of that

for the rest of the family. Even if the professional
group home or institutional settings, the experi-
alent because the professional was paid for the
n vacations and spent more time away from the

...... hand, it is difficult for many parents to understand the stress many professionals are under — particularly in
these times of tight money and large caseloads — from working
with so many families whose problems are extremely varied and
whose needs are often so much greater than the resources available from several agencies, much less one individual provider.
(Sue Duffy, 1984, p. 37)

Although both parents and professionals are concerned with the child's
care, their perspectives are quite different. The contrasts are illustrated in
the accompanying figure (Figure 1). The professional typically centers his
or her attention, skills, and knowledge on a disease process, disabling
condition, or other therapeutic concern. The professional may be involved
with large numbers of similarly affected children. His or her knowledge
includes general information about a condition or illness. Focusing on a
specific problem during an office or clinic visit, the professional often sees
only a snapshot of the child's life. In clinic or hospital settings, many
caregivers are part of the child's and family's life for an intense, but
relatively short period of time.

Professionals unprepared to work with families may anxiously take
refuge within their own area of technical expertise and dare not venture
forth to meet parents as real people with a distinctive, holistic view of their
sick child. This stance deprives caregivers of participating in the total life
of the child and family; of supporting and nurturing those who are most
committed to the child's well-being, happiness, and progress. Parents
appreciate professionals who are able to be flexible, to subordinate their
agenda to the care of the whole child within the family. A mother
delineates her goals for her children and frankly recognizes that her goals
differ from the more limited objectives of individual professionals working with her youngsters:

Few professionals seem to understand how to work side by side
with parents to develop a long-term, comprehensive plan for the
child's treatment or care. Instead, they focus their attention
exclusively on the single domain of their expertise, ignoring
other aspects of the child's needs such as his personal growth and
psycho-social development. As the mother, I see the totality of
the child. I look at my children for their present needs, but I must

World Views in Conflict
Complementary Areas of Expertise
Different Perspectives

PROFESSIONAL VIEW	PARENTAL VIEW
Deal with a large number of children with similar diagnoses (similar diagnostic categories; experience with a broad range of children)	Care for one unique, loved child
Particular area of concern focuses typically on child's problem; specialization; unidimensional	Relationship to whole child; parents serve many roles in child's life
Typically trained in "cure" or "fix" model—focus is on the child-patient's illness or imperfection	Focus is on overall daily care and nurture of the child within the family unit
Hospital-based training may overlook home setting	Hospital is an unnatural, hostile environment
See child and family in circumscribed, time-limited and time-specific visits; snapshot of child's life	Twenty-four hour exposure; long haul
Authoritarian tradition; control through knowledge and skill; paternalistic tradition emphasizes power	Look to partnership with professionals who are "consultants"; prefer joint decision-making power; will bear ultimate consequences of decision
Have chosen their roles	Have not chosen to have a child who is anything other than healthy and whole

also concern myself with their future, well into adulthood. My goals include helping my children function just a little bit better tomorrow, but always with an eye to what this improvement might mean for their lives in general. (Madelyn Iris, *Participating Families*, December, 1988)

Parents urge professionals to be aware of the gap—at times, chasm—between the parents' body of experiences and emotions and the professional's vantage point. Recognition and appreciation of the parents' ongoing struggles will enable professionals to respond with compassion. Parents share the following:

> How many caregivers have breast-fed a baby with heart disease? Lived with diarrhea and diaper rash? Shopped for groceries with a shrieking infant in a backpack? Sat alone in a cold waiting room trying to calm a terrorized child. . .? Tried to ask urgent questions over the din? Gone out in public (without armor) as the parent of a child who was clearly "not okay?" (Laura's mother)

* * * *

> [Vanessa's] face and head begin to heal. The time arrives for the last traumatic event on the road to recovery—the stitches and staples need to be removed. At four and a half years old, this is a very scary event. It is not fun to see someone coming at your already tender nose and head with scissors and tweezers. (On second thought, this may be frightening at any age.) To keep her still and immobilized. . .she has to be strapped into a "papoose."
>
> It is *very* tough to see the fear in your child's eyes and not be able to do much to help them. By the time we get through with this ordeal, it is hard to tell who has been more traumatized—the child or the parent! Vanessa gets very upset and cries, and, of course, I get upset then, too. I just want the fear and the hurt to be all over with. I just want it to be over with. . . (Colette Lau, *Facial Expressions Newsletter*, November, 1988, p. 3)

* * * *

> The nurse part of me was able to use my knowledge as a valuable tool. The defense it provided helped me to maximize my sense of control in a situation where I basically had so little control. The pregnancy itself and ensuing birth of Joshua and Miriam were an emotional crisis for me and my husband. Professionals must understand that parents *are* undergoing a crisis if they are to respond appropriately. (mother of Joshua and Miriam, premature twins)

As professionals begin to understand such experiences, to learn what a particular medical or disabling condition means in the life of a family and in the lives of the individual members of the family, they come to respect parents as experts, learners, decision-makers, and partners. Despite inevitable differences, professionals can enhance their understanding of the parents' world, the parents' point of view (Sassaman, 1983). A father and organizer of a parent support group speaks to both parents and professionals:

We provide a support mechanism to that portion of our population that recognizes the significance of learning the alphabet by a ten-year old with Down syndrome or the meaning of a smile on a child who has not smiled in a year. The rest of the world may not understand achievement on that scale. You do. So do we. (Kenneth Fussichen, One Man's View, *The Advocate*, Vol. 3, No. 1, March/April 1988, p. 9)

Areas of complementary knowledge and expertise emerge as parents and professionals recognize and begin to understand their differing emotional and physical perspectives. Professionals benefit from the parents' unique knowledge of their child; parents benefit from the professionals' general knowledge and skill. Laura's mother writes:

There are professionals, too, who are involved in giving Laura the best outcome possible, and who take the long view with me. In particular, I think of the orthopedist, as he and I both know that Laura will likely have at least two surgeries at his hands eventually. I depend on this, in fact, that he can "invest" a bit in Laura's future, thinking about how she will grow, planning for what he will want to do just at which right moment; if she is not "real" enough to him, he cannot possibly do right by her. Some. . . specialties are long-term projects, too, just like child-rearing.

Disagreements, differing points of view, need not be destructive. When respect defines the parent-professional relationship, differences of opinion enhance communication, choices, and the ultimate care of the child. Within a framework of respect, parents and professionals share their observations, skills, knowledge, and goals.

Keep being a student of medicine. The families of sick children will appreciate your "learning stance" in a very special, unique way. Parents and professionals have much to learn from each other. Our areas of expertise are different, but compatible. (Sherelyn Campbell, *A Few Words to Young Health Professionals*)

* * * *

Over the years I have thought about the difficulty encountered in the uneven relationship between a parent and a professional.

The inequality between a parent and a professional is not in their inherent worth as human beings, but is a difference in what they have spent time studying. I see it as two containers—the parents, filled with knowledge about the child, and the professional, filled with knowledge about the specialization he has chosen. Had the parent the interest, inclination and time, he could have "filled himself" with the same material the professional has absorbed. So when I approach a professional of any sort, I do not see an authority figure in the sense of someone of whom I should feel awe, but someone with whom I can share information. And if I am very fortunate, that person feels that way also. (Bill's mother)

Parents such as Bill's mother recognize that there is often a reluctance among parents to "be equals and communicate." Reasons for this are wide-ranging. For many parents, it is difficult not to feel intimidated by professionals treating and assessing their child. Parents are afraid and vulnerable as they seek help for their child from powerful strangers who possess the technical knowledge and skills that can make an enormous impact on their child's life. Attitudes of awe and passivity toward care-givers are common as parents struggle to find their way in a new, threatening world.

Historically, patients and their advocates have not been encouraged to assume active roles in their care. Health care professionals have traditionally not viewed themselves as "educators," "consultants," or "partners" of families. For many professionals, such roles are unfamiliar, distant. During a time of burgeoning consumerism, parents and professionals are charting new territory in areas of parent education, collaboration with parents, and joint decision-making power. Challenge offers opportunity.

You, as professionals, carry the ongoing burden of continual support. You share in the family's successes as well as failures. You are a part of the problem-solving team; one who *must* be aware of the emotional bonds which pull the family together in times of crisis. Your role is essential and paramount to all others, with the exception of the parental role. You are forging a new frontier in home health care. (Julianne Beckett, Comprehensive Care for Medically Vulnerable Infants and Toddlers: A Parent's Perspective, *Equals in this Partnership*, NCCIP, 1985, p. 10)

* * * *

Realize that you have the opportunity to make us stronger and better people by sharing of yourselves and your knowledge. Most of us can cope if given any impetus to do so, but the only outside reward we may ever receive is your regard - if you express it. (Keough's mother)

Professionals who welcome parents, actively teach parents the most effective ways of advocating for their child, and invite parents to participate as assertive team members know that involved, responsible parents are a professional's most important asset. Parents who, through their questions and concerns, work with a professional to set goals for their child's care enhance and broaden the professional's contribution.

> I feel that my daughter's pediatrician is her advocate. He supports me in my quests to get the best possible services for my daughter, listens to and acts on every concern I have. He has never brushed aside any of my worries, and I appreciate that. He values my opinion. (Cari's mother)

Pioneering professionals are offering guidance to parents as they assume their central place within the health care team, as parents become "full-fledged members of the team." (Carla Lee Lawson, *Prescription for Participation*, Iowa Pilot Parents, Inc.) A developmental pediatrician writing for parents sends an important message to professionals as well:

> Remember what you have that the professionals lack - a total commitment to the child and to your whole family, allied to uniquely complete knowledge of the child and the responsibility of making decisions and choices in regard to every aspect of your child's management. . .
>
> The assertive parent is not the "boss" of the treatment team, nor just their "client" (although use of this term reminds us of who is hiring whom) but a "partner" - and the partner whose ultimate responsibility for the success of the whole project has the deepest roots and will be exercised long after the professionals have forgotten the "case." (A. Mervyn Fox, How to Be an Assertive Parent in the Treatment Team, *Participating Families*, Feb., 1988)

Openness to partnership with parents emerges through a process of growth, through a process of enlarging one's view of the child's world, through a process of examining one's assumptions about parents. A clinician and researcher shares her evaluation of ten years of work with families:

> There is a very strong, overriding belief in any educational community that when parents say a child can do a skill, if we the professionals have not seen it happen, of course, the child cannot do it. There is almost this belief that parents lie to us. I have never figured out why they would lie to us; I have never figured out what they have to gain by lying to us; but we hold parent opinion

as suspect. We hold parent opinion as not valid. . .

[Current research shows us that] parents do know what their kids can do. They are reliable observers. They do differ from us. One thing that the parents do that the professionals do not - and it's personally one of the things that I find most delightful about parents - is give children credit for emerging skills. They see children starting to do things and maintain the hope that budding trials will evolve into full blown skills in the future. I certainly hope as professionals that we reinforce parents in that kind of optimism and that kind of quest. (Lisbeth Vincent, Family Relationships, *Equals in this Partnership*, NCCIP, 1985, p. 37-8)

ATTITUDES AND VALUES: WHERE THE WORLDS CAN BEGIN TO MEET

Reframing a model of care

A model of "acute" illness has guided the training of most health care professionals. Such a model fails to capture the distinctive needs and realities of children and families living with chronic conditions and/or disabilities. For example, when children with chronic conditions must be repeatedly admitted to the hospital, usual hospital practices may disrupt the parents' efforts to safeguard, as far as possible, the "healthy" aspects of these children's lives—their "normal" daily routines. Appreciating and supporting parents' long-term perspectives and goals are important even as children receive acute treatment (Robinson, 1987).

A physician describes how a model of "acute" illness affected her earliest clinical experiences:

My pediatric clerkship rotation was almost entirely composed of experiences in acute settings: inpatient acute admissions, the pediatric emergency room, outpatient clinics dealing with acute problems. We did see children with chronic conditions such as cystic fibrosis, sickle cell anemia, leukemia, and neuromuscular disorders. However, we were typically concerned with the child's acute hospital stay, the pathophysiology of the disease process, and biological treatment of the acute exacerbation.

There was precious little time devoted to an understanding of the child's care at home or of the long-term impact of chronic illness on the child's development and/or emotional well-being. Although parents were grudgingly allowed to stay with their children, they were often seen as peripheral to the child's admission. Parents were even viewed as nuisances by some staff members. We gained very little knowledge of the parents' concerns and needs. I now see how narrow our training was and how poorly prepared we were to help children and families. (PTL)

Different models of care are required, a reorientation of professional practice (Myers, 1984; van Eys, 1985; Lipp, 1986; Chesler & Barbarin, 1987). A model of acute illness with its focus on cure of biological disease fails to address the full role of professionals caring for children with long-term conditions. Such a model also fails to clarify the caregivers' sources of gratification.

Despite the harsh, pressing realities of chronic illness and disability, health care professionals can derive satisfaction from their interactions with parents and children. Parents and professionals working together maximize the child's care and nurture family bonds of love and commitment.

In order to withstand the crushing blows chronic illness and/or disability will bring, parents, children, and professionals alike must take pride in "their best efforts" in the face of enormously difficult circumstances. Although the child may need many months or years of treatment and may never be made totally perfect or whole, the support, guidance, and steadfastness of caregivers do "heal" the hurt child and family in powerful, significant ways. Contrasting her pediatric clerkship with another model of care, the physician continues:

> During my internship, the pediatric hematology/oncology attending developed warm, open relationships with parents. I vividly remember how parents would seek him out in the doctors' lounge during their children's nap times. Together they would share information over a cup of coffee. He would answer questions and talk with parents about tough decisions and tough therapies.
>
> Many of his patients were very sick. Parents in great pain felt able to cry in his presence. In a quiet way, he would offer his support, caring, and concern. This doctor taught by his example. Years later, images and memories of how he calmly and compassionately reached out to parents in intense distress remain with me.
>
> I wish, though, that he had also formally talked to us about his philosophy of care. We really needed such a perspective. Unpretentious and genuinely caring, he valued his relationships with parents greatly and derived much satisfaction from knowing that he was helping families as much as he could. (PTL)

For children coping with illnesses such as cancer, parents and professionals hope for cure and work toward cure. However, given the state of current knowledge, children must endure years of painful, invasive treatments, debilitating side effects, possibly amputations, and other major surgeries. Many of these once fatal diseases have become chronic conditions touching every aspect of the child's and family's life and development (Chesler & Barbarin, 1987). Attention to the child's emotional well-being during treatment and follow-up is critical as children fight to build self-esteem, overcome the scars of illness and treatment, adjust to permanent disability, and manage their darkest fears of recurrence. Parents and children need the regard and support of caregivers while they carry on with life.

A "care" model—caring for the child and parents as they struggle to create a healthy family life despite the unrelenting demands of chronic illness and/or disability—broadens both the caregiver's healing identity and sources of professional satisfaction and self-esteem. For those who help children with long-term difficulties and uncertain futures, relationships with children and parents become a major source of professional fulfillment.

> The rules are simple: forget the rules! Especially the one about distancing yourself from your patients and their families. It doesn't work with children, and it rarely works with the chronically ill. What our children need from you is something entirely different than what you are asked to give your other pediatric patients. They need an ally, a knowledgeable and caring friend outside the family; one who will help them understand and learn to live with their illness. In most cases, you can't "fix" a chronic illness, but the teaching, support, and resources you provide will enable the family to accept the diagnosis and move forward. (Sherelyn Campbell, *A Few Words to Young Professionals*)

Many decisions that must be made in the lives of medically fragile children are profoundly difficult and painful. A "care" model understands that such choices, conflicts, and decisions defy simplicity and certainty. Distressing questions may far outnumber clear-cut answers and solutions. "Care" of children and families facing these painful dilemmas embraces the child's hurt spirit; listens to his cry for rest; supports the parents as they stand by their child. A young teen's parents and his pediatrician are struggling together to address his despair and fatigue, to "care" for him as a whole person:

His pediatrician and I both think that he's not emotionally strong enough to undergo such a major surgery. He is weary and doesn't seem to have much of a will to fight any more. Some is past history, no doubt, and some is fear, but he is "all out of courage." We have decided to postpone the surgery for now (as long as his medical stability holds out, anyway) and work on the mental health. We have a good counselor. . . and we are planning some fun things to look forward to in the upcoming weeks and months. Hopefully, he'll find some inner strength and some reasons to keep going. We were all kind of afraid he'd just give up and die.

At 13, he's been through more than most people in much longer lifetimes. . . and medically, he has had every difficulty in the book. He's a survivor, but even those hearty souls get weary. We thought it was an important message to give him: that we value his emotional and mental health as well as his physical well-being, and that it's worth a major restoration effort. Also, we have heard *his* deeper message of desperation. (mother of Jesse and Doug)

A "care" model values and respects the pivotal commitment, quest, and responsibility of the family (Shelton, Jeppson, & Johnson, 1987). A "care" model nurtures, supports, and empowers parents as they meet ongoing crises, face difficult decisions, and work together with the many professionals in their child's life. A mother emphasizes:

Progress toward a system of care which is family-based and coordinated can come only when everyone, parents and professionals, realize power is not the issue but empowerment. Empowerment occurs in effective parent-professional collaboration. Professionals give up power and control in order to empower parents to advocate for change. Parents who are leaders give up power to empower other parents. . . We are strong not when we seek to control others, but when we seek to strengthen others. . . (Kathy Odle, Parents are Saying. . ., *ACCH Network*, Vol. 6, No. 4, Spring/Summer, 1988, p. 4)

Early intervention strategies and programs have highlighted these issues. As professionals increasingly work with infants, toddlers, and very young children in need, "care" of the child becomes intimately involved in nurturing, supporting, and empowering parents (Dunst, Trivette, & Deal,

1988). A mother describes how her daughter's early intervention specialist strengthened her during a time of intense stress and uncertainty:

> The first thing Jan *did* when she initially came to our home was get down on the floor and play with our daughter. It made me feel good. Most of our friends, though very supportive of our daughter, treated her somewhat gingerly when it came to physical contact since she still had a feeding tube inserted in her stomach, but Jan launched right in.
>
> She has told me since that this was a calculated move and something she tries to do each time she begins working with a new family. It tells them she likes their child, it puts her physically at a lower level than the parents and it demonstrates that she's an informal, non-authoritarian person. It's very effective. More professionals ought to try it. (Sue Duffy, *Acceptance is only the first battle*, MUAP, 1984. p. 43)

Human values and the less-than-perfect child

Mental and physical defects, crippling injuries, catastrophic illnesses are all part of the human condition. Parents struggle for perspective under the painful impact of these events in their children's lives (Park, 1985; Simon, 1987). The mother of Rachel, who has a form of dwarfism, shares:

> When the diagnosis was first made, my husband and I felt full of pain and helplessness. Our minds ran the gamut of sorrow, hurt, anger, disbelief, and pity for ourselves, our family, and our daughter.
>
> Our minds went a step further and projected the whole picture into the future. . .
>
> I spent a great deal of time holding Rachel; I loved her so much. But there were so many questions — How would our society accept her in a world conditioned to accept not less than close-to-perfect? . . .Would she have a hard time making friends, getting a job, finding true love? My emotions were snowballing too far down the road, and I knew I must accept things one day at a time . . .
>
> My husband and I realized that our daughter needed our hearts. She was throwing a world of rainbows at us and all we could blindly envision were the thunderstorms . . . We could either show her a cold, cruel world full of defeats, misery, unhappiness, tears and sorrow or we could show her a world full

of warmth, laughter, happiness, challenges, victories, songs, and, most of all, love. (Debby Moosreiner, *Families and Disability Newsletter*, Vol. 2, No. 1, Spring, 1990)

Parents and professionals alike are products of a society that has devalued and stigmatized persons with disabilities. An adoptive mother of a child with a cleft lip and palate explains:

We soon realized that we were totally unprepared to face the reactions of those in our everyday life. Despite our wealth of information on the treatment of cleft lip and palate, we had not spoken to those who really live it day by day - the parents and the families themselves. As obvious as it might seem, I was totally unprepared for the negative response of others to our daughter. I expected that because *we* were accepting of Lauren and her facial disfigurement - everyone would be. I was totally taken aback when we encountered staring and rude comments from strangers, heart-broken by the rejection shown by a portion of our family members. (Jane Richardson, *AboutFace*, Vol. 4, No. 6, November/December, 1990)

In the face of society's harsh, largely negative images of children and adults with chronic illnesses and/or disabilities, parents consistently and repeatedly speak of their love of their children. Parental love, complicated, richly textured, "ordinary," is the cornerstone, the rock upon which their relationship with their child rests.

So many times people have said to me, "I don't know how you do it." The simple truth is they would do the same. You love the child you are given. I don't want anyone to pity me or my child. (Cari's mother)

* * * *

Children with handicaps, mental retardation, developmental disabilities are *children* first. Treat the *child*; then treat the disability. Treat the family of that child as you would the family of any child. Know that parents care for their disabled child as deeply as they care for any of their children. (Ben's mother)

* * * *

I was blessed by having Katherine 17 years. I grew as a human being and as a parent. I know I see life differently. She lent compassion and love. I sometimes think that our children with severe disabilities are a beacon and bring out the good in people.

She left her mark. And it is a compliment to her that she could be so loved. (Katherine's mother)

* * * *

I am taking the time out to answer your questions because I honestly believe that sick children can become valuable members of society ... Wanting things to be different for Joel is a selfish act - - I can't undo the damage his illness has caused him. I can do my best to give him a loving life. Joel is living proof of the value of love. He is a warm, considerate, active child who is pleasant as can be. He is constantly making progress, and we hope that in the future he can be in the world without his ventilator, oxygen, trach and g. t. . . . . Joel is loved for himself. (Joel's mother)

Parents emphasize that love transcends disability, illness, and the stares of an often unwelcoming world. Parents love their children with challenging needs as they love all their children: each child holds a special, unique place within their lives and hearts. The bond of love is strong, not fragile. Although there may be pain and frustration, love is the wellspring from which parents derive strength and courage to push forward.

I am the parent of three sons. The youngest is deaf and chronically ill. My vision is no different from that of other parents. I want my child to be happy, productive, loved, in love, and accepted. (parent writing in *Families and Disability Newsletter*, Vol. 2, No. 1, Spring, 1990, p. 2)

* * * *

None of us has to be perfect to be loved, or to love. People who are not parents, or parents only of healthy children, doubt others because they cannot themselves imagine loving such a child. They imagine that it is somehow different from loving the normal child everyone hopes for. Our children are very real to us before they are born: imperfection is a grievous shock, but pain is not the sum and total of what one feels. (Laura's mother)

* * * *

Some years before my son was born, my beloved Golden Retriever was hit by a car near my rural home. Although I rushed Jeb to the veterinarian half an hour away, the doctor told me there was nothing he could do but "put him to sleep." This vet had cared for Jeb and performed surgery for a minor disability. As I cried, the vet countered, "Don't cry. He wasn't right anyway."

"He wasn't right anyway." "He-wasn't-right-anyway" rings in my ears. For many years I heard that silent declaration every time my son came under the care of a new physician, and, in those early years, it was frequently. . . Health care professionals have often been criticized by parents for refusing to recognize the very real, the very natural love of parent for child; for excluding from their concept of unconditional parental love children with disabilities. (Sam's mother)

* * * *

Remember, please, the strength of human love, which even the weakest, most mentally handicapped human being is capable of giving. This special child is a human being, not an object, a burden, or a monster, and parents will benefit from this subtle change in attitude, for they, too, have doubts. Health care professionals can encourage those doubts and cause them to grow into crushing nightmares, or they can ease the doubts with human gifts of compassion and information. (Ted's mother)

* * * *

. . . We [my husband and I] are incredibly lucky in that we have a child capable of giving back in love 10 times anything we can give her. . . (Sue Duffy, *Acceptance is only the first battle*, MUAP, 1984, p. 35)

Parents urge professionals to reflect seriously and challenge prejudices and fears concerning a child's appearance, the chronicity of many conditions, the fact of retardation. Professionals open doors of understanding when they carefully examine superficial, culturally acquired beliefs about human value and love in the face of disabling conditions. By suspending judgment and learning from parents and children, professionals begin to build bridges.

I think the most important thing is that you shouldn't make assumptions about how the parents feel about their baby. I got the feeling that many health care people thought that we thought Patty's birth was a disaster . . . It's important to remember that people respond differently. Some parents might be devastated; others not.

A lot of health care personnel communicated in some way that a baby born with a cleft lip would be a disaster to them. We never felt that Patty was a disaster: we loved her from the beginning. People working with parents should try to find out how parents actually feel by listening and not project how they would feel onto the parents. (mother of Patty, a baby with a cleft lip and palate)

* * * *

Although our pediatrician did not tell us to put Sara in an institution, neither did he put much credence in early intervention programs. However, he was always willing to note Sara's progress and listen to our reasons for believing in early stimulation and has since become enthusiastic about Sara's development. He now believes the stimulation program has made a difference and I applaud him for being open enough to change his mind. (Jan Mariska, *Acceptance is the first battle*, MUAP, 1984, p. 29)

Behavior springs from values. Parents are acutely aware of the underlying attitudes which shape a professional's interactions with their children.

Many health care professionals do not feel it is necessary to talk directly to Jill and often behave as if she is not even in the room with us. Some professionals avoid making any physical contact with Jill, acting as if she has a condition that might be considered "catching." There is often a reluctance to make eye contact with her. This form of rejection is subtle but is very painful to parents when they consider their child a much-loved and valuable member of their family. (Jill's mother)

* * * *

Know who you are, what your philosophy is on the place of people with disabilities/chronic illnesses in society. It makes a big difference. For example, Thomas has had two teachers with conflicting visions. In the area of teaching signs for communicating, the summer school teacher decided to challenge Thomas to see if he could learn to sign accurately; she discovered that he could. Thomas' previous teacher during the school year accepted approximate signs as adequate. I see this as a difference in philosophy that can make a major impact. Instead of seeing Thomas half-empty, he was seen as half-full. (Thomas's mother)

* * * *

And Dr. J, as my daughter calls him, did far more than discuss her life-threatening medical conditions when we first met; he helped us to begin loving her by revealing himself as a philosophical and profoundly loving man. Without that, he'd have been of far less help and importance to our family. In fact, without the kind of support and hope he gave us, I doubt I'd have ever gathered up the nerve to have a second child—and we now have a healthy 6-week-old girl for our eldest to be a big sister to. (Keough's mother)

People first language

The language one uses to describe children with special needs also shapes behavior. Language may unintentionally limit society's vision of what is possible for people with disabilities. Patrick's mother, an orthopedic nurse, points out:

> The term "wheelchair-bound" is often used when talking about a person's capacities. "Wheelchair-bound" focuses totally on the negative; there is an image of someone shackled to a wheelchair. In reality, the wheelchair enhances mobility and thus provides greater freedom and independence for children with certain kinds of physical challenges.
>
> I prefer the term "wheelchair-abled." "Wheelchair-abled" is definitely closer to a child's or adult's experience. Such positive terminology also helps to change attitudes of the larger, non-disabled community.

A parent who describes herself as ". . . the mother of a charming, warm, caring, family-valuing 14 year old son with several disabilities" discusses the importance of "people first language" in the life of her child.

> By people first language, I mean wording which mentions the person first and the disability second as in a *child* with disabilities, a *person* with mental retardation, or a *toddler* who is ventilator dependent. I know that using this form of language can make sentences syntactically difficult; but I feel very strongly that we need to mention the *person first* to eradicate the notion that people are their disabilities or that all people with a similar disability are alike.
>
> I also shun words that evoke pity or horror, such as affliction, suffering, or wheel-chair bound. I realize that often people with disabilities do suffer and that the need to use a wheelchair can circumscribe a person's parameters; but these words place an emphasis on the negative aspects of the person's life. If we hear most often how negative and problematic are the lives of persons with disabilities rather than how joyous or productive, we will cling to the perception that the lives of people with disabilities are sad and worthless. (Sam's mother)

Parents encourage professionals to speak, think, and act in terms of "people first" language. Children, beyond diagnostic categories, disabling conditions, needs, and challenges, are children first. Parents stress this crucial message and share their thoughts concerning value, love, and imperfection:

> My children with special needs, two of whom are labeled mentally retarded, have had to work extremely hard to reach goals that come easily to "normal" children. Their motivation comes from within; from people who love, nurture, and accept them; from adults who create environments for their learning. Are these not the same resources necessary for the development of all children? . . . Children and adults with special needs have feelings that are no different from our own: they want to be valued and respected for themselves. (mother of Lisa and Nancy)

* * * *

> A label means nothing of any importance or usefulness. It does not tell you about the likes and dislikes of my kids, or what turns them on or off. It doesn't tell you anything about their future or what it will take for me to keep my family together. All it does is tell you a label that is generally very meaningless and even deadly. (father of two children with special needs)

* * * *

> I will always cherish and remember those who celebrate Lyn for what she can do for herself and others. (Lyn's mother)

Expanding one's world

Health care professionals have grown and developed within the arms of their own families. Disability and chronic illness may have touched their lives in very close ways. Medical students share their own poignant, private family dramas.

> People often ask me why I went into medicine. I immediately think of my brother. My retarded brother was such an important person in my life. I watched him struggle and succeed as only he could. As children, sadness and joy were interwoven throughout our lives. Since I was little, I've always wanted to be able to help others. (personal communication: first year medical student)

* * * *

> It was rough growing up with an autistic brother. Years ago before any legislation or programs, my mother struggled with every imaginable community institution. She just wouldn't give

up. And my brother was able to live at home and attend local schools.

Personally, I struggled to deal with many ambivalent feelings. I loved my brother, but I hated his destructive tantrums that would turn our house upside down. I remember a mixture of confusing, conflicting feelings: resentment, guilt, love, closeness, humor. Now as I work with kids in the developmental center, my own experiences have deepened my approach toward kids and parents: I can listen without fear. (personal communication: child psychiatry fellow)

* * * *

My father was dying after a massive stroke just as I was beginning my clerkships. I took a leave of absence to be with him and to help my mother. My father had been *both* a wonderful father and positive role model for me. He was a sensitive family doc and friend to his patients. I was angry and bitter that his life should end so terribly in such humiliation. He became totally dependent on the hospital staff. Some of the nurses and doctors were condescending and treated him as if his life had never mattered.

When I came back to school, I began to see my father in every patient. It was *very* hard for me. I once started screaming my head off in the middle of the PICU when a nurse was brusque and matter of fact with a little girl. The nurse wanted to throw me off the service! The attending and I had long conversations. She never judged me. I came to realize that I could have handled the whole thing with much more tact. The nurse was just another hassled human being, not the evil witch I had envisioned. My emotions for my father overwhelmed me, and I could not advocate for the patient in an effective way. (personal communication: third year medical student)

Parents feel a special affinity with professionals who themselves are the parents of children with challenging needs.

When we were in the hospital after I gave birth to Thomas, there was a doctor who called a patient of his and asked her to come in to talk with me about her son who was born a year before with a cleft palate. This doctor also shared with me that he had a child with learning disabilities. (Thomas's mother)

* * * *

Since Lisa's birth, we have had an excellent pediatric neurologist. He has something which many others do not; he is the father of a child who is deaf. (Lisa's mother)

Parents realize that few health care professionals will have such direct, personal experiences with childhood disability and chronic illness. Professionals can expand and remold values by seeking experiences that may lead to personal growth; by studying the real children beneath the labels; by deliberately reflecting on patient and parent contacts; by responding to feedback. Parents who love and value their children can help professionals reorder priorities and learn about the depth of parental love and commitment. The care of children who are not perfect presents professionals with the opportunity to enrich their professional lives. A mother poignantly observes:

> I'm excited about the changes I've seen in recent years, and especially to watch the vision become one shared by both parents and professionals. How fortunate for the families who are yet to come; whose chronically or seriously ill children are entrusted to the care of a physician who is able to focus knowledge, skill, and compassion into a relationship with a family rather than a disease. . .who doesn't see the chronicity of an illness as a personal or medical failure. And lucky the physician who has at least one such special child and family in his or her practice. They teach some of the best lessons of medicine, and of life. . . those of courage, trust, and hope. (mother of Jesse and Doug)

Parents value professionals who strive to grow in understanding and awareness. Willingness to listen, openness to parents' lives outside of clinical settings, observation of parents with their children pave paths toward enhanced sensitivity and appreciation of the world of parents and children. Such expansion of one's world comes through struggle and work; grappling with preconceived ideas and values. In the following vignettes, both "young and old" professionals describe such a process — its difficulties and ultimate rewards.

A pediatric intern's story:

> Today on rounds I stopped to play with one of my patients with cerebral palsy who is recovering from pneumonia. The child, spastic and nonverbal, looked up and smiled. His smile, genuine and real, contrasted sharply with the flip remarks I had made last night about having four "gorks" as patients. Flip remarks - desperate, if futile, attempts to limit the pain inherent in working with such severely, severely damaged children. Am I making empty excuses? When the baby looked up at me, made contact with me, pierced through flip comments, thoughts, and values,

the barriers to pain collapsed. Had this child, this "gork," brought me to a special space within me?

Four severely damaged babies—four children suffering as few adults would ever suffer. A young mother gently hugs her rigid, motionless baby. Her eyes are filled with love and longing. I watch her caress her child. She does not know how much she will teach me.

A third-year medical student recounts:

When we had to work with a child during a six week human behavior course, I initially was not thrilled about working with Joe, who is a mildly retarded boy with spina bifida. I heard the words "mild retardation" and "paraplegia" and could not imagine the great, cheerful, caring kid Joe is. The labels really stood between me and Joe. I'm so glad that we met and talked and played together. The child life specialist was a great help to me in breaking the ice and showing me what activities Joe enjoyed.

Joe's mother would tell me about Joe's role in the family. She could always count on him to help the young ones, crack a good joke, and enjoy her cooking. He was in the hospital because his family could not afford a lift to get him up and down the stairs. He would develop terrible abrasions and ulcers while dragging himself up and down the stairs.

I became very involved with the family and very angry at the bureaucratic system that made Joe's life so miserable. I even wanted to get my friends at the local TV station to do a story about Joe! Joe taught me to be wary of labels and to value people for whom they are.

A family physician shares this story:

I was working at a large HMO. One of my first patients was a woman with hypertension. She shared with me that she was a special ed teacher with two children of her own who had many problems. She was very upset during our visits and began telling me about her son Timmy who had severe developmental disabilities. The repair of Timmy's hypospadias was a focus of much distress. My patient was in the midst of fighting with the HMO to provide a pediatric urologist. She also was very worried about how Timmy would cope with the surgery and hospitalization.

I began to dread our visits. I was terrified by the stories she told me about her children: both boys needed so much. I couldn't understand why she was so concerned about the hypospadias repair when Timmy had so many other serious difficulties. But I suspended judgment and listened. As she spoke, I remembered my introduction to child life when I was a medical student. Through a friend I was able to contact the child life specialist and refer Timmy and his mother to her. The child life specialist prepared Timmy for the operation and provided support throughout the hospitalization and after.

My patient was very grateful. *And* I learned a great deal: my views and feelings of helplessness were no more than *my* views that I had no right to impose on my patient. I was wrong to make snap decisions about parents' priorities for their children. My patient's success in helping her son urinate as other little boys could was a plus for the whole family. I was glad to be part of this positive experience.

Sharing one's humanity

Many external forces place enormous stress on the parent-professional relationship: bureaucratic settings that emphasize "number of patient or client visits" rather than quality of time spent with children and families; insurance policies that reward procedure and technique over education and counseling; the complexity of institutions serving children with special needs; the intricacy of the interrelationships among such institutions; embattled funding sources for such programs as respite care and home care. Given such problems, the core human-to-human contact between parent and professional becomes the keystone that gives strength and cohesion to the relationship.

Health care professionals often struggle with how much of themselves to reveal and share as they meet parents and children in distress: As a "professional," is it appropriate for me to cry in front of parents? Should I share my own anxieties and worries about the child's status? Shouldn't I be strong in parents' eyes, in control? Can I meet the expectations parents have of me?

Parents repeatedly emphasize that open caring and concern are basic elements of helpful parent-professional encounters.

I think it is important for doctors and other health care providers to feel comfortable baring their human side especially when families are undergoing significant emotional trauma. It won't erode the professional-client relationship; if anything, it will enhance it. (Cari's mother)

* * * *

Share something of yourself such as a hobby or a little about your family. Dr. C told us that his family would sometimes meet him at the hospital for dinner so they would have time together. I thought that it was a nice thing to do. Sharing makes you more real, touchable. (Thomas's mother)

* * * *

We as parents need to understand that doctors and nurses are human, too. Don't be afraid to *sit* and talk to parents. Even crying is OK. Parents need to know you really care about their child. Parents will be more understanding and accepting if things go wrong if you don't abandon them or avoid them. You may even avoid legal action if parents feel you did all you could and really cared. It also helps parents through the grieving process if they feel they can still talk to you and look for support after a child dies. (Emily's foster mother)

* * * *

Having a sick baby makes you feel so helpless. Dealing with your own unspoken fears about the baby's survival is critical. Like all new mothers, we need to talk about the delivery as a way of processing and beginning to resolve all the painful events.

One night while I was in the hospital with my babies, a nurse who was pregnant and I talked for a very long time. We ended up both crying and laughing. . . it felt so healing. Healing occurred when anyone of the staff — my obstetrician, a nurse, the social worker — showed genuine kindness or concern for our feelings; when caregivers emotionally and/or physically touched us. (mother of Joshua and Miriam)

* * * *

My son was two and a half years old when he developed bacterial meningitis. He was in a coma for five days and was not expected to live. Our most helpful encounter within the health care system occurred during that time. The medical care he was given was wonderful as was the support my husband and I received. The first time Stan regained consciousness and held his arms up to his Dad the nurses cried right along with us. (Stan's mother)

* * * *

Ten years from now, I may not remember the particular tests or therapies administered to my son, but I will most definitely remember the interaction I had with you as a health professional. I will strive to remember your name and especially the way in which you spoke with me and my child - the compassion and realism you exhibited. (Greg's mother)

Parents speak of the friendships and close, meaningful ties that have defined their most positive relationships with professionals caring for their children.

First and foremost, then and to this day, the friendships with those who have helped Bill over the years have sustained me, helped me grow, and helped me to help Bill. At the time Bill was young, I had precious little positive reinforcement and having caregivers who encouraged me and saw me as being someone with whom they could be friends meant everything!

Bill has been particularly blessed to have worked with people who have cared about him as a person and who have stayed with him over the years. I think he has responded in great measure to this. I know I have. What has distinguished all these relationships has been mutual respect and caring and growth over the years... I do not feel that the personal nature of these relationships has diminished their effect on Bill in a therapeutic way; in fact, my feeling is that it helped. If Bill needed anything, it was connections with other humans. (Bill's mother)

* * * *

I've thought quite a bit about the "best of times" and "worst of times" in the 11 years of being a Medical Mom. The best has come from those health professionals who are now my friends. The recollections are really rather personal, and while I don't mind sharing them, I was surprised at the very deep emotions that accompanied my attempts to write them down for you. They are truly poignant moments . . . moments when people shed their professional veneer to be with us.

On the other hand, the moments I recall as being most troublesome were (are) those in which the veneer thickened to an impenetrable depth. The doctor or health professional involved either could not or would not make a human connection with us . . . and it was the distance that hurt most. (mother of Jesse and Doug)

A mother describes how a very human, caring connection between her and her sons' pediatrician forged a healing bond during a time of enormous emotional and physical turmoil:

Frequently during the early days of my sons' care, I was at the pediatrician's office twice daily. We were working together as a team trying to avoid hospitalizations. On one particularly rough day, the pediatrician called me at home after an office visit. To this day I remember his words of kindness and concern: "I wasn't comfortable with the way you looked when you left the office." (mother of Barry and Bobby, twins with multiple needs)

Students and young professionals share their perspectives as they reached out to parents and parents reached out to them.

It was tough going to Kevin's funeral. But inside I felt I must. I had grown so close to him and to his family. The 2:00 A.M. talks with his parents were special to me. We shared so much together. I can't say that I will be able to go to other funerals. But with Kevin's family, I know it was right for me and for them. Sounds crazy, but I hope his parents will be able to come back and visit us. Should I write to them or call? Would it be too painful for them? (personal communication: pediatric intern)

* * * *

I remember my coffee breaks with the mother of one of my patients. We would find a private corner of the cafeteria and quietly talk about her child's illness and its effects on the family. Mrs. K spoke movingly about the sudden onset of Susan's disorder. She longed for her spunky, active little girl. Mrs. K had many worries. She worried about Susan's future. She feared the powerful, potentially dangerous medications that were absolutely necessary to keep Susan's debilitating illness under control. She constantly fought the guilt within her and confided that she often wished that illness had struck her and spared her daughter.

Mrs. K told me that her family had been great but that she didn't want to burden them with her constant worries and questions. Our time together gave her the opportunity to ask her questions over and over again. She knew that many of her questions had no answers. I listened and learned. The birth of my first child helped me to listen. I was experiencing first hand what parental love was all about. (PTL)

In summary, parents and professionals both gain from such open communication. As professionals send a message of caring—"I'm concerned about you; hang in there"—to parents, their own professional and personal horizons expand.

Building Bridges

Under the best of circumstances, parents come to health care professionals with both hope and fear. They entrust caregivers with their most precious gift: the lives and futures of their children. Tension is inevitable. Health professionals have the opportunity to share in parents' struggles; to impart the sense that "one is not alone;" to nurture courage, commitment, and hope despite the vagaries of chronic illnesses and/or disabilities. Parents' experiences and observations will help young professionals as they embark on their professional paths. Both Dave's mother and Dave's neurologist invite young health care providers to participate as the "partners" of parents in the care of children like Dave whom they will meet professionally:

> My child's neurologist has learned that I am going to ask questions and that I have definite opinions about such things as Dave's seizure medications. He knows that I will faithfully carry out whatever we agree to do about Dave, but I need to feel that he and I made the decision together - his knowledge and experience as a doctor and my knowledge about my child and view of what works for him. Because this neurologist is sensitive, considerate, and a good listener, we have worked together well—we are a team. (Dave's mother)

Conclusion

The importance of a parent-professional partnership is inescapable. Despite its overriding role in the care of children with chronic conditions, the parent-professional relationship may be fraught with tension, stress, and misunderstanding. A community-based system of care demands a reassessment of barriers to communication and appreciation of the expertise both parents and professionals bring to the care of children in need.

Parents and professionals do see the child from different points of view. The parents' unique, intimate knowledge of their beloved child enhances the professional's general knowledge and experience. In optimal situations, parents and professionals recognize that they are involved in a common endeavor—to provide the best possible services for children. Parents' concerns and observations augment the professional's specialized focus; the professional's skills augment parents' choices and goals. Mutual respect develops and defines the parent-professional relationship. What factors nurture this common purpose? What factors encourage the development of mutual respect and understanding?

• **Identification of the stressors confronting both parents and caregivers provides the basis for improved parent-professional understanding.**

Parents of children with serious, chronic conditions find themselves in a strange, threatening world where they are largely out of control of their children's lives. They depend upon professionals caring for their children to help them regain self-esteem, maintain active roles in the care of their children, and establish a vital place on the decision-making team.

Just as vulnerable young professionals are confronting the needs of parents and children, they also face powerful, painful feelings within themselves. Sadness, fear of failing children and parents, fear of failing idealized expectations of themselves become "occupational hazards" of their challenging work. Peer support and guidance from senior professionals are critical in enabling young professionals to reach out to parents and children.

• **Through exploration of contrasting world views, parents and professionals discover complementary areas of expertise.**

The parents' intensive, daily experiences with their child add to the professional's general skills and awareness. When respect defines the parent-professional relationship, the parents' knowledge about their child and the professional's knowledge about his or her area of study work synergistically. The outcome is improved care and satisfaction for children, parents, and professionals.

• **Attitudes and beliefs greatly affect how professionals define and value their work with children who cannot be made perfect or whole.**

Models stressing cure of "acute" illness fail to grasp the realities of families and professionals caring for children with chronic conditions and/or disabilities. Although children may need many years of treatments and therapies and may never be made perfectly whole, professionals "heal" the hurt child and family in highly significant ways. Professional support, steadfastness, and "caring" help children and families create a healthy family life despite the unrelenting challenges of chronic illness and/or disability. Professionals caring for children with uncertain futures and long-term difficulties can derive heightened professional fulfillment from their commitment to the well-being and integrity of the family.

• **Parents of children with chronic conditions urge professionals to challenge cultural stereotypes that have often stigmatized and devalued people who are chronically ill and/or disabled.**

Parents urge professionals to understand that parental love is broad and inclusive, not narrow; parents love their children with special needs as they love their well or non-disabled children. A child's accomplishments and struggles are viewed within the context of the child's personal best; parents value and derive pride from the efforts of their children with special needs.

• **Through expanding one's world, the caregiver can better understand and appreciate the parents' perspectives concerning love, value, and disability.**

Such broadening of one's experience comes through carefully listening to parents as they talk about their children and themselves and through suspending preconceived judgments. There is no substitute for actively listening to parents as caregivers grapple with societal prejudices and strive to understand that children with chronic conditions are "children first."

• **Listening to parents' hopes and goals as one commits one's energies and skills to the care of their children begins a process of "building bridges;" parents ask for partnership, dialogue, and honest discussion.**

In appreciating the struggles and triumphs of children and families who require special services, professionals create a legacy of care and concern that counteracts despair. By empowering parents; by welcoming parents as active members of the health care team; by acknowledging parents as equals in the decision-making process, professionals enhance their own healing identity.

Parents and professionals are charting new territory on behalf of children in need as they share their skills. Such dialogue challenges traditional views; a parent-professional partnership based on equality may develop. The ultimate rewards of rethinking and reformulating the critical role of parents include improved care of children, improved relationships with parents, and improved satisfaction with one's challenging, difficult work.

HANDLING THINGS BETTER

Situations to ponder

STRESSORS ON STUDENT CAREGIVERS; REACHING OUT TO PARENTS IN EMOTIONAL PAIN

In the following vignette, a student explores her feelings as she attempts to reach out to a parent whose daughter has recently been admitted to the ICU. The mother's grief, intense distress, and inner turmoil are overwhelming. The child life intern expresses her fear of not meeting the mother's needs; her own pain as she cries with the mother; her embarrassment and shy withdrawal as senior professionals approach the mother. Overriding the student's own anxiety is her strong desire to develop a caring bond with Sarah's mother, to listen, to help. The student returns to Sarah's mother and joins her as the long vigil continues. Encouraged by her supervisors to share and thus begin to understand her responses, she writes in her journal:

Sarah

I saw her sitting alone on a broken down wheelchair left in the hallway as I hurried to do an errand. Afraid to ask, "How's Sarah?," I greeted her. She motioned her head away from the court yard to the purple doors behind me.

"Sarah's in ICU," she said. "I can only stay in there a short time. Then I have to come out. I can't stand it, to see her like that. All those tubes; she's got those tubes down her nostrils to help her breathe. It just hurts me bad to see her like that." Tears rushed to the surface. She wiped them from her face with a moist and crumpled tissue.

I stared, and I held onto my own tears. I couldn't speak.

"I'm sorry to upset you," she said.

"No, no," I said. "Sometimes it's good to cry. I just wish I could do something." The white floor and white windows glared. I felt uncomfortable in my body. I wanted to touch her, to comfort her, but I didn't know how. I became aware that I was standing above her. I sat beside her on the windowsill.

She told me all about Sarah, and several times she said, "She was never sick before this. I never saw her sick before. Sixteen years old and I never had her to the doctor except for her shots, you know. I don't know where this leukemia came from."

She told me how they had discovered that Sarah had leukemia, the exact date that she was diagnosed, and about all that had happened since then. I didn't know what to say. I watched intently.

The social worker approached us with a psychiatrist. Sarah's mom stopped in the middle of her story to respond to them. I didn't want to leave before she had finished. I wanted her to know that I had been listening - not to appease her until someone else came along, but because I cared. At the same time, I felt incapable and embarrassed in front of the social worker and the psychiatrist. I felt awkward and moved myself away from the windowsill. I told them that I had to return to the clinic.

I took a box of tissues from the clinic and brought them to Sarah's mother. I handed them to her, and she continued her story as if we had never been interrupted. Her father had died of leukemia here in this hospital one year ago. She didn't know whether to tell her mother that Sarah had been moved to ICU. "Sarah's my baby - my baby." (child life intern: journal entry)

The child life intern, through her steadfastness, handles herself well.

Perspectives

WHEN HUMANISTIC CARE DOES NOT EXIST: AN ADULT SPEAKS

The memories of an adult whose childhood was touched neither by emotionally supportive care nor modern surgical techniques underscore what these advances have meant in the lives of children and families. For this child and her family, choices were limited. Attempts to fortify and strengthen the child and family were marginal, at best, or completely nonexistent. Psychological and developmental issues were simply not addressed.

This adult articulates, decades later, what she suffered silently; expresses now what she could not express as a needy child. If children are to grow up "whole," "unscarred," "healed," the urgent goals of parent-professional collaboration must emerge clearly and powerfully.

My own experience represents one whose life has been permanently affected by facial disfigurement. I was born with a unilateral cleft lip and palate during the years when advancements in reconstructive technologies were being developed and refined by surgeons operating on disfigured victims of World War II. Born too soon to have benefited from those procedures, some of my surgeries actually worsened rather than improved my condition.

What would have been traumatic due to the invasiveness of the medical procedures themselves also became an experience of emotional abandonment and social isolation. Parents could not visit their hospitalized children. There was no Association for the Care of Children's Health, which is working to ensure parental and child rights during hospitalizations; there were no play therapists, team psychologists, child life specialists or patient representatives. In essense, psychological help for children and parents was nonexistent.

Coping mechanisms for achieving the emotional and developmental tasks necessary for a healthy childhood were acquired, if at all, by coincidence or good fortune. Though it surprises me now, I became so resigned to being the passive and compliant object of other people's desires to make my appearance, teeth and speech "acceptable," it never occurred to me that life's choices could or would ever include my own.

Due in part to early technological limitations, I had to undergo a series of surgical orthodontic and prosthedontic treatments in the early 1980's. As I was nearing the end of these procedures, repressed childhood traumas awakened within me. Painful memories haunted me.

Riddled with anxiety and depression, I began a long, painful journey back through my isolating and terrifying childhood experiences, through panic attacks, night terrors and flashbacks of traumatic surgeries without general anesthesia. Again, I felt the paralyzing powerlessness of the little girl who years before had longed to be known by more than her outwardly visible shell. (Elaine Wynn, Adult with cleft lip and palate seeks information from LFI members, *Let's Face It*, Vol. 2, No. 2, Spring, 1989)

Perspectives

WHEN BARRIERS TO COMMUNICATION FALL

In the following section, parents and professionals share situations in which parent and professional met as people struggling together. Barriers to open, honest communication had fallen. Moments of mutual understanding deeply affected both parent and professional; profound experiences touched parent and professional in unexpected, unique, healing ways. Powerful feelings were involved. A mother, a student, and a physician discuss such encounters: how their lives were enriched and views of "the other" expanded.

Eddie

After examining our son and trying to answer my many desperate questions, Dr. P hung his head and was very quiet for a few moments. When he lifted his head, there were tears in his eyes and a look of real pain on his face. With a faltering voice, he explained his position.

He said that he had gone to medical school to learn how to heal children. To do this he had to investigate and uncover the causes of their problems. He found the whole process very satisfying. But, he explained, with our son, it was not to be. He had been unable to determine the cause of Eddie's symptoms, and, therefore, was unable to effectively treat the problem.

He felt that he had failed himself, his training, me, and, most of all, putting his face into his hands, that he had failed our son. Several times he stated, "I am sorry. I am sorry."

For the first time, I was struck with how involved others had become in Eddie's care; in fact, they probably felt the same emotions I did in a different degree. The tears, fears, and frustrations we shared that day have bonded a relationship that will never end. (Eddie's mother)

Janie

Today was by far the saddest I have had at the hospital thus far. I began my day, as I usually do, gathering art supplies, opening toy cabinets and energizing myself for the morning. Today we were to make masks. Sue asked me to help, and I agreed eagerly, for I knew most of the children in the clinic this morning. The children and I were laughing and playing only a little while before the screaming started.

The screams were not the screams of an infant but rather of a young girl just off to the side in the finger-sticking room. From my vantage point I could just make out the child thrashing about. The children and parents saw it as well; it left a horrible tension in the room.

What happened after that left a real pit in my stomach—it was the first time that I saw one of the parents cry. Janie's mom, who always seems so collected and strong, just started to cry. Very casually I walked over and told her that she should feel free to take a break if she needed one—that I would look after Janie.

Then she started to talk. She said that she was upset because on Friday the doctors did a spinal tap and bone marrow procedure on Janie. It killed her to watch her baby have to go through all of this. She said that she felt bad for the child in the room and for all the parents and children in the clinic. She said that it was awful that these children had to face things that many adults would never have to confront. (I have often had similar thoughts and feelings. These children must deal with horrors that many adults will never see.)

I told her that Janie was a great kid, and she responded by telling me that Janie liked me a lot. That meant a great deal to me, but still I felt so bad for this mother. I guess it goes back to something my mother has always told me when I have been sick. She has felt helpless because she loves me so much but cannot alleviate my suffering. My mother has said that this is one of the most difficult parts of being a mother. (child life intern: journal entry)

Linda

The hospital's fluorescent lighting renders a bitter glow to the long, uninviting waiting area. Despite the bright harshness, children play tag and jokingly tease one another. Several of the younger children, clutching their parents, dare not move.

Linda is happily chatting with her favorite pediatrician. Today is just a "check up" and rest from her long, arduous chemotherapy regimen. Her father, who has come with her to every clinic visit, barring none, since the ordeal began, wistfully glances at his child. He is relieved that Dr. M is with her.

For the first time in several months, he and I are alone. Linda is safely joshing at the other end of the hall, and he is able to reach out to me. We talk about how well she has done; her returning to school; her hair growing back.

Am I spouting forth empty talk? Father nods his head, but his words come as a shock, a grim surprise: "Yes, it is going O.K., but I can't relax. Years ago my best friend in high school died of Hodgkins disease. Three years after diagnosis and treatment, he died. I watched it all, I saw it all."

We talk about the circumstances surrounding Linda's diagnosis and first hospitalization one year ago. Father has held a deep, abiding memory of the staff involved with her diagnosis and the survival statistics quoted at that time. He cringes and cannot believe that the year has gone well.

We talk about his care and concern. Mom and dad both work. Dad's schedule allows for clinic visits. Mom is present for each hospitalization and spinal tap. We talk about his easy going humor with his daughter and the family's embracing love. I thank him for sharing a part of his past that may help us to understand a bit more of his world. I thank him for his trust. "No one knows until you've been through it," he states. I agree.

I later approach the pediatric staff. We talk about Linda; how well she is doing; how important it is to share Linda's new status and more hopeful prognosis with her parents. The sensitive pediatricians meet with Linda's parents to reassess Linda's prognosis. Several weeks later Linda's mom is in the clinic. Mom crosses her fingers as she quietly, whispering, tells me that Linda is now in the 70 per cent group — 70 per cent chance for a total cure.

As I leave the clinic, I think of Linda's father: Thank you Mr. G. for sharing your most dread thoughts with us. Once the pediatricians knew of your deep and lonely fears, they could make attempts to allay the nightmare. Feeble attempts, yes. No father wants a "per cent survival" tag placed on his child. Does "70 per cent", magical number that it is, dare to invite breathing room for hope? Hope — despite the grueling two year treatment; long, long clinic waits for blood count lab results; endless probes and needles; hair loss and fatigue. Hope. Perhaps, hope edges her way in slowly, slowly like a tiny rootlet greedily burrowing a path into the earth. (PTL)

Contrasts

VALUES; CONGENITAL DEFORMITIES AND FACIAL DEFECTS

Parents of children with congenital deformities and facial defects emphasize their love of their children. There is also much pain: Will my child endure rejection by others? Will barriers of prejudice and fear constantly confront her? Society's emphasis on a stereotyped picture of physical beauty adds to the burdens families bear. The following vignettes contrast a health care professional's anxiety-ridden comments with a parent's point of view.

Connie

For us, destructive experiences with health care professionals fall into two categories — total insensitivity and. . .giving an opinion that is out of their expertise. On the total insensitivity side, we have had several experiences so destructive that we have subsequently avoided those doctors. For example, one medical geneticist said when Connie was only a few weeks old that he "could not imagine an uglier face." Frankly I disagreed with him, but saw no possible reason for his making that statement to new parents. (Connie's mother)

Livia

When Livia was born with a severe cleft lip and palate I wanted to see her just as strongly as I imagine I would have had she not had the cleft. When the doctor brought her to me I examined her face as any mother would. I was filled with curiosity about her misshapen mouth and nose. Far from disgust or repulsion, I fell in love with my daughter's unique face - the only times I felt the shock of her differentness was when I saw her in the mirror, in a photograph or in the reactions of stranger when we ventured out in public.

When Livia had her first surgery at 10 weeks of age, I was by no means looking forward to the surgical repair of her nose and mouth. Certainly I wanted her to have the repairs to improve her functional ability and of course to help her look as much like other kids as possible. However, as Livia's mother, I loved her face just the way it was. I grieved at the thought of losing the precious face that my baby was born with. I wasn't sure how I'd feel about the face to come.

I discovered after Livia's first surgery that I went through the same process of falling in love with her new face as I did when she was first born. During recovery I held her constantly and gazed at her face, again with curiosity about the changes. When we returned home after a week in the hospital I went directly to the photo album to see Livia's newborn pictures. To my surprise, for the first time I felt the impact of the shock that others felt when they initially saw Livia. In five days I had released my attachment to Livia's newborn face and had thoroughly fallen in love with her "new look." This pattern repeated itself in subsequent surgeries; each time bonding with Livia after surgery enabled me to release my attachment to what was and to embrace her new face and embark on the next phase of the reconstructive journey. (Jill Saunders writing in *Let's Face It*, Fall, 1988)

When parents look at their baby, cuddle and caress their child, they do not see a deformity. They see, touch, and love a whole child beyond external appearances: they see with their hearts. Society has only rarely provided a framework to appreciate parents' perspectives. Health professionals may experience initial fear and shock when caring for children with deformities.

Before approaching parents and children, it is crucial that young professionals begin to understand such initial reactions: Do my values extend beyond superficial perceptions and images? What is my vision of what is truly beautiful about people and life? Does my view of children include more than "cleft palates," "absent ears," "deformed bones?" These difficult questions challenge myths and fears and bring caregivers closer to parents and children. A medical student, who was fortunate to have had much guidance and support as she struggled with these questions, writes about her experiences with Jimmy.

Jimmy

During my first session in the playroom, Jimmy, a scarred and disfigured 6-year-old, angrily threw toys into the water table, squirted water around the room, and grabbed toys away from other children who dared to come over and play. He was impatient, shouted at both the children and child life workers and demanded more and more soap to create angry "volcanoes" in the water. Imaginary "victims" were dying in Jimmy's raging storms and seas; they could not be saved.

The intensity and anger of this child haunted me. I was shocked, horrified by the scars that twisted his face and hands. I wanted to learn more about Jimmy. Supervisors encouraged open discussion of our feelings about the children. Sharing my fears helped me a great deal. I began to talk with Jimmy while he was playing at the water table. As we played together, running the soapy water through our fingers, making bubbles and watching the ships go down under the stormy waves, we made a game out of guessing all the new and different things the bubbles could become. In time, we discovered that the seas could be calmed — the foamy bubbles could also become soft clouds and cooling snow as well as horrible engulfing flames. The tension in Jimmy's voice and body relaxed as "water play" became a focus for our beginning friendship.

As time went on, I began to notice Jimmy's compassion for others in the playroom. He would make his paper airplanes for the very ill children and take younger children by the hand to help them around the hospital. He tried to master his own fears by caring for the younger, less experienced children in the hospital.

Anger and hurt were part of Jimmy's reality. One afternoon, a 13 year old patient, Peter, who had previously befriended Jimmy, began to tease Jimmy. Peter, angry and frustrated by his own multiple hospitalizations, tugged and pulled at Jimmy's clothes. Jimmy exploded, and with all his strength, struck out wildly at Peter. Peter, twice Jimmy's size, just laughed. Enraged, Jimmy began throwing chairs at Peter.

Chaos reigned. We separated the boys. Screaming that he hated the playroom and everybody, Jimmy pulled away and turned to the wall in the hallway. We waited with Jimmy. He slumped to the floor and, with his face buried in his hands, began to whimper.

He could not hold back his tears and cried deeply. We sat with Jimmy as he sobbed and wept. Tears welled up in my own eyes as I gently put my hand on his shoulder. When he was ready, Jimmy turned to us, took our hands, and asked us to stay with him as he went to his room. (a medical student/summer child life intern)

Situations to ponder

VALUES; WHEN PHILOSOPHIES CLASH

Parents urge professionals to state their values and philosophy concerning the treatment of children with challenging needs and disabilities clearly, directly, unequivocally. When the professional's belief system clashes with the parents' values and wishes, clear, open discussion of opposing points of view is critical. The professional may, after communicating his or her position, want to withdraw from the case. Parents, too, may seek out other professionals who share their own orientation and values; professionals who will be their allies when difficult decisions must be made.

However, if the professional does remain with the family, he or she is obliged to work within the family's value system. The professional cannot pursue his or her own beliefs furtively without the parents' consent. A mother of a child with many challenging needs writes of an extreme situation in which parent-professional values not only clashed, but the professional secretly worked against, undermined the parents' stated wishes and desires for their child.

Keough

The most destructive and painful experiences we've had with medical personnel were due to our original pediatrician who, 20 minutes after our daughter's birth, informed us that she had Down Syndrome and an unformed esophagus and offered to let her starve in the hospital's nursery. We declined and had her airlifted out of state for surgery. She remained out of state for 2 1/2 months, but came home healthy with a repaired esophagus.

When we began having trouble with cyanotic spells a month later, this pediatrician told us it was nothing to worry about and that she would "grow out of it." After two months of this, with cyanotic spells about three times weekly and me calling the doctor after each one and doing CPR on her twice, we drove the 500 miles to Salt Lake City and admitted our daughter to the tertiary hospital where a faulty stomach sphincter was diagnosed and repaired. An unfortunate by-product of her having to be placed on a ventilator following the surgery was that she had to come home with a tracheostomy, which defied all efforts at removal for 6 1/2 years.

We changed pediatricians immediately on returning home and found that when our daughter's records arrived from the first pediatrician, there was absolutely nothing noted about my calls or office visits about the breathing problems. We later learned from his receptionist that he had been telling his staff that we were fools to be wasting time and money on a baby who would grow up to be a "gork" and have usefulness only as a "pet."

It has taken me years to forgive him for his initial suggestion regarding starvation, but I will *never* forgive him for his lack of action after we got Keough home. We had made our decision regarding her life, and he was still trying to let her die for what he saw as our own good - when he no longer had any business doing so.

Perspectives

VALUES; WHEN MUTUAL GOALS OVERCOME DESPAIR

Valued relationships with parents and children may develop under circumstances fraught with apparent hopelessness and fear that little can be done. Despite such anxiety, support of parents' decisions concerning their children may lead to relationships that deeply enrich the caregiver's professional and personal worlds. A child psychiatrist working in a developmental evaluation clinic tells of such an experience:

Tony

Before meeting Tony and his mother, my only contact with people who had severe autism had been with very young preschoolers. Tony was eighteen. Upon first meeting Tony and his mother, my heart sank within me; I was shocked by the degree of Tony's impairments. He was nonverbal, often flapped his hands when under stress, and could tolerate little change in his environment. Tony would repeatedly line up cups and endure terrible tantrums if their order were changed in anyway.

Tony's mother, a smiling, perky woman, was totally committed to having him home with her for as long as possible. She sought out summer programs and Saturday respite care and became a great resource for our parents' group.

Life with Tony was stormy. Any change whatsoever—either external or internal—was traumatic. He required several brief psychiatric inpatient admissions; his mother and I worked together to adjust and fine tune his medication. Our goal was to prevent the panic that sent Tony into fits of uncontrollable rage.

Despite Tony's overwhelming problems, one fact was clear: Tony loved his mother. I would see his eyes light up around her. Many times her gentleness would calm him. Frequently, her concern and devotion would calm those caring for Tony throughout his rocky course.

Was I helping? Was I doing any good at all? Was I giving Tony's mother the concrete tools she needed to manage his rages and outbursts?

Were we, in fact, doing "all" that could be done given the depth of Tony's disability? Together we tried our best. Tony's mother and I had come to appreciate each other's efforts. We both were trying to keep Tony in his home for as long as possible.

When I left the clinic, I learned that our meetings, phone calls, and many prescriptions had become symbols of our relationship. As a good-bye gesture, Tony's mother gave me a lovely gift—a plaque—"a treasured memory." On it rest a rose and a message of friendship.

The rose and memory of friendship are now with my own little boy who often asks me about the "pretty picture" hanging in his room. (PTL)

Through the parent-professional partnership, Tony's mother and doctor created a "space" in which sharing and respect flourished—a barrier against despair and helplessness.

Diagnosis

Bad news is bad news. Nothing can make the announcement of a serious problem light-hearted or painless; it is neither easy to hear nor easy to give such news. (Laura's mother)

* * * *

The time surrounding the birth of a baby who is very ill or who has disabilities is terribly sensitive. For a lifetime, parents have planned for and dreamed about the birth of their child. Suddenly, hopes are shattered. The loss is one of enormous proportions. Parents grieve. Few people seem to understand. (Cari's mother)

* * * *

At two-and-a-half, Rosemary had many delays but progressed nicely in school. She learned some sign language and used a communication board. She had names for all of us and fed herself. Rosemary was loved by everyone who knew her. She played like any other child. She loved other children and would smile and get excited when the school bus picked her up! She was far from deaf or blind or a vegetable - "who wouldn't amount to much" - words hospital staff had used to describe Rosemary on her first day of life. (Rosemary's mother)

Introduction

Parents and health professionals begin their dialogue at a time of great stress for both (Tarran, 1981; Wolraich, 1982; Moses, 1983; Simon, 1987; Turnbull & Turnbull, 1987; Leff, Chan, & Walizer, 1989). The sharing of the initial diagnosis sets the stage for all future parent-professional encounters. It is at this intensely painful point in the parent-professional relationship that issues of trust, caring, and mutual respect are emblazoned in bold relief in the family's memory and consciousness. The following chapter will present six areas of mutual concern as parents and professionals begin their journey:

Impact of the Diagnosis

Meeting Critical Needs

Caregiver Stress: Bearers of Bad News
Guidelines for Caregivers
Parent-To-Parent Support
The Meaning of Hope

IMPACT OF THE DIAGNOSIS

The diagnosis of a serious illness and/or handicap in one's child presents parents with a crisis of overwhelming dimensions (Olson, Edwards, & Hunter, 1987; Leff, Chan, & Walizer, 1989). Previous ways of viewing and integrating reality are challenged. Parents describe the magnitude of their pain in terms of an existential crisis, a gripping confrontation with the unfairness, injustice, and fragility of life. It is a time of disequilibrium, grief, and intense emotional reaction (Poyadue, 1988; Leff, Chan, & Walizer, 1989). Ted's mother writes:

> Frequently, the first people to tell parents about the child's problems are the health care professionals. While it is true that there is no easy way to destroy a dream, there are better ways to initiate people into the new world they will now inhabit. Far too many parents report these first experiences to be mishandled with the very poorest of manners. Health care professionals should write this down when they doodle, underline, or highlight: Listen and look carefully. A parent's world is falling apart. He or she is strong enough to put together a new world with a little hope and direction.

COMMON THREADS

Parents may experience any or all of the following under the impact of a diagnosis:

Fear

For parents, fear is the common thread that twists and knots itself throughout all diagnostic crisis points. Fear is projected onto the future. How will my child be accepted by others? How will we financially meet her needs? What will be the quality of his life? Fear is felt throughout the child's life as parents deal with new programs and transitions.

Isolation

The diagnosis of a serious illness and/or disability in one's child may drive deep, painful wedges between parents and their families and friends. Parents may feel isolated, bereft of support, bereft of those upon whom they had previously depended. A mother shares her painful experiences and discusses the new social network that developed during her daughter's first year of life:

Just Be There

As I sit back and relax after cleaning up from my daughter's first birthday party, I can't help but reflect back on this past year since that devastating day when the doctor diagnosed my newborn daughter as having Down syndrome. But even more devastating than her diagnosis were the people in my life who let me down after her birth. I have had some family members and friends whom I counted on for support in those first horrible months who just were not there for me.

My message is that if you know someone who has given birth to a baby with Down syndrome or is going through any type of crisis in their life, be there. The people I will never forget are the ones who said nothing, but just held my hand while I cried. I will never forget the letters of support from people in my community saying, "You can handle it". . . or even the phone calls from people who called to say, "I don't know what to say."

On the positive side, I have made new friendships throughout the year, and the people who did stand by me through the tough times are sharing with me the joy of a precious, precious little girl who has brought more happiness in my life than I ever imagined was possible that day one year ago when the doctor said, "There is no doubt in my mind; your daughter has Down syndrome." (Joan Crater, *Down Syndrome News*, September, 1987, p. 96)

Emotions and Reactions of Grief

Parents express the powerful, often overwhelming, emotions of grief they experienced upon learning of their child's serious illness and/or disability. A more detailed discussion of the meaning and significance of grief work in the lives of parents and families will follow in the next chapter.

SHOCK. My most painful experience was the initial evaluation that our son was impaired neurologically. The grief, crying, pain, anxiety, *loss* were awful. There are still times when waves from those first few days of formally knowing return. However, I feel that no professional could or should have cushioned these feelings. Support, yes; cushioning, no. Our distress was a necessary human reaction that helped us push forward to investigate appropriate programs. I must add that the bad news was coupled with specific recommendations for treatment and programs. We were able to focus our grief and anger in ways that helped our child. (Larry's mother)

DISBELIEF. I knew Rochelle had problems, but I couldn't face up to the fact that this could be a life-long disability for many months—at no fault to the many doctors, friends, family, and professionals that tried to help me. I just wasn't ready. (Rochelle's mother)

ANGER. Shocked, angry; I was so careful before and during my pregnancy. We were tortured by his sufferings. I longed to put him back inside me where he belonged. No one is so naked as a premature baby. I was angry at science's ineffectual interference; my baby was saved to be tormented. (IVH Parents Newsletter, p. 2)

FEELINGS OF BEING OVERWHELMED. I was a basket case. I came home from the hospital to a house with a bassinet, crib, baby clothes, flowers, but no baby. I cried throughout the day every time I thought of my daughter. When the doctor called with the news about the hemorrhage, I thought my heart would break. My husband just rocked me till I calmed down. We prayed a lot. (IVH Parents Newsletter, p.1)

A SENSE OF LOSS OF CONTROL. This diagnosis was really crushing, and not for ourselves, but for what it meant for Laura. One hopes for goodness and mercy for one's children. (Laura's mother)

ATTEMPTS TO PLACE GUILT AND BLAME. I have also come to realize the burden I have escaped by having Lauren as our daughter through adoption, not through birth. I am guilt free! Just as I have no part in her conception, development or birth, I have no part in her facial deformity.

. . .In working with parents in the Hamilton Area Chapter of

AboutFace, I have come to realize just how difficult that guilt can become. With each operation or invasive procedure, guilt can come rushing back, robbing parents of energy and hope. With no specifics as to the cause of a cleft lip and palate, *every* action during pregnancy becomes a possible, even probable cause. Thus grows the ever widening circle of guilt. (Jane Richardson, *AboutFace*, Vol. 4, No. 6, November/December, 1990, p. 2)

PESSIMISM OVER THE FUTURE. Expect us to have some true depression, sorrow, anger, fear about ourselves and our child. Our parent roles have suddenly changed, and we are scared and uncertain of our responsibilities . . . (Carla Lee Lawson, *Prescription for Participation*, Iowa Pilot Parents, Inc.)

DISTURBED SLEEP. The dozen nights that passed before we could bring Laura home were even longer than the days. I was exhausted, yet I had trouble sleeping. I am ashamed to say that I gave in to the compelling impulse to take a little cloth diaper from Laura's hospital bassinet, which had sat forbiddingly empty next to my abandoned bed. It smelled of her; at night, in my own bed, I clasped it to my shoulder and slept a fitful, dream-filled sleep. (Laura's mother)

TIMING

From parental accounts, four rough groupings emerge which describe common timing scenarios for learning of a child's serious illness, disability, or problematic condition:

- during the neonatal period, in the delivery room or during the hospital stay immediately after birth;

- after a period of dawning recognition and worry;

- after a trouble-free beginning, when the child has been healthy until stricken;

- after previous troubling diagnoses, when a new concern has shown itself or been confirmed as an additional problem, (one which may be more serious than initial concerns.)

Each of these scenarios carries its unique burden of power and pain. In each case, parents must recover from the shock.

IN THE NEONATAL PERIOD. A new child is, in all cases, a child of hope and possibilities; parents can only wait to see how their child grows and develops, though they will have dreams for him. Inevitably, all parents must give up unrealistic hopes, but this can happen slowly, and in the context of other gifts that emerge. An ill or disabled newborn has been deprived outright of some of life's possibilities. As yet, the compensations are question marks. Thus, parents of a newborn with difficulties are now bereft and vulnerable in special ways. Great care must be taken to give truthful information in a compassionate way that strengthens parent-infant bonding (Clyman, Sniderman, Ballard, & Roth, 1979; Leff, Chan, & Walizer, 1989).

The silence of a delivery room staff fearfully avoiding contact with the new mother or father may be the parents' first sign of trouble. The moment of birth, rather than being joyous, holds tension, uncertainty, even terror itself. One mother recalls:

> After I pushed Patty out, I didn't hear any cry, and everyone was silent. When I asked if the baby were OK, no one said anything. I started to get really frightened and asked what was wrong with the baby. *Still* no one said anything. Finally after I said something like, "I know something is wrong so you better tell me what it is," one of the nurses told me that the baby had a cleft lip. I was very grateful that she finally told me the truth. I was sure that the baby was stillborn or had some horrible deformity by the way everyone was acting. It was actually a relief to hear that she had a cleft lip after what I had been imagining.

Parents may be told of their baby's problems as they are recuperating from the delivery during the first hours or days of the baby's life. It is a time of intense vulnerability. A mother speaks to caregivers:

> If my child is diagnosed at birth, let me love my child as a child, but in privacy without other new moms who don't understand how I'm feeling and may want to enjoy their child without feeling guilty. Let me decide if I want rooming-in, siblings, visitors, or a private room: I'll tell you—just make these options available. Let me change my mind, too. At that time, I am very mixed up emotionally.

Even in the best of outcomes—normal labor, uneventful birth, healthy baby, warm bonding—the neonatal period includes physical discomfort and exhaustion, hormonal mood swings, and the anxiety of new roles and responsibilities. Parents of ill or imperfect newborns experience all of these normal strains at the same time that they may be faced with urgent decisions and crushing pain. At the time they most need protection, reassurance, and the pleasure of shared joy, these parents encounter alarming demands, fear which cannot be comforted, the necessity of informing others of their unhappy news, and, often, separation from their infant. The mother of a child with a facial deformity describes her experience:

> After Victoria's birth, I was obviously put on the maternity floor. This caused much pain when the other mothers would get their babies for feeding, and I had nothing. I would also hear the babies crying, and this would make me want to hold my baby terribly ... Even though the birth of our daughter was very traumatic, one nurse took a picture of our baby (which is normally routine). That picture was all I had as our daughter was immediately transported to the medical center, and I had to remain at the community hospital.

As dramatic technologies increasingly "push back" the limits of viability, parents of extremely premature babies with grave or uncertain prognoses encounter excruciatingly difficult ethical, psychological, and financial conundrums (Farrell & Fost, 1989; Rosenthal, 1991). Profound questions and dilemmas confront these parents at every turn in the care of their extremely ill and premature babies: How long will our baby suffer? Can our family endure the pain and anguish? What will the future bring? Who will support and guide us as we struggle with unbearable choices and decisions? Who will be there to help us cope with the consequences of our decisions—whatever they may be?

Such agonizing questions are among the most difficult parents and professionals must face. The mother of a baby who spent the first 80 days of his life in the neonatal intensive care unit explains:

> Nobody at the NICU seemed to understand our feeling that technology had taken over...
>
> For the sake of parents trying desperately to do the right thing and to make plans, provide them with a summary of latest literature. Take the time to convince them that you care about what happens after their infant leaves the NICU. (Ronnie Londner, IVH Parents, 1991)

These complex issues and painful conflicts call for open, thoughtful discussion. Parents ask that they—those who will shoulder the ongoing care of their children long after the NICU doors have closed behind them—

participate consistently and fully in this process. In a climate of growing concern for the long-term outlook for children and families, parents ask that they be valued as critical members of any decision-making team (Farrell & Fost, 1989; Kolata, 1991).

AFTER A TIME OF DAWNING RECOGNITION. For many parents, weeks, months, or years of growing awareness of their child's "difference" may precede official diagnosis. Jim's mother hopes for change since her earliest years with her son:

> In my case, the most destructive experience was not being told that there were concerns about my son when he was born. I took him home, only to go through three long years of "dawning recognition" which was painful and bad for both of us. As a neuro nurse, I saw these things but tried to suppress them, just as his pediatrician did—"Go away and play with him more." But Jim wouldn't play, or couldn't, as other children could.

Health care professionals may "suspect" problems but fear talking about their concerns with parents. Parents, however, may sense from how they are treated or regarded by hospital staff that serious issues are at stake for their child. Neil's mother describes such a situation:

> I had personally felt something was wrong . . . mother's instinct? I just wasn't sure what. Every time I had gone out to see Neil through the nursery window at the hospital, the nurses were always listening to his heart. They also moved me into a four-bed ward all by myself!

Parents greatly appreciate professionals who, at the earliest time possible, offer clear explanations of suspicions and worries. A mother of three children with special needs emphasizes:

> I realize that it is not easy to share information that is not all good. With Len, his pediatrician said, "Maybe there are some problems!" There was nothing definite said. I feel that it is best to be as honest as possible. Lack of honesty delays and prolongs the grieving process. With Thomas there was denial on the part of his physicians in response to my questions—my many questions. It left me confused and unable to trust my own feelings.

Parents gain nothing from false reassurance. Confusion and lack of faith in one's own judgment result when parents' worst fears are not addressed openly, compassionately, honestly. Dennis's mother recounts her "first negative experience" as she began her long journey to understand and help her son:

> When my son was nine months old, we switched pediatricians and had our concerns regarding his development, or lack of, recognized. Our first pediatrician kept assuring us that there was no need for any diagnostic procedures to explore why Dennis was so delayed in his gross motor development. After we had begun to deal with his problems, we contacted her, and one of our questions was why she hadn't given us more direction. Her reply was, "The first six months are so special. I wanted you to to enjoy them. You'll be dealing with him for the rest of your lives."

Parents may meticulously observe their child for signs of "typical" growth, anxiously measuring their youngster against a "normal" sib or neighborhood toddlers. Fear and dread are daily companions of such parents long before a health care professional validates their deepest concerns. Attempts, however well-meant, to protect parents from harsh realities—to "soften the blow;" to "allow time for bonding"—cause much distress. Dennis's mother continues:

> The new pediatrician confirmed our fears and while my heart "stopped" when he said, "You really *do* have a problem," he also *directed us* to county services and *made contacts* for us that brought us into the California Children's Services System. He also has continually stressed that the key to Dennis' future lies with Dennis—that no limits should be set for him based on the progress of children with similar conditions.

Parents may react strongly when information is not shared immediately and openly. Trust in the parent-professional relationship is eroded. Deeply pained over their child's troubles, parents have also lost a helpful alliance. Hank's father states:

> In keeping the "bad news" from us they are also exercising power over us and the circumstances that we find ourselves in. This is unacceptable to us.

AFTER A TROUBLE-FREE BEGINNING. A catastrophe may befall a previously healthy or stable child. Accidents will happen to children of even the most careful parents. All children develop fevers, aches, and minor rashes, but in some instances innocuous symptoms are the presenting signs of serious, even life-threatening crises. In an instant, lives are forever changed. A mother shares:

> I am the mother of three wonderful children. Never in my darkest nightmares could I have imagined that one of my children would become seriously ill. The leukemia came as a grave shock. (mother of a child with acute lymphocytic leukemia)

Parents in these circumstances may feel robbed or unfairly punished. Suddenly, their lives are filled with frightening choices and overwhelming demands, and the stakes may be very high. Susan's mother expresses her painful feelings:

> All I want is for Susan to be "bad" again—the active, bright, mischievous little girl she once was. The weakness, fatigue, and swelling all started so innocently. The doctor, at first, gave her Benadryl for "allergies!" Things went from bad to worse. At the low points in her illness, she could not move - simply could not move. If she fell, she could not push herself up. I see her lying on the floor—helpless, weeping. I see her struggling to breathe—choking on her own saliva—the panic in her eyes. (mother of a young teen with the insidious onset of a rare neuromuscular illness)

AFTER PREVIOUS TROUBLING DIAGNOSES. Many parents of children with challenging needs may repeatedly endure the stress and pain of "diagnosis." Parents are never immune to new difficulties, new onslaughts, new blows. Jeffrey's mother speaks of the need for continuing awareness of the meaning of "diagnosis" to parents:

> Throughout the life of a child, there are many "initial diagnostic situations." Whether it be as simple as an ear infection, as serious as the recommendation for surgery, or as devastating as the need for using life support, the basics of good parent-professional relationships should not get lost or forgotten. . . Parent vulnerability never goes away. It is important to be a good listener—sensitive and non-judgmental —throughout the child's life.

The most experienced and competent of parents are not "prepared" to see their children once again in pain, suffering through additional treatments, procedures, adjustments. Professionals wisely avoid treating these parents like "old hands" when they refrain from taking short-cuts in sharing information or expecting rapid adjustment to the latest blow. Jesse's mother chronicles:

Since I wrote last, my oldest son, Jesse, has added yet another specialty clinic to his rounds. While doing a lower GI to look for the source of some persistent abdominal pain, the radiologist found a very large bone cyst in his left femur. The initial steroid injections were unsuccessful, so the orthopedic surgeon performed an experimental bone marrow graft from Jesse's hip to his femur. We're anxious to see the X-rays to see if there's been any improvement. If not, the surgeon says he'll repeat the marrow graft 2-3 more times before resorting to the standard bone graft with 8-12 weeks in a bodycast. Jesse has so many other medical considerations that no one is particularly thrilled about that option.

Meanwhile, he's still in much pain (referred from his femur into his pelvic area), taking narcotics, and on crutches to prevent a fracture. The frustration of chronic pain and doctors who hate to prescribe narcotics for kids has recently been eased. We were referred to the university's pediatric pain clinic. They've been wonderful, and our doctors are delighted that someone else is now managing his pain meds. We started him on Elavil last week, with the hope of reducing his need for analgesics and treating the depression that comes with chronic pain. What a learning experience *this* has been.

Parents of children with multiple serial difficulties bear cumulative burdens. Parents may doubt their ability to summon energy for dealing with yet another problem. However knowledgeable they may be concerning "all" possibilities, new problems or exacerbations strike with power and pain. Autumn's mother describes her despair around a hearing test, an examination which many health care professionals might consider a relatively minor event:

Autumn has a hearing test at the hospital (a Cleft Palate Team suggestion). They put her to sleep and evoke responses from her brainstem. *I am so nervous I can't even sit still.* She has never taken a test yet where they came back and said, "She's just fine."

This is no exception. The nurse tells me that Autumn has a mild hearing deficit in both ears. It's probably due to a lot of fluid in her ears, indirectly a result of the cleft palate. I call the plastic surgeon. He sets a date to close the palate and put tubes in her ears. (Janet Troy, *Facial Expressions*, August, 1988)

These scenarios are not mutually exclusive. Each situation represents a point of stress and vulnerability. Reflecting on ten years of seasoning, Laura's mother writes:

I can see our own experience in each of these "categories." I can bear remembering, but I cannot forget, the dreadful fear when my beautiful two-day-old baby turned blue in my arms. It was so horrible to call the celebrating family members and let them know that she was terribly ill, that no one knew what it was yet, that she might die. We were actually relieved to learn that it was a heart defect; at least the enemy had a name.

And then, after she lived through the surgery and we were all just beginning to recover, an additional diagnosis was made with far-reaching implications for her future. It hit us like a ton of bricks.

Still, we were managing all of that; then came her second heart surgery, when she suffered the crippling complications. We had trustingly handed over this lively, jolly little baby girl, expecting that this was the last hurdle before she would be perfectly healthy, and we got back this sick, angry, limp infant with her legs pulled out like a frog's. And we lived through a year of false reassurance, while we grew more and more concerned because she did not walk, could not even stand.

After that was clarified, we still had several new health concerns that reared their ugly heads unexpectedly. Many of these later problems have been more frightening and far-reaching than the original problem of congenital heart disease.

No matter what, you never get used to getting bad news.

MEETING CRITICAL NEEDS

Just as parents are beginning the complex, difficult journey through the normal grieving process, they are also being introduced to the pressing demands of caring for their child with special needs (McCollum, 1981; Simon, 1987; Poyadue, 1988; Leff, Chan, & Walizer, 1989). Professionals who understand the meaning of the crisis to parents, who listen to parents, who offer guidance and support, set the stage for building a healing relationship. A mother writes:

Recognize that the parent is an integral part of the care team. As soon as it is feasible, get the child back into the mother's arms. Help the bonding take place. Often times because they have relied on the professional to "make their child better," they feel they no longer can add anything to the child's life. Help them to realize that isn't so, that they make the "educated" decisions—

that the child is their child. This will only help to strengthen them through the years to come. If they feel supported from the onset, they can become strong, loving parents. (Julianne Beckett, Comprehensive Care for Medically Vulnerable Infants and Toddlers: A Parent's Perspective, *Equals in this Partnership*, NCCIP, 1985, p. 11)

Parents' struggles do not occur within a vacuum. If the child is a newborn, parents are immersed within a hospital system that may either aid their efforts to bond with their infant or, through ignorance or thoughtlessness, unwittingly erect additional barriers and burdens (Steele, 1987; Leff, Chan, & Walizer, 1989). Mothers of infants with special needs describe how staff nurtured and respected the parent-child relationship.

Nurses who decorated the crib, had contests for who had the cutest stuffed animals, talked to parents and shared information with parents, were valued and appreciated. These nurses made the parents feel as if their babies were cared for as babies, not as objects with tubes and machines. (mother of Joshua and Miriam)

* * * *

A nurse provided me with an option for breastfeeding, the use of an electric breast pump so that I could provide Thomas with breast milk. My husband has allergies, and I felt that breast milk would be best for Thomas. At that time, I did not know that Thomas was severely allergic to dairy products and soybean products, nor that I would be using the pump for two years. (Thomas's mother)

* * * *

The nurses in Neonatal ICU were helpful. The majority of them were patient and relaxed as they worked with us to figure out how to feed Patty and teach her how to suck. They had a "you'll figure it out eventually" attitude which was reassuring. They didn't minimize the difficulties of caring for a baby with cleft lip and palate, and they didn't act as if it were a tragedy either. They went over aspects of baby care like bathing, etc., and didn't just focus in on Patty as a "cleft palate baby." They talked about how beautiful Patty was: they saw the whole baby and not just "THE CLEFT." (Patty's mother)

* * * *

My child was born in a small mountain community. . . After the initial shock of my child being born by Caesarian section, I noticed how purple, yellow and tiny she was. One nurse helped me with the bilirubin light schedule for my baby's jaundice. But more importantly, she would hold, massage and talk to the little bundle I didn't, as yet, know I could love. She taught me how to encourage my baby to nurse and told me about her five-year-old niece with Down Syndrome. I kept in contact with her for several years. I remember that she asked her sister and ex-brother-in-law to write to me and tell me about Down Syndrome. I now see how the nurse provided a model for me and nurtured my bonding with my baby. (Sandy's mother)

When lack of knowledge or carelessness interfere with the helping process, parents experience despair and doubt. They feel deprived of the support they so desperately need from their child's caregivers. Such early negative encounters will affect parents' faith and trust in their child's future health care.

Professionals were unfamiliar with our daughter's condition. Because of their inexperience, they put her in isolation and did not allow us to touch her. To my knowledge, there was no medical reason for this separation, and it caused much anxiety and depression for me. (Victoria's mother)

* * * *

Like many parents, my first negative experience occurred during the hospital stay when Jeffrey was born. A nurse told me he couldn't be breastfed because he was retarded. I didn't listen to her. I expect these experiences will never end. (Jeffrey's mother)

Parents are immensely vulnerable at the time of diagnosis, the beginning of the crisis. Parents are attuned to and dependent on the environment—both positive and negative. Perhaps at no other time are environmental supports as crucial to rebuilding hope and confidence as they are at this juncture in the family's life (Leff, Chan, & Walizer, 1989) . Ron's mother stresses:

The medical people who were the most supportive and helpful let their caring and feeling come through to us. They would warm the stethoscope, wrap the baby after a procedure, give me a hug when I needed it. They were always professional, but treated us with kindness, care and respect for our abilities to cope.

...Some painful events at the hospital still haunt me. At times, interns would interrupt my breastfeeding to do tests on Ron. After the tests, he would be left naked, covered with Betadine, on a table. This prompted me to scream, "Hey, my son is not a pork chop!"

For people in turmoil, the importance and value of apparently simple helping acts are magnified many fold. Basic support, such as quietly listening to parents' worries and concerns, goes a long way in encouraging parents to regain strength and faith in themselves (Moses, 1983; Leff, Chan, & Walizer, 1989).

> There have been nurses who will come in and sit with me during their breaks—not to talk—just to "be there" after a poor prognosis has been made. This gives me time to "soak" up the prognosis and try to to see how it fits into my future. At the same time, it allows me to absorb some of the strength that flows from these special people. (mother of Eddie, Janet, Tracy, and Lori)

> * * * *

> The professional does not have to feel that there are "right words" to say to parents following a devastating diagnosis. Often the professional's "being there" is what is most helpful to parents. After my son was born, my obstetrician would call me in the evening and ask if everything were all right. He was a quiet, sensitive man who knew I needed his support. Four or five years later I returned to the hospital to thank him once again. (mother of Patrick, a child with Down syndrome)

Many health care professionals, working in acute care settings with limited time exposure to parents and infants, experience difficulty in appreciating the far-reaching significance and consequences of how parents are treated during the diagnostic phase. Years and "lives" later, parents vividly recall, in exact detail, the setting and tone of how they were told of their child's diagnosis.

Kind, nurturing acts become powerful therapeutic tools. Health care providers reinforce parents' self-esteem with caring responses, such as referring to parents and infants by name and gently wrapping or touching the infant. In the technological, life-saving, busy hospital environment, these simple gestures of respect may appear small and inconsequential. However, from the parents' perspective, physical and emotional support will be remembered long after the child's hospital stay (Leff, Chan, & Walizer, 1989).

> I'll never forget a very kind surgeon who stood silently with me at my baby's bedside and gently put his arm around me. I was,

and remain, most grateful to him for this simple gesture of support. (Cari's mother)

* * * *

There was a nurse who said, "I'm sorry," when she entered the room and saw a hospital gown hanging over the picture on the wall of a mother and a very normal looking baby. (Thomas's mother)

Innocent lapses in care and poor communication among staff members loom large in the hearts and memories of vulnerable parents.

At times, nurses coming onto a new shift would be uninformed about our daughter's birth defects. One came into my room and asked where my baby was and if I wanted to feed her. She did not know that my baby was at another hospital. (Victoria's mother)

* * * *

After several weeks of having our daughter in one spot in the nursery, she was moved without anyone's informing us. When I walked in and did not see her, my heart sank with anxiety and fear. Please give parents information regarding changes in their child's care before they actually arrive at the nursery. (mother of Joshua and Miriam)

Parents derive comfort from knowing that health care providers have faith in their resilience even though they may be temporarily overwhelmed. Such faith and positive regard will have long-lasting effects on the parent-child relationship (Clyman, Sniderman, & Ballard, 1979; Wikler, Wasow, & Hatfield, 1983; Leff, Chan, & Walizer, 1989). Through respect for the family unit and open, sensitive communication with parents at the time of diagnosis, health care professionals lay the groundwork for a positive parent-professional partnership (Shelton, Jeppson, & Johnson, 1987).

It is extremely difficult for parents to deal with any difficulties their child may encounter. Nevertheless, the health care professional's ability to approach and handle the situation appropriately can make a great deal of difference in the way the parents (and ultimately the child) react. Don't dwell on the handicap. Treat the child as a child first. Be honest and knowledgeable. Give us facts on our terms, but don't talk down to us. Give comfort and support: "We're all with you." Take time for details and questions. We have so much to absorb, and we are scared. Be positive and friendly—it helps. (mother of Tammy, a child with a diagnosis of autism)

CAREGIVER STRESS AS THE "BEARERS OF BAD NEWS"

Professionals who must "bear the bad news" often experience to some degree the fear, uncertainty, and pain gripping parents (Leff, Chan, & Walizer, 1989). Anxiety is common. Diagnosis creates a crisis situation for the family; for the professional a different sort of ongoing crisis is present (Doernberg, 1982; Wolraich, 1982; Shonkoff,1983; Olson, Edwards, & Hunter,1987). What happens when health care professionals find that the baby or child is terribly ill and/or seriously disabled? What happens within the health care professional when his or her patient or client cannot be made "perfect," "whole?"

Feelings of hopelessness and helplessness may overwhelm some professionals and interfere with their ability to reach out compassionately to families in great need. In the face of the parents' intense distress, caregivers may feel inadequate, unable to comfort, fearful of the parents' pain. Guilt, uncertainty, distress, and doubt in one's identity as a healer all contribute to the professional's discomfort and anxiety. A pediatric resident speaks of how his own inner turmoil affected his relationship with a parent:

> One of the most difficult parts of my job is telling parents that something is wrong with their baby or child. My hardest time was talking to the mother of a baby we had evaluated. I had to tell her that her child was really delayed, severely impaired. *Nothing* in my training had ever prepared me for the pain in her eyes, her shock and despair. I was shaking inside. I was all alone. I didn't know what to say to her. It was even hard for me to look at her. I just wanted to run away. (personal communication: pediatric intern)

Young professionals may feel totally helpless in such a situation. The emotional costs of conveying painful information truthfully with compassion can neither be minimized nor ignored. Witnessing the grief, tears and anguish of parents and children is excruciatingly difficult (Leff, Chan, & Walizer, 1991). Professionals who "bear the bad news" need support and understanding from colleagues and peers.

It is crucial for young professionals to understand that through their presence and involvement they are able to recover their "healing" identity. Parents consistently emphasize that while caregivers may be unable to make the child perfectly whole or well, they can help the parents and child in meaningful ways. In offering information, concern, and availability despite pressing anxiety, caregivers participate in the life of the family in a very special, healing way.

By embracing such a difficult role, however awkwardly and hesitantly at first, professionals, both young and old, actively join parents in their struggles for dignity and self-respect—"health" in the midst of devastation and pain. Accepting this important role involves the "risk" of sharing painful moments with parents rather than withdrawing and creates unique bonds that deeply comfort parents (Leff, Chan, & Walizer, 1991).

> When the neonatologist told me about my second son's intraventricular bleeding, I flipped out—screamed and cried. The neonatologist sat with us and took the time to stay with us. I know that he must have been incredibly uncomfortable. I later wrote to him to thank him for his special kindness. I will always appreciate the support he gave at that crucial moment. (mother of Barry and Bobby, twins with serious neurological problems)
>
> * * * *
>
> It's hard to communicate when you're so vulnerable, and, in this case, everybody's vulnerable—parents, staff, and the kids. And to risk pain and exposure when you're in pain—that's as tough as it gets. (Bill's mother)

As parents endure the trauma of discovery, they will experience a broad range of intense, often conflicting emotions. Professionals must expect to meet parents whose feelings and reactions fluctuate: the turmoil of diagnosis may propel parents from peaks of rage to the depths of sadness and despair.

Parents ask caregivers to be the steady compass during the storm. Parents ask caregivers to understand that with guidance and support most families will "make it," will integrate the painful reality into their ongoing lives, will experience the day-to-day victories. Patrick's mother, an experienced nurse, shares:

> In our role-playing sessions with the nurses, we throw trays, cry, and scream. I want our nurses to be prepared for a wide spectrum of parents' reactions to "bad news" about a child. I realize that nothing truly prepares a young nurse for the despair and panic in a father's or mother's eyes—the despair and panic in one's own heart. Our role-playing brings home the reality of parents' grief and encourages new ways of approaching parents in crisis.
>
> I want our staff to know that there are no magic words to say to parents. Honest "people talk"—"I'm sorry. I don't know what to say, but I do want to help in any way that I can"—is far better than empty cliches. Steadiness—not running away from troub-

led parents, not dismissing parents as crazy—is tremendously important. I also want our nurses to understand that despite the devastating news, they *can* be of great help and support to parents. Listening to parents is at once the most difficult and most rewarding aspect of their work.

Maintaining a "steady state orientation" may be particularly difficult for inexperienced professionals who have not had the opportunity to participate in the growth of families and to nurture the strengths and abilities of parents. Parents urge young caregivers to believe that most families will emerge from the crisis; unfaltering professional regard and respect can be a driving force in fostering family "success." Lyn's mother makes the following suggestions:

> I think it is important for students to hear from parents one, two, five, ten, even fifteen years down the road from diagnosis. All too often professionals who must tell parents about the child's problems only see parental pain and anguish; young professionals need a broader perspective, one which stresses how parents and children do find their way along their journey of love and commitment. . .Your readership would like to know that having a child with special needs at home within the community can be a joy for all concerned. . .

GUIDELINES: CONVEYING PAINFUL INFORMATION TO PARENTS

Parents offer the following guidelines for professionals who must "break the news:"

• **When the initial diagnosis is given, make every effort to inform both parents together.** They need the opportunity to meet adversity as partners (Poyadue, 1988: Leff, Chan, & Walizer, 1989). Ken's mother, currently involved in establishing parent-professional seminars, hopes that her experience will never be repeated.

> The most painful experience was the way I was told Ken had Down Syndrome. The doctor came into the hospital room with a nurse and blurted flat out, "Your child has Down's. Do you know what that is?" When I said, "Yes," (praying not to cry), he said, "OK," turned on his heels, and left. I had to tell my husband alone and saw this bear of a man shrink in front of my eyes.

Laura's mother emphasizes:

> Grief is lonely. We each wanted comforting desperately, but we couldn't ease one another's pain as we struggled with our individual devastation. Informing only one, or informing separately, drives still more of a wedge. Too many men report that they were expected to "be strong" and take the news and then tell their wives and comfort them; it took them much longer to be able to express their misery for fear of failing everyone. At least if the parents were told together, there is one less hurdle to get over in the process of surviving and renewing the partnership.

Too often the pain, despair, and crushed hopes of fathers are minimized: their emotional needs for support and understanding go unmet; perhaps are not recognized at all. Myths die slowly: "Men-must-always-be-in-control;" "Men-do-not-show-their-pain;" "Men-are-not-emotionally-attached-to-their-babies." A father describes how such myths affected the way he was informed of his newborn daughter's problems:

> I remember the doctor saying, "Your wife's child is brain damaged. You're going to have to help her." My reactions were of a man who had always tried to be in control: I was devastated. The reliance on knowledge that I had counted on to guide me did not help here. As a man, I had received little or no training in dealing with the flood of emotions that. . .occurs when you do lose control. In coming to grips with the trauma, I have come to understand the different expectations for men and women in our society.
>
>   In effect, the doctor's words told me this child was not mine. She was brain damaged, and I was responsible for taking care of her and my wife. The assumption was that the important emotional relationship was one of mother-child, not father-child. His words also conveyed an expectation that men have better skills than women for dealing with emotional upheaval. We are expected to be stronger, not to need emotional support ourselves, to be able to hold things together. Men pride themselves on being able to do this, but they need help. The lack of support for my emotional needs was to be repeated many, many times. (Phillip Davis in Remarks Made by Fathers of Children with Special Needs, *ACCH Network*, Vol. 8, No. 2, Spring, 1990, p. 8)

• **See parents in person at the earliest opportunity. Arrange for a quiet, comfortable setting.** *Privacy is crucial.* If possible, ask the parents if they would like the presence of a supportive professional, a family member, or a comforting friend. This is likely to be an emotional time. Protect the parents' dignity by granting them time alone together to regain their composure after the painful conversation (Leff, Chan, & Walizer, 1989).

• **Set aside time for the parents only.** Avoid interruptions. If possible, turn off beepers and request phone calls only for emergencies. For an office visit, the end of a workday or a "day off" may be preferable. Leave time for discussion. As one parent says:

> Don't make people feel that they are an inconvenience. Parents may want time now, but that doesn't mean they will always need your time. (Ken's mother)

Parents are acutely aware of the many responsibilities of professionals and of the multitude of demands on their time. Yet at a moment when they are desperately needy, your time is an irreplaceable gift. Stay with them.

> . . .Imagine that words used in normal, everyday conversations weigh two pounds each. When you are telling parents that their baby has had a brain hemorrhage, or irreversible retinopathy, or any other horror, your words weigh 1,000 pounds each. The breaking of bad news may be a difficult, but not unusual event for you. You know you have to do it, and you want to get it over with. For many parents, the way they receive that news is seared into their brains. The smells, the sounds, the pattern on the floor, the color of your shirt—those things are remembered in some special place in the brain reserved for calamity. When you talk to parents, find a quiet place. Sit down. Sit back. . . (Ronnie Londner, IVH Parents, 1991).

• **Good communication skills are essential.** Introduce yourself. Sit at eye level with the parents. Address the parents by name: Mr. and Mrs. Be aware of the parents' level of fatigue and physical discomfort. If the child is a neonate, the mother may be recovering from a difficult delivery; the father may be exhausted. Gentle touch is a powerful nonverbal way of expressing your concern (Clyman, Sniderman, Ballard, & Roth, 1979; Doernberg, 1982; Leff, Chan, & Walizer, 1989).

Communicate regard for the child as an individual. At a time when parents are fearing that their child has somehow been diverted from the mainstream of life, your behavior may powerfully communicate a message of acceptance and inclusion. Using the child's name is one such means.

The nurse who was present at Sara's diagnosis realized that parents of special kids need to hear good things about their children just like any other parent. She spent a lot of time with me telling me how beautiful Sara is and pointing out such things as her long eyelashes. (Jan Mariska, *Acceptance is only the first battle*, MUAP, 1984, p. 29)

• **Choose clear, direct, accurate statements.** A simple sketch or drawing is often helpful to parents. Be direct and open about what is known for certain. "Considering the magnitude of the decisions involved," Jill's mother states, "only the best—[most current and most accurate] —information will do." Parents need to be told the truth, however painful. Parents need to be told the *whole* truth. The truth can be told in a caring way and with hope.

Certainly those who are concerned about how much parents should know and when they should know it operate out of generous concern for families. But they should save their support to help one *handle* the whole truth, not use it to shield parents from the whole truth. (Minna Nathanson, Family Roles in Medical Decisions, *The Candlelighters Childhood Cancer Foundation Newsletter*, Vol. 6, 1982, p. 3)

* * * *

I remember as most helpful the doctors at the hospital who told us everything that was going on—even what they weren't sure about. A wonderful surgeon explained the procedures in understandable, lay terms with drawings. Doctors who felt they had to "protect" us by keeping information from us caused much pain. The unknown was far more terrifying than being told the hard facts. (Ron's mother)

* * * *

Don't lie or sugar coat. Be straight out. Give options when possible and include parents in decisions . . . . . it is *their* child. Tender and considerate "frankness," human concern, touching, hugs, etc. are most appreciated. (mother of a young man whose death was due to trauma)

* * * *

Our initial meeting with Patty's plastic surgeon was helpful. He laid out in detail all the steps of repair. He showed us photos of other babies after their repairs, and this was very reassuring. He also acknowledged that the whole process could be very draining and that we would all be driven crazy eventually. He presented everything with a good combination of hope and reality. (Patty's mother)

• **Be sensitive to problems of conflicting information.** In reality, there is often a great deal of uncertainty concerning diagnosis and prognosis. In such situations, frequent communication with parents decreases anxiety (Leff, Chan, & Walizer, 1989).

> There is no easy way to tell parents. For us, it was a day to day trauma, and we had frequent discussions about the prognosis for our daughter. I wanted answers, and I didn't want to wait. The doctors couldn't give me those answers, and it was difficult for me to live with that uncertainty. I am grateful that they did not make any sweeping judgments and that they taught me to take it one day at a time. (Cari's mother)

• **Never be afraid to say, "I don't know" to parents when difficult questions arise.** Parents value professionals who are able to acknowledge the limits of personal knowledge and help parents seek out appropriate resources.

A professional who must respond, "I don't know," could also add, "but I will find out and call you within the week." He or she could also respond, "Perhaps, the speech therapy people or child life department can be of help to us." Parents view such honesty and openness as a sign of caring and concern. Not only does the professional thus assist parents in answering their many crucial questions about treatment protocols and programs for their child, but he or she also "takes care of" the parents as well. The message is clearly, "We are in this together. We will work together for your child's good."

> Our pediatrician was up front and honest as soon as he recognized Sara's problems. He answered questions I had right away. If he didn't have answers, he looked for them and scheduled a conference with us for the *next day.* The timing was crucial because I wanted to know so much and informational delays were maddening. (Jan Mariska, *Acceptance is only the first battle,* MUAP, 1984, p. 29)

> * * * *

> Our current pediatrician . . . has no ego problems with saying, " I don't know," when he doesn't, and is happy to call [our expert] for advice. And Dr. J himself . . . has no problem in telling us that he doesn't know when he doesn't—but he keeps looking and asking at medical conferences. (Keough's mother)

> * * * *

> I would like to believe that professionals are now being taught that there is no shame in asking for help and in no way does this asking reflect on their competence. (Ken's mother)

* * * *

I have most appreciated, "I don't know. We might get an answer from this source." If answers to our many questions have not been known, I have valued the health professional who has honestly said so. "This is not known" has been hard for us to accept but ultimately kind and helpful to our adjustment. (Larry's mother)

* * * *

So. . . openness: it hurts, and it can be discouraging, or it can inspire families to keep looking and trying instead of being lulled into thinking that we have done everything we can. The professionals have to be honest and, what must hurt them, especially the inexperienced ones fresh out of school, is that sometimes they have to tell families that they don't know, they don't have an answer, and the family should get a second opinion. (Hank's father)

• **When the family must embark on a long journey of diagnosis, several sessions may be required as the child completes a series of tests and procedures.** Parents urge professionals to take one step at a time and refrain from deluging parents with worst-case possibilities that might or might not apply. Cross bridges as you come to them; try not to project too far into the journey through this illness. There is a delicate balance between conveying information and overwhelming parents.

The neurosurgeon we saw on the first day gave us too much "information." Although all he said turned out to be true, as far as I know now, the tumor could have been a benign one, and lots of what he said wouldn't be true. It was so much at first that we felt flattened. (Wendy's mother)

* * * *

A few minutes after I was told that Patty had a cleft palate, a pediatric resident came in and said, "She may have heart problems, kidney problems and she may be retarded. We have to do an echocardiogram and a renal scan and probably some other tests because if a baby has one anomaly, it probably has others." This was too much. His litany of problems and the thought of my newborn being zapped with radiation was terrifying. True, a pediatrician has to check for associated problems, but it was too much to assimilate at one time. I told him he didn't have our consent to do anything until we [met with our] private pediatrician and consulted with her. (Patty's mother)

• **Be wary of making predictions.** The health care professional who gives the broad spectrum of the child's possible capabilities without making long-range predictions conveys hope. Joan's father points out how absolutes—"never," "always"—have negatively affected both his family's life and his relationships with professionals:

> The most destructive and painful experiences with health care professionals have been: "Your daughter will not live a year; take her home and make her comfortable. Your daughter will not live to age 5, your daughter will not live to age 12, your daughter will not live to age 16, your daughter will not live to age 21. A state institution is the best place for your daughter. A state institution is the best place for children like that. The state institution is a wonderful place. She will never do that. There is no money. Take her around to the back; she is upsetting the normal patients. In my professional opinion, God has chosen you. God only gives you what you can bear. You already have a special place in heaven. We can't do that. We won't do that. You don't understand. You would be better off if she had died. NO!"

No two children are alike; even those sharing a disabling condition will differ in significant ways. Dennis's mother reflects that ". . . the most helpful encounters are those where the health care professionals remind us to keep an open perspective."

Outcomes in many situations are unpredictable. Balance truthful information with hope.

> We don't want to hear crystal ball predictions of what our children won't be able to do. Allow us to hope, and remember that most parents of kids with disabilities have a story of at least one incident where their child proved a professional wrong on his/her prediction. (Kim's mother)
>
> * * * *
>
> Parents too frequently are given predictions of their child's far-off future. Parents count such predictions among their most destructive experiences. For example, parents of an eight-year-old boy with arthrogryposis, who now walks with crutches, rides an adaptive bike, and swims, were told, "He won't walk." Parents of a ten-year-old child, who now is only two years behind in language development, were told, "He won't talk." I was told that my son, who currently talks too much because it is difficult for him to modulate himself, would never speak. (Larry's mother)

• **Expect strong emotions and reactions.** Parents are utterly vulnerable to their children's misfortune. Under extreme stress, parents may deny or distort information and/or display hostility or anger. Health care professionals must expect and accept strong emotions as part of the grieving process. Parents need to be reassured that intense feelings are aspects of mourning— an individual process (Moses, 1983; Leff, Chan, & Walizer, 1989).

Caregivers who neither flee nor minimize parental grief offer comfort and support that parents will never forget. Parents acknowledge that it is painful for health care professionals to witness their grief, anger, hurt, fear. Anxious professionals, at a loss for words, may grope for something "right" to say. Empty cliches or random, gratuitous comments may be blurted out (Leff, Chan, & Walizer, 1989). Say less rather than more when searching for something to say. Simple, honest statements, such as "I am sorry that this has happened" or "This just isn't right or fair," send a message of concern and caring. Moments of shared silence may comfort and heal.

Parents appreciate caregivers who openly acknowledge and share their distress and discomfort (Leff, Chan, & Walizer, 1991). Reflecting the parents' feelings is often helpful to parents in distress. "Eye contact, touching, tone of voice, and body language all contribute to our continued communication." (Carla Lee Lawson, *Prescription for Participation*, Iowa Pilot Parents, Inc.) Value the potential healing impact of your presence on the lives of parents in crisis.

> When the doctor informed us, he was quite certain of the diagnosis. We knew it was not easy for him. This was a doctor, though very reserved, who was passionate about his work and cared very deeply about the babies under his care. This was comforting to us. (Cari's mother)
>
> * * * *
>
> Take time to acknowledge the shock. Don't be afraid to show a little emotion. We felt soothed to hear our doctor say that it wasn't fair. (Wendy's mother)
>
> * * * *
>
> We acknowledge your discomfort in the "telling parents" role. However, if we see only your "professional self" and hear only your objective terminology, great distances will be between us forever. (Carla Lee Lawson, *Prescription for Participation*, Iowa Pilot Parents, Inc.)

* * * *

Being able to share my feelings with professionals and then having them cry with me touched me deeply. (Rochelle's mother)

• **Follow-up is critical.** Parents often need several meetings with the professionals involved in the diagnosis of their child. Discussion over time enables caregivers to evaluate parents' reactions and possible misconceptions. Careful, sensitive listening to parents' unique worries and concerns should guide practitioners. Parents need to hear information many times. Strong, painful emotions can make it difficult to take everything in and recall it later (Vining & Freeman, 1985; Olson, Edwards, & Hunter, 1987; Leff, Chan, & Walizer, 1989). Provide written information if you are convinced that it is accurate and appropriate.

> Many times even two people participating in one of these meetings can hear different sets of information. A brief, written statement of the situation will confirm the parents' understanding. . . It could be child-specific or simply information about the disease. Parents need to know that they are going to meet again [to ask questions and clarify their concerns]. They need to know when. (Barbera, et. al., 1988, p. 6)

• **Give parents something to take away from the meeting,** whether an outline of a treatment plan, a pamphlet, or simply a slip of paper noting their next appointment to talk. A written statement confirms the parents' understanding and can be shared with family members and friends. Parents in a state of shock need tangible evidence that action is planned, that they have something to do that expresses their feelings of helpless, anguished love, their desire to protect their child, their hope for a partnership with those caring for their child.

• **Hold out a hand of courage and hope.** Support and empower parents with concrete aid. From the first moment a serious difficulty is confirmed, needs spring up. Professionals implicitly acknowledge parents' desires to care for their children when they at once offer referral to appropriate service systems, respite programs, financial resources.

> Parents need to leave with hope; not false hope, but hope for what is going to happen to their child in terms of services and support. (Barbera, et. al., 1988, p. 6)

* * * *

Don't destroy my vision of my child as a human being. Give me the normal hope of love between a parent and child for however long, short, retarded, gifted, normal, physically impaired, or chronically ill our relationship may be. I don't need extensive medical details as much as I need information about how to live my new life. If the health care professional can't provide this, it really is his or her responsibility to put me in touch with someone who can. This is my first contact with the vulnerability of life. (Ted's mother)

* * * *

Parents NEVER forget what is said at the time of diagnosis, and often it sets the tone for the child's medical experience. Choose your words carefully, and let the message be as hopeful as you dare. It's OK to say you don't know, but be sure to follow it up with reassurances about what is known and what can be done. Feeling helpless is bad enough without feeling hopeless as well. (Sherelyn Campbell, *A Few Words to Young Professionals*)

GUIDING PARENTS TO SOURCES OF EMOTIONAL SUPPORT

Of great importance is the professional's role in guiding these parents, these families, to sources of emotional support. Again, the more quickly this occurs, the better. A mother covers many points in discussing the significance of emotional support:

One of the best things anyone has ever done for us happened very early in our story. Perhaps that is why it was so very valuable: it came at once, while we were reeling with pain and shock and desperate fear for our child.

We were just beginning to recover from her near death and heart surgery as a newborn when the diagnosis of Turner Syndrome was made. My background gave me pessimistic insider's knowledge. . .

One of the research doctors who had been called in because of the Turner's made a special point of meeting us along with our pediatrician—on his own time, at the pediatrician's office. And here is the most important part: he arranged for us to meet a woman with Turner syndrome (TS). It was just unbelievably heartening. What it gave us was tangible hope—a person with a graduate degree and a career and a positive adjustment, even though she had been born well before any of the standard hormone therapies were available. What her presence gave us was the feeling that Laura, too, could grow up! (Laura's mother)

PARENT-TO-PARENT SUPPORT

Parents vividly recall and appreciate these earliest supportive contacts with "senior families." Families are given hope that they, too, will survive, even flourish. A mother emphasizes how her conversation with an "experienced" parent altered both the way she saw her child and the way she viewed her own personal goals and possibilities.

> We were referred to a pediatrician whose youngest child has Down syndrome. In his waiting room, we saw a large poster of a man with a little Down's girl riding on his shoulder — both of them laughing their heads off—with the legend "Children value themselves as they are valued." The man in the poster turned out to be the pediatrician we'd come to see.
>
> [Several] things stand out in my memory of our conversation with this man—first, that children with Down syndrome look like their parents. This seems obvious to me now, but at the time it was a revelation. When I held Keough in the hospital later that day I examined her in a new light and saw my husband in her. She stopped looking like Winston Churchill and became part of the family. . .
>
> The pediatrician mentioned in passing that his wife is a judge—a brief remark that reopened my personal world. It said to me that parents' lives can continue to grow, that Keough was an addition to—rather than a termination of—our dreams and plans, that my career goals might be slowed but would not have to be completely sacrificed to Keough's needs. I really needed to hear that. (Sue Duffy, *Acceptance is only the first battle*, MUAP, 1984, p. 32)

The role of parents helping each other, supporting each other through formal and informal networks, is singular and unique. Parents repeatedly and movingly emphasize, stress, the power of parent-to-parent support—from informal discussions with other parents in the hospital parking lot to membership in ongoing groups that meet regularly and consistently over a period of many years. Self-help networks offer parents the opportunity to share, cry, and laugh together without the onus of outside judgment; within the safety of fellow-feeling. The anguish that isolation and loneliness bring is diminished.

Other parents. . . provided me with a context—often just by listening without trying to reassure me; sometimes by reinforcing half-formulated plans of action; occasionally by confiding fears that mirrored my own. My own healing during Nicky's illness began with those parents. . . (Ann Oster, *Equals in this Partnership*, NCCIP, 1985, p. 30)

* * * *

One is never more alone than after one's child has become or has been found to be ill or disabled. One encounters rejection and distancing from others—even those from whom one has a "right" to expect better. One withdraws, bruised and hurt. A support group, no matter how small, helps not because "misery loves company," but because one is no longer alone! . . .

And don't worry too much about a perfect match. I have long-standing friendships made "in the trenches"—in hospital corridors, in budding support groups—and they have been priceless to me. (Laura's mother)

* * * *

When I saw a copy of the *Let's Face It* newsletter, I read a story about a little boy who, like Derek, was born with a deformity. In the story a mother described her relief when she met a parent whose child had a similar condition.

At [the hospital] I met, for the first time, a mother whose ten-year-old son had microtia, and I can't tell you what it was like for someone to say "I know how you feel" and realize that she really does know how I feel. (Andrea McGuire quoted in Brotman, M., New ears for Derek, *Let's Face It*, Vol. 2, No.1, Fall, 1988)

Parents discuss the reluctance of some professionals to help them "find" one another, to encourage parent-to-parent support.

But it can be a complicated task for families of disabled and at risk babies to find their peers—particularly during the first few months or years when the future is a list of unimaginable possibilities rather than a clear diagnosis. Nick was nine months old before I met a mother whose baby had similar problems . . .

Through policies of confidentiality and professional territoriality, the system impeded our access to each other instead of encouraging this crucial human contact. (Ann Oster, *Equals in this Partnership*, NCCIP, 1985, pp. 30 & 32)

* * * *

On this point, what I would like to say to professionals is: build bridges between people. Understand that support for the parents gives strength and courage in the long struggle to help a needful child. Don't be afraid to do something out of the normal scope of official duties. . .

There are just a lot of things that never come up during office visits, yet parents need to talk about them, and one's spouse cannot be IT all of the time. Parents of ill children may be more so, but I think all parents need supports of this sort. This need really seems to become imperative with the additional strains of birth defects or illness.

Even our very best pediatrician, whom I would otherwise hold up as an ideal, was unaware of such basic groups as Compassionate Friends. To his credit, when I provided the information, he did pass it on to a family who had lost a child. This was a very caring thing for him to do. (Laura's mother)

Perhaps, lack of knowledge and understanding of the goals and effectiveness of parent-to-parent support have in the past contributed to this practice of not helping parents join together. Parents repeatedly and movingly emphasize, stress, the value of mutual support along their journey.

The great thing about a strong parent network is that when you are feeling isolated and alone, it doesn't take too many calls to find someone else who has experienced exactly what you have gone through. (mother of Eddie, Janet, Tracy, and Lori)

* * * *

It may help to know that we do a lot more laughing together than crying. Although we often come in the door frustrated, angry, bitter and feeling helpless, we rarely leave that way. Support group is generally *not* a place where people come and fall apart at the seams. If and when that does occur, we can almost always patch the seams to hold for another couple of weeks. (Jan Mariska, *Acceptance is only the first battle*, MUAP, 1984, p. 13)

* * * *

The most beneficial encounters I have received in the "medical" portion of the care of my daughter have been through the medical training we parents receive at our national, state and local conferences and meetings. Our speakers are neurosurgeons, eye surgeons, orthopedic surgeons, urologists, brace specialists and others who cover all phases of the medical care of children and adults with spina bifida. (Amber's mother)

* * * *

At the top of my list is support. It's been important to me to be in touch with other parents who have children with special needs. We share common frustrations, rejoice together about the achievements of our children and understand the significance of the small victories. When our children are together, we don't feel quite so odd, stared at and misunderstood. (Cari's mother)

Professionals may fear that parent-to-parent support will threaten parents and add further burdens to parents of newly diagnosed children. Parents speak directly to this fear:

Unlike our social worker, who was extremely sensitive and supportive, some want to keep families of children who have died or who are not doing well away from others— particularly newly diagnosed families. They fail to understand that from the moment of diagnosis [of childhood cancer], every parent inside is facing the death of his or her child. Parents who demonstrate that they are coping or holding on in spite of this can be of real comfort and strength to newly diagnosed families. (Minna Nathanson, Family Roles in Medical Decisions, *The Candlelighters Childhood Cancer Foundation Newsletter*, Vol. 6, No. 1, 1982, p.1)

* * * *

For some reason, professionals can be very reluctant to put parents in touch with one another. Maybe they are afraid it will be upsetting, spread erroneous information, or turn into professional-bashing. . . Parents are quite able to assess the relative value of input, to spot the aggressively bitter, and to avoid pitfalls—and we have never forgotten the doctor who was not afraid to help us meet another person who might have something to offer us. (Laura's mother)

Parents greatly appreciate those professionals and institutions who actively aid them in their quest to meet and join together (Leff, Chan, & Walizer, 1989). There are ways to protect confidentiality while encouraging this vital form of parent and family support. Parents, children, and professionals reap the benefits of such efforts.

We went to the one person we thought could help, . . . the social worker at the [Children's Hospital]. Becky said she would look into the possibility of starting a support group. In August 1987 she called to tell us she had four other people who wanted to join a support group for Crouzon Syndrome, and in October of that year we had our first meeting.

The room was filled with energy and enthusiasm. It was great to be with people who understand the fears, isolation and prejudice that happen when a family member has a facial anomaly...

The group had a family picnic in June and in my daughter's words: "It was so neat to go some place where you didn't have people making fun of you or calling you names or staring." (Dianne Wachendorf, Indianapolis comes Face to Face with people who care, *Let's Face It*, Vol. 2, No. 1, Fall 1988, p. 5)

* * * *

My support group for CAH, the Congenital Adrenal Hyperplasia Support Association, Inc. (the acronym being CAHSA, pronounced "CASA" like "house" in Spanish), held its first meeting last Sunday. This meeting was beautiful! Practically everyone who attended had never before met another person with CAH. One patient was 35 years old!

It was so rewarding for me to see these people respond with such enthusiasm and gratitude. There are 70 patients on file at the university health center; they range in age from 8 months to 35 years. Twenty people responded to the letter the university sent out for me. (Beth's mother)

* * * *

Parents need to be needed: parents need to help others avoid the pitfalls, cope with the enormous stress and despair. For example, our hospital has encouraged a "veteran parents" program in the NICU. Parents of a baby who has been in the NICU for at least ten days are hooked up with parents of a baby who has been recently admitted. We bring our parents a rose. We share our phone numbers and help make the initial contacts with community agencies. We are a resource for doctors and nurses. (Patrick's mother)

The emotional needs of fathers of children with chronic and/or disabling conditions have only recently been acknowledged and openly discussed. Fathers, too, need each other. Peer support—sharing the pain, joy, successes, and challenges of day-to-day family life—reinforces and strengthens men as they reorder priorities and commit themselves to the care of their child (Meyer, Vadasy, Fewell, & Schell, 1985; May, 1991). A pioneering organizer of self-help support groups for fathers shares this experience:

> One way to deal with our pain is to deny that we have it. A glib "I'm fine," or "Everything's great" masks the confusion and concern men feel regarding their families and the struggles they are going through.
>
> I think of the man who installed my storm windows a few months back. His manner was gruff and hard, and we made little eye contact. Upon completing the job, he used a phone in my office. On the desk was a copy of a book about families of handicapped children. When he saw it, he brusquely asked me, "What do you know about handicapped kids?"
>
> Upon my telling him about my job, he unloosed 20 minutes of unbridled anger about the past 15 months of his life since his special needs child was born. He complained bitterly about the medical costs, the stresses experienced by his wife, and the loss of a job.
>
> It was evident that this was the first time he had openly shared these thoughts with anyone else. What was also evident behind the frustration and anger was the immense love and concern he felt for his child.
>
> Not daring to interrupt, I let him share his stories, and when he was through I told him about groups of men who meet to share similar feelings and help support each other through their struggles. He was dumbfounded to learn that such groups existed. Like so many other men, he needed a place to vent his frustrations, share his joys, and reach out for assistance. (James May, *Focus on Fathers*, Vol.1, No. 7, May, 1987)

For their own reasons, professionals themselves may join support groups for families of hurt children; such groups almost always accept as members "any interested person." Caregivers thus gain a different perspective of family life, children with serious illnesses and/or disabilities, and their own role in caring for these persons.

> Health care providers would benefit from attending support group meetings. Their own perspectives and ways of seeing children with severe disabilities would grow. They would better understand the quality of life possible for children with conditions thought hopeless. (Ted's mother)

* * * *

We have been happier running our group ourselves with very little professional help. We sometimes invite professionals in to speak or to listen, and we are told by them that they have grown much in their understanding of our needs simply by listening to us. (Jan Mariska, *Acceptance is only the first battle*, MUAP, 1984, p. 13)

* * * *

Our support group met with two doctors from the pediatric clinic of our children's hospital. It was great! They explained what we could do to help them be more efficient, and we told them what we wanted. Guess what? They listened, and there has been change. (Ellen's mother)

Parents helping parents—be they two or three parents meeting over coffee to share their daily triumphs and struggles or organizations that are heard at high levels of policy-making and administration—serve several functions that extend well beyond the initial diagnostic period. Ongoing mutual support, exchange of information, and avenues that lead to advocacy and outreach to the general community are among the contributions made by the self-help movement. A father and social psychologist explains:

> Self-help groups promote... active participation by parents in the care of ill children. In such groups the strength and wisdom of every parent is multiplied by the efforts of many others. By meeting and acting together we share our pain and our joy, teach each other many important lessons and help each other through the hard times. These are all ways of improving the care of ill children and the quality of life of all parents and families. (Mark Chesler, editorial, *The Candlelighters Childhood Cancer Foundation Newsletter*, Vol. 10, No. 2/3, 1986, p. 2)

THE MEANING OF HOPE

An effective way of understanding what hope means to parents is to explore what it is not. Hope is not denial of the child's difficulties; hope is not withdrawal from treatment; hope does not come at the expense of the truth.

When Ron was initially diagnosed, I was told that I was in a state of denial. I often told Ron's therapists that I was in a state of hope and just to work with him and not to tell me about all the things he wouldn't be able to do. Ron's neurologist now says that my son does more than we would ever have dared to hope. (Ron's mother)

* * * *

One nurse upset me terribly the day my daughter was born. Although this is no longer the [policy], I was placed in postpartum after my daughter was born. They did their best to place me in a corner in a room of my own, but it was easy to overhear other parents calling their relatives and joyfully announcing the arrival of their new babies. It was very hard for me. At one point when the nurse came to check me, I mentioned that my baby was doing well. She said not to hope and reminded me that my baby was very tiny. I needed to hang on to every thread of hope I had, and these words of discouragement were devastating. I left the hospital the day my daughter was born because I could not bear to remain around the new parents and babies and "not hope" that mine would live. (Cari's mother)

Hope is addressing the child's problems with courage, energy, and faith in oneself. For parents, hope embodies the belief, the conviction that their love, care, and hard work will help; will help build the best possible life for their child in need. Parents of children who had suffered from intraventricular bleeding (IVH) episodes were asked, "Was anything particularly kind said?" One parent responded, "Nurses . . . said the baby is a fighter" (IVH Parents Newsletter). This positive comment was treasured, a sign of honest alliance in loving their child.

Seeds of hope sustain parents as they create a new life for themselves and their child; as they heal. Professionals who nurture hope leave parents with a lifeline.

The most helpful experience I can remember was with an older doctor who told me a story. He had been the family doctor for a family with three children who had Down Syndrome. The oldest child was very high functioning, able to attend regular school, graduate, find a competitive job, live in an apartment and lead a completely normal life. The second child was lower functioning, attended special education classes part of the day, had a job that was part of the school work program and lived in a group home. The third child was the lowest functioning of the children. He had many physical needs and was draining the parents. In turn, the parents were considering having him placed outside the home for the well-being of all.

After he told me this story, he asked me if I understood what he was saying. He wasn't able to tell me if my baby were going to be like the first, second, or third, but that I would be able to tell in time. My first thought was I wanted Ken to be like the first baby and lead a normal life. I was able to hang onto that hope while the healing process continued. I gave up the ideal life slowly over a long period when I was ready. This doctor didn't push me into reality because, in our case, there was no need to. (Ken's mother)

Hope is the hub around which family life revolves: hope is an absolute necessity. Parents urge professionals to appreciate the power of hope as they reorganize their lives and homes to meet the needs of their children.

> Provide me with some ray of hope. Robbing me of hope is the worst thing you can do to me. Remember that after I leave your office, I will create an atmosphere at home of hope or despair, and surely one of hope is better for my child. You can give me hope through your attitude and through what you say. Your belief that my child could defy the statistics will soften the facts you must tell me. Never hide these facts, but do not write the facts in concrete by using "never," "always", or other absolutes.
>
> For example, two doctors who had been evaluating my child used a bad news/good news approach. One told me the diagnosis, the bad news, and the other one occasionally added a few words of encouragement, such as "You can never tell— children learn to compensate in amazing ways." At the time, I heard only the bad news, but during the following months I remembered the encouragement more clearly and drew great comfort from it. When a parent is in despair over a child's condition, the slightest suggestion of hope goes a long way. Give me some small ray of hope before I leave your office. (Alexander & Tompkins-McGill, 1987, p. 362)

* * * *

> Most of all, we hope you will share a vision for our children who experience a disability; that they will be integrated, productive citizens, accepted, recognized for their strengths, and have a life filled with the same opportunities available to their non-disabled peers. (Cari's mother)

In the well-known legend, Pandora opens a forbidden box to satisfy her curiosity. All of the ills and sorrows of mankind are loosed, never to be recalled. Pandora's folly is kept from devastating the world because a small being — whose name is Hope — remains. The nature of humans is such that, given the slightest toehold, parents will climb up from despair to love and nurture their hurt children. The tool with which they chip away at their mountain of troubles is hope.

HANDLING THINGS BETTER

Contrasts

CARE DURING THE NEONATAL PERIOD

Parents are particularly vulnerable at the time of the birth of a seriously ill baby. How staff regards parents, how information concerning their baby is conveyed to parents will play a major role in their views of themselves, their baby, and their new struggle. The respect and care shown to parents during this period of shock and despair will be long-remembered and valued.

In the following section, Carl's parents describe the support and concern from the NICU staff that enabled them to face weeks of uncertainty in their baby's battle for life. For Dave's parents, however, information was conveyed brusquely, on the run, with little attention to the parents' needs. A legacy of pain and anger has remained over many years.

Dave

My child was in a neonatal ICU for 10 days after his birth. The first encounter we had with the head neonatologist was memorable and horrible. She had very bad news for us, and she delivered it quickly, bluntly, without giving us much hope. In 5 minutes she was gone , and we were left to cope - without a place to be alone, to sit down, to go, with no one to talk to, with no kleenexes!

I hated that doctor after that, and yet, I don't really know if she could have told us the news in an easier way. Maybe the news so colored the encounter that I can't be fair about it.

I do believe that there should have been some kind of immediate support system offered to us as well as a longer term support system . . . a place to go, someone to talk to, someone to give us more information, maybe a softer technique by the doctor talking to us. At least, the physician could have invited us out of the ICU to talk in private, where we could have sat down. I've always felt very angry about that encounter.

Carl and Stuart

Stuart died about 30-45 minutes after he arrived at the tertiary neonatal center. We had the most sensitive, caring head nurse and doctors. We were asked (thank God, I *never* could have asked) if we would like to hold him. We checked his tiny, perfect body; touched his soft, velvet skin; cried; and kissed him good-bye. When our nurse came to take him away, he asked if we would like a picture of Stuart that he had taken. We clung to that picture. As we were mourning for Stuart, Carl continued his up and down road, and we were told that he might die, too.

We went on the roller coaster for the next three months. Carl was intubated for six weeks, had a PDA, a blood exchange, pneumothorax so many times that I lost count. He needed five chest tubes in at one time! He weighed only one kilo and was only 14 1/2 inches long.

The social worker at the hospital was invaluable. She came to see us everyday, called, told us whom to contact. The nurses held our hands and guided us through. Everything was always explained very clearly. We were encouraged to ask questions; visit; call; cry; and laugh.

We met with Carl's primary nurse, primary doctor, and the neonatologist daily and discussed what was happening. Our other children felt welcomed. They touched their brother; asked questions; put up pictures for him. I can not say enough for everyone at that hospital . . . The nurses and doctors we had taught us not to be afraid.

Both Dave's parents and Carl's parents encourage professionals to explore ways of communicating with parents of sick newborns that open rather than close doors of caring. "Bringing bad news" is a job rife with tension and anxiety. There may be a wish, a strong pull to avoid or flee parents—their tears, their questions, their neediness. By holding firm, by remaining with parents during a period of deep pain, the healer's own role is reaffirmed. The hurt family is supported and nurtured.

Parents understand how difficult it can be *not* to run from their distress. However, the positive ramifications of steadfastness and availability will last long beyond the neonatal period. The lingering anger and hurt Dave's parents express are replaced by memories of support and concern. The staff caring for both Stuart and Carl helped the parents to recover their strength despite catastrophic circumstances. The staff caring for Carl helped his parents to value their role in their son's care and enabled them "not to be afraid."

Contrasts

INFANCY AND THE DIAGNOSIS OF DOWN SYNDROME

Both Neil's and Sandy's parents endured a long, complicated waiting period for results of chromosomal studies. Despite the anxiety surrounding the parents' long wait, Neil's parents and their family physician were able to develop a trusting, caring relationship that would support the family through the crisis. Unfortunately, this was not the case for Sandy's parents.

Sandy

At first the doctors joked with my husband and asked if everyone in our family were that "funny looking". Then possibly realizing that there may have been a problem, nothing else was said until one doctor later came in and told us that our baby could have "trisomy this or trisomy that"—all of which were fatal—or a number of other syndromes. He asked us to call our insurance company—I think the hospital office could have done that—to see if a chromosomal analysis were covered. He bluntly, coldly stated that my little girl would probably never walk or talk. All this was very frightening—terrifying.

My baby had the blood drawn one week later: it took two times before the sample got to the lab. Three *months* later our doctor called us. He refused to talk to my husband. He then told me *over the phone* that my daughter had Down Syndrome. He gave me no hope, no current information about children with Down Syndrome, no guidance concerning the role of early infant stimulation in improving the lives of children in the '80's.

In the three months, we had built up false hopes that the early dire predictions were not true. When I cried over the phone, he snapped, "We obviously have two patients." . . . Here again is the matter of communication. The phone call didn't make it as far as being sensitive and helpful—let alone the long, long wait for test results and others in the community seeming to know about my child before I knew.

The family physician caring for Sandy has failed Sandy's parents in serious ways. He has withdrawn from dealing with the painful situation for as long as possible. His own anxiety, fear, sense of helplessness seem to have massively interfered with his ability to reach out to the parents—to reach for the best within himself.

Sandy's parents hope that their story will encourage young professionals to examine "what went wrong"—the long, lonely, unconscionable wait for test results after agonizing fears had been aroused by hospital staff; the brusque telephone call; the insensitive response to a mother's natural emotions; the excluding of Sandy's father. Perhaps, the physician saw himself as a failure—unable "to fix" Sandy's chromosomes. Did this narrow view of himself as "fixer" deprive him, rob him of the gratifications of his potential "healing" role as a physician who cares, guides, supports?

Neil's parents invite caregivers to ponder these questions as they present their own contrasting experiences.

Neil

I was twenty-four years old when Neil was born. My husband... was twenty-five. We brought Neil home from the hospital three days after a normal delivery. Our family practitioner was concerned about his muscle tone and said he was going to do some tests, but it was nothing to worry about so we thought everything was fine. He had told us to call him in a couple of weeks for the test results.

A couple of weeks turned into about a month, and he called us in on a Saturday morning with no one else around to tell us that Neil was born with Down Syndrome. The three of us cried together. (I had personally felt something was wrong... mother's instinct? I just wasn't sure what. Every time I had gone out to see Neil through the nursery window at the hospital, the nurses were always listening to his heart. They also moved me into a four-bed ward all by myself!)

The day he called us in the doctor told us that the nurses at the hospital were the ones who suspected Neil had Down Syndrome. The nurses brought this to his attention, and he requested a chromosome study. He himself had not suspected Down Syndrome.

Our doctor said that he didn't want to tell us earlier about the nurses' worries for fear that we would run to the library, look up

Down Syndrome, and find out-dated material. This way we had a month with Neil knowing that he was "normal" (except for a few motherly instincts), and our bonding took place. The doctor went on to say that he thought we could keep Neil at home and that he had no health problems. If the time came when we thought we couldn't handle Neil any longer, all three of us could get together and talk about what to do.

He assured us we could call him anytime, and the three of us would get together for a beer and discuss any of our concerns about Neil. We are still very close with this doctor and feel he handled it the best way he knew how.

Although initially unable to talk openly with the parents about staff's worries and suspicions about Neil, the family physician in many ways compassionately demonstrated his availability and concern. He respected the parents' need for privacy and gave of his time as he shared the painful news. He validated, accepted, and shared their emotional distress as he conveyed information that he understood would shatter dreams. He was honest in discussing the missed diagnosis. Most importantly, he offered sound, current data concerning the development of children with Down syndrome and hope for the integrity of the family. He affirmed the parents' love of their child and their ability to care for him at home for as long as they were able. He made no judgments and encouraged Neil's parents to call him whenever they felt the need.

The parents, observing these qualities in their physician, are able to forgive his initial inability to confront and help them cope with staff's fears. Neil's parents look back to this very early period in their family's life with pain and sadness. There is the wish that their physician could have been able to inform, guide, and support them at the earliest time possible, when "mother's instincts" had alerted them. Nevertheless, Neil's parents have accepted their doctor's humanity, his human flaws and imperfections. At that point in his professional and personal life, ". . . he handled it the best way he knew how." Neil and his parents have appreciated and valued their doctor's best.

Contrasts

TODDLERHOOD AND THE DIAGNOSIS OF AUTISM

The diagnosis of autism or other severe pervasive developmental disorders strikes a harsh blow against parents' dreams and hopes. Many parents describe the profound impact of the diagnosis as a time of crisis— a watershed, historical moment in the family's life. Past ill-conceived theories concerning the etiology of these conditions have cast additional shadows over parents encased in uncertainty and doubt.

Increasing knowledge of the neurobiological basis of such disabilities has eased the burden of blame thrust upon parents. Unfortunately, residues of "the-cold-rejecting-mother" hypothesis remain and may continue to affect professional attitudes toward parents.

The following parental vignettes illustrate two very different ways of approaching the parents of children with severe developmental disabilities. Both families would be told that their toddlers were autistic. In each situation professionals played a critical role in the lives of parents and families.

The first account stresses the long-term consequences of the blame-the-parent model—a legacy of blame and judgment hurled at worried, vulnerable parents seeking care for their child. In contrast, the second narrative describes how sensitive professionals can gently initiate parents into their "new world" and support parents as they begin their long, often lonely and frustrating, journey to understand, nurture, and advocate for their child.

Penny

When my eleven year old daughter Penny was two, we sought help in understanding why she was "different." After receiving very little information from our family doctor, we took Penny to our local university for evaluation. We were frightened—frightened for our daughter, frightened for ourselves—and in a great deal of pain and distress.

During the evaluation, we had contact with many professionals. Our most painful encounter within the health care system occurred with a clinical psychologist at the university. After a half-hour discussion with us about Penny, she bluntly turned to us and condescendingly asked, "What did you do to cause this child to be like this?"

We had just learned about Penny's autism, and our fears and anxieties were overwhelming. We went home and began to ruminate and wonder, ruminate and wonder: What had we done wrong? We pondered over the details of our life together, over our life with Penny: What had we done wrong?

Now, of course, I would have had a totally different reaction. At the time, however, the psychologist's brutal condemnation was devastating—a dagger through our hearts.

Penny was our first child. We had waited until our lives were set. We loved her and doted on her. Needless to say, it was a very, very difficult time.

Fortunately, the director of the speech and language clinic at the university became "our guide through the maze." However, the psychologist's horrifying question wounded us deeply, and nine years later, I remember her words as if they were etched in stone.

Ryan

In our case, the most helpful encounters within the health care system were with the very people who diagnosed our son Ryan, now six years old. When Ryan was almost two, we took him to our local university for evaluation after our own pediatrician refused to take our concerns seriously. A wonderful group of doctors, therapists, and counselors guided us through a lengthy, painful diagnostic period.

A psychologist did most of the testing including the first evaluation in our home. She was very professional, and yet we knew from the start that she cared about Ryan and our family as a whole. Since I was four months pregnant with my second son at the time, we not only were scared for Ryan but terrified for our unborn child as well. The doctor's sensitivity and thoroughness were a great help to me during those nightmarish days.

After informing us of Ryan's diagnosis, she gave us material about autism and recommended schools in our area. Most important of all, she introduced us to some very special counselors—counselors who would be a tremendous comfort to us when no one else could be.

One of the "special" people was the mother of an autistic child who understood in her heart my fears, pain, and feelings of utter helplessness. All of these fine individuals have truly been my strength, direction, and inspiration. I owe them much more than I can ever say.

Both families learned of their children's autism through a long, difficult evaluation process in university settings. Penny's parents and Ryan's parents invite caregivers to compare and evaluate their differing experiences. Their narratives present striking contrasts. They starkly illustrate the power health care professionals hold.

- Choose words carefully, for they may become weapons of destruction inflaming parental guilt and despair.

- Understand the impact of values and attitudes, for they may impart comfort and support to distraught, embattled parents.

Both Penny's and Ryan's parents began their journey by seeking help from their family physician or general pediatrician. The parents' experiences with their primary care physicians were sadly similar. Both physicians did not take the parents' observations seriously. Both physicians minimized the parents' concerns.

Parents see their child's primary care physician as their first line of defense. They turn to their doctor for referrals, for support when the painful news comes, for steadfastness as their child enters community programs. When ignorance or anxiety interferes with this role, physicians lose the opportunity to become healing allies of parents. Marilyn's mother contrasts her experiences with those of Penny's and Ryan's parents.

Marilyn

> When Marilyn was two-years-old, our pediatrician who had worked so well with me in understanding my son's severe allergies, noted that Marilyn had significant developmental delays. He alerted me to his concerns and referred Marilyn to a fine testing facility. His caring attitude helped me a great deal as he spoke to us about the need for testing and the seriousness of Marilyn's problems. He and his entire staff have been incredibly supportive through the trauma of learning the diagnosis of autism. He has been Marilyn's physician and advocate throughout our uphill battle to work for her advancement.

Perspectives

CAREGIVER STRESS AS THE "BEARERS OF BAD NEWS:" AN INTERN'S EXPERIENCE.

Rosa

> The case conference droned on. . .and on. Clumsily suppressing a yawn, I quickly glanced at my watch—5:00 P.M. My mind was

overflowing with tasks yet to be completed before "home" was even a faint possibility. It would be another 8:00 P.M. night—lab reports, X-ray reports, IV's, chart notes, new orders. Tomorrow would be another 26 hour day.

The case: Rosa, 12 months old, with major developmental delays; many questions concerning her ability to see. The discussion had touched upon intrauterine development, central nervous system infection, neuroanatomy. The mystery surrounding Rosa would be solved: "All the data - CAT Scan, EEG, ophthalmologic exam, blood work - point to intrauterine infection. This child is blind and most likely severely retarded."

The attending's words roused me from my stupor. I shuddered. What kind of life lay ahead for this beautiful baby and her adoring mother? What could be done for her? I felt thoroughly helpless.

As students, interns, residents, and attendings trickled out of the conference room, the senior resident caught my eye: "No need for this baby to remain in the hospital any longer. She'll just pick up whatever's going around. Sign the discharge order with a follow-up appointment for the developmental disabilities clinic."

Her mother knew that Rosa would be discharged after the conference and was waiting eagerly by the nursing station for the final discharge papers. She had dressed the baby in a bright pink sweater and was happily tickling her. The baby was responding with joyful coos and giggles.

Good robot that I was, I followed orders *exactly*— discharge note and referral. When Rosa's mother, in broken English, asked me how the baby was—what all the doctors had said in the important meeting, efficient robot disintegrated into a bumbling, anxious fool: "Ms. Rivera, the baby is blind and very, very delayed . . ."

Tears welled up in her eyes. She clutched Rosa close to her and desperately held back sobs. There was no place for us to go; to sit down; to be alone. I didn't even have a tissue for her—there in front of a busy, late Friday afternoon nursing station. "The special clinic will help you," I stumbled and blabbered as my beeper shrilly rang.

I did not know how to comfort her; how to be with her. I wanted to run as far away as a routine call on my beeper would propel me. In my truncated state of awareness, the call to check an IV became "an emergency," and I left Rosa's mother alone as she struggled to maintain dignity and pride.

Weeks later, after the clamor and din of that crazy afternoon had begun to fade, Ms. Rivera's face remained locked within my memory. We hadn't meant to be cruel, but we were. And I had played a major role. We hadn't set out to be thoughtless and insensitive. . .

During the case conference we had discussed everything to the "nth" degree of differential diagnosis except the most meaningful intervention of Rosa's hospitalization—how to tell a young, loving, poorly educated mother that her baby was disabled, multiply handicapped; how to destroy dreams without destroying hope; how to demonstrate our respect for her love.

I was angry at myself, at the system that had permitted me to minimize—to flee—a mother's grief and tears. A depressing story—yes. A horribly memorable story—yes. No heroes or heroines of modern medicine graced our halls. We were simply scared, anxious humans who had much to learn—much to learn from a young, caring woman who could tell us of her love. (Leff, P., excerpts from diary, 1979)

Situations to ponder

CHOOSING WORDS CAREFULLY WHEN CONVEYING DIAGNOSTIC INFORMATION; REMAINING "STEADY" IN THE FACE OF PARENTAL DISBELIEF AND ANGER

Rochelle's mother endured months of shock and disbelief as she struggled to process painful information concerning her baby's serious problems. Currently a consultant to state agencies, Rochelle's mother plans programs for health care professionals. In articulating her own past depression and intense suffering, she seeks to help professionals "choose words carefully;" attempts to protect parents from the full facts only increase confusion during a time of overwhelming distress.

Rochelle's mother shares her thoughts with caregivers who must inform and support distraught parents and families in crisis:

Rochelle

Rochelle was delivered by C-section and then transferred to another hospital to investigate and treat her seizures. Rochelle was treated by several neonatologists over a three week period. At no time did the social service department speak with me about how I and my family were doing under the stress. . .

On Rochelle's discharge, the doctor informed me that my daughter was going home "within normal limits" except for the NG feeding tube. He referred my daughter to our regular pediatrician and added, "Watch her development." Follow-up CAT scans and EEG were suggested. Rochelle's seizures had stopped, and she was on phenobarb.

One week later I saw my regular pediatrician. He stated that Rochelle had had an intracranial hemorrhage and would probably have cerebral palsy. He could not tell me the extent of the involvement or how she would be affected.

I thought my pediatrician was crazy. The neonatologists told me that Rochelle was "within normal limits." I tried to remember back to Rochelle's hospital stay and recalled the day a doctor gave me the results of the CAT Scan. He was looking for the cause of her seizures and stated that all they had found was a "small intracranial hemorrhage." This was not an uncommon finding with premature babies, and he didn't seem alarmed or concerned.

I felt our doctor was crazy. My daughter wasn't going to have cerebral palsy. How dare he say such a thing.

The point I want to make here is that we have to be careful how we describe a child's condition. Yes, Rochelle was "within normal limits"—the seizures were under control. But she had suffered severe head trauma and had had an intracranial hemorrhage. The term "normal" blocked out all the other information given to me. I had extreme difficulty talking to our pediatrician . . .

When Rochelle was four-months-old we returned to our doctor's office for her immunizations. He stated that he felt spasticity in her arms. He very carefully explained what this was and how it could or couldn't have an influence on her development. His gentle clarity brought me back to reality. The time he spent discussing all of the possibilities really had an effect on me. The information was factual, but also gave me room for hope. . .

Although Rochelle's mother thought that her child's pediatrician was "crazy," she did not seek another doctor for her daughter. Despite her anger and negative reaction to his expressed expectation that Rochelle would show some degree of cerebral palsy, she remained with his practice. What were the underlying bonds of trust that enabled her to continue with this pediatrician?

Answers to this question emerge at Rochelle's four-month check when the doctor renewed his mention of cerebral palsy. Rather than being impatient with this mother's denial, he took the time to go into detail about his observations and the implications of these problems for Rochelle's development. Whatever his private exasperation may have been, the mother's experience of him was "gentle clarity." He did not spare himself by backing off from the painful subject with the excuse that "mother is unaccepting and not ready for the facts." He continued to work *with* mother and child.

The physician's rewards are this mother's readiness for early intervention with her daughter, a parent's undying gratitude, a partnership in care.

Perspectives

PARENT-TO-PARENT SUPPORT; LINKING NEWLY DIAGNOSED FAMILIES WITH "SENIOR FAMILIES"

Professionals who value and believe in parent-to-parent support provide a service that parents deeply appreciate. Allan's mother describes how a caring nurse gently and patiently guided her to a crucial source of help—another parent who had endured depression and fear and was now able to reach out to others.

Allan

All of the experiences I have had in special education and psychological assessment in no way prepared me for my son's diagnosis of cerebral palsy.

The weeks following the diagnosis will always be vivid to me. My family called daily. We are very close—consequently we feel each other's pain. At least three times a day, I would pick up the phone to a weeping voice asking, "What's new?" In retrospect, we laugh about it. Friends responded with cards and phone calls of support and sympathy, with offers to babysit and with home-cooked meals. These well-meaning and sincere efforts were greatly appreciated, but they almost intensified the reality.

Throughout those weeks, a very supportive nurse. . .called to see how we were doing. Each time we spoke she mentioned Nancy and Nancy's son, now 11, who was diagnosed with cerebral palsy at 6 months of age.

My first phone call to Nancy was not easy to make, but that contact and our subsequent relationship have been vital to my continued growth as the mother of a child with a handicap. For many weeks Nancy was a voice on the phone who always seemed to call at the appropriate time. For example, the day after Allan had his CAT Scan, I was feeling very sad, scared, and angry. Nancy called. After I explained the process to her and shared my frustration, her comment, "I know what you're going through," was more helpful than I can ever tell her. . .

From that point on, Nancy continued to be a resource who encouraged me and gave me "permission" to articulate all of my anger, sadness, and fear. . .

Whenever I call Nancy and mention the fear of "the clenched fist" or "delayed gross motor ability," she quickly reminds me [that it is not the CP, but] the positive and lovable characteristics that are Allan. . .

CHAPTER

3 Grief, Coping and Renewal

Being aware of the stages of grief, I thought: "I am going to get through these stages and have it done with and get on with life." I know now that I was being unrealistic. The grief never really goes away; certain rites of passage trigger the grief cycle, although usually not as severely. (mother of three children with special needs)

* * * *

We could not have survived all of this without the support and counsel of our friends and families. In counseling I have come to see that all my fears about Autumn's future are really my own fears that I've never resolved—fears of ugliness and rejection, of imperfection, of loneliness. I have yet to see anyone turn away from Autumn in disgust. On the contrary, she is constantly met with smiles and delight, because that's what she offers people. I've struggled a lot with the concept that the world will judge our worth by the "product" we offer—as if a child is a commodity or something—and that I would be "tried and found wanting." How screwed up can we be? Having and loving Autumn is setting me free from a lot of that kind of garbage. (Janet Troy, Facial Expressions Newsletter, August, 1988, p. 8)

* * * *

Parents can and must "strike out on their own," so to speak, to make a place for their contributing member and to change the perspective of society. One way is to do helpful things for others. (Lyn's mother)

Introduction

The preceding chapter has discussed many of the overwhelming feelings parents initially experience when learning of their children's problems. This chapter will further clarify such feelings, discuss the concept of "grief work" as it applies to parents of children with difficulties, and illuminate the process of integrating a child's difference into the lives of parents and families. Most parents describe a long, complicated process of grieving, coping, and renewal.

Grief Work

Parents react to the diagnosis of a serious illness or handicapping condition with a constellation of complex feelings and painful emotions— normal grief over the loss of the "healthy" baby they had hoped would be; wrenching sadness for their child's pain; despair over the limitations illness has imposed.

> At the time of his birth, my husband and I asked ourselves why. We still have no reason. But that question was soon replaced with many practical ones - can he hear; how will I feed him; what are people going to say and how will they react. Can I take this child out in public; can I ever leave him with a sitter? . . . (Mary Gabriele, mother of a child with congenital facial deformities, writing in *AboutFace*, Vol. 4, No. 2, March/April, 1990)

Parents may cling to irrational guilt since it is often easier to accept blame, with its fantasy of control, than the total loss of control with which they must grapple. "Why my child?" is a frequent, if unanswerable, question. Professionals can play an important role in countering irrational, painful guilt and blame that sap energy from parents and families. A mother and nurse who has organized many workshops for professionals emphasizes:

> Parents need to hear a professional say that they have done nothing wrong. Sometimes parents take on guilt because, by taking the blame, it gives them some sense of control of their situation. They are feeling a real loss of control at this time because everyone is taking care of their child, calling the moves and telling them what to do. The professional can give them some sense of control by inviting them to participate in decisions and in the care of the child. This participation will instill confidence in the parents. (Poyadue, 1988, p. 84)

Grief is an individual process rife with intensely personal meaning; lonely, subterranean passages as well as the growth and flowering of new, unanticipated values, strengths, capacities, and friendships. Parents love, protect, and advocate for their children in need as they simultaneously grieve for lost dreams and possibilities. A couple writing in *Participating Families* share their family's story:

> Our son will be four years old in March, making this the first year we have not dreaded the occasion of his birth. As each year has passed we have become stronger. The pain is no longer there daily, only sadness occasionally when we see the beautiful autumn colours; a bright cornflower blue sky with the brilliance of a yellow sun shining down on the many varieties and colours of flowers; green grass; white snow. All these wonders we take for granted our son will never see with his eyes. However, through our descriptions and the feel of crunchy leaves in autumn; soft velvety flowers in spring; spiky grass in summer; soft, cold snow in winter, he can "see" all these miracles of nature in his mind's eye. . .
>
> Within days of his birth, we learned there would be problems. We cried and held each other tightly, questioning ourselves a hundred times - why - why - why? Why me? Why us? Then the inevitable - why him? What did we do wrong? A hundred questions flying through our minds.
>
> Those first weeks before our baby came home were stressful to say the least. We both had mood swings but were fortunate in that when I was in the depths of despair, my husband came through for me and was so strong. I was able to reciprocate during his hours of anguish. Our marriage became stronger due to our mutual heartache and, ultimately, our love for each other and our children.
>
> Because of our limited experience with handicapped children, we even wished our son dead if he couldn't lead a perfectly "normal" life. Since then we have both come to realize that the word "normal" is greatly over-rated. Who dictates what "normal" is? The bottom line is that we have two beautiful sons. When we go to bed at night and check each one, love spills over for each child. They are individuals and should be treated as such. One is not favoured or loved more for being "normal" or "special". They are both unique and special in their own way . . . (Linda and Bob Jeffery, *Participating Families*, Vol. 1, Issue 2, February, 1988, p. 9)

The varied paths of "grief work" must be respected. There is no right way to grieve, to cope with massive change and loss. Individuals and families react to painful situations in widely differing fashions. For every parent who finds solace in the notion of "God's special purpose," there is another who is outraged by such a sentiment.

There is no formula for categorizing parents, nor is such a practice useful. The parameters of "normal" adaptive response are broad, not narrow. By actively listening to individual families as they begin their journey, professionals enhance their sensitivity to the unique needs and responses of "normal" parents meeting extraordinary challenges within their child, within themselves, within their communities. Frannie's mother explains:

> I cried inconsolably, inconsolably when my baby's heart rate could not be controlled. I want to be with her in the NICU, but it kills me to see her so sick: her body thrashing; needles piercing her perfect head; machines glued to her tiny frame; my utter helplessness. Even when I go home to rest at night, my mind is filled with dread, no peace.
>
> Frannie's nurses and doctors have let me cry and scream. So many questions float through my mind over and over again. The cardiologist and chief resident came to me and listened to me for the hundredth time. I am learning the impossible: to deal with Frannie's condition one day at a time, one hour at a time.
>
> The uncertainty is a knife through my very being. I'm angry, sad, frightened, exhausted all at once. Anger grips me but knows no focus. With whom can I be angry? Myself? My innocent baby? The doctors who practiced sound medicine? Guilt, heavy and dark, is a weight on my heart. A terrible sadness for the baby I love and adore overwhelms me. I need my baby's doctors and nurses to understand. And they have. As much as they know, they communicate to me. They come to me when I can't go to them. They are not afraid of my tears. They care for her, too, and are "with" my little fighter. All of this helps . . . really helps. I don't feel so alone.

Health care professionals will encounter dysfunctional individuals — parents, for example, who are severely mentally ill, who abuse drugs, or who maltreat their children. Such parents do require intensive supervision to safeguard the well-being of the child. These pathological situations differ greatly from normal grief work.

A Model of Grief

The diagnosis of a chronic and/or disabling condition in one's child shatters cherished parental dreams; a symbolic death has occurred (Moses,

1983; Simons, 1987; Turnbull & Turnbull, 1987). A theoretical model of the stages of grief is often presented to make sense of the surge of painful, conflicting feelings parents experience as they set aside deeply held wishes for their child; as they cope with enormous loss and change. For most parents, new hopes and dreams for their child, for themselves, and for their family will slowly emerge as they simultaneously grieve for images and fantasies that cannot be (Darling, 1983).

A model by its very nature reduces unique, complex, interweaving psychological phenomena to generalized terms and abstractions. Such conceptual handles as "shock," "denial," "anger," "guilt," "sadness." "involvement," and "resolution" have been used as landmarks to help guide parents and professionals through a maze of hurt and pain (Linda Wurzbach, in *Ed-Med*, 1985).

Important issues emerge: What do each of these terms, abstractions, mean in the lives of real parents and children? How are parents experiencing the stream of confusing, at times ambivalent, emotions, confronting them? Is a model true to their reality over the span of their child's life?

The stages of grief are, in reality, states of feeling that often coexist and will be re-experienced throughout the child's life (Moses, 1983). Parents' journeys should not be viewed as a linear progression with a final goal to be reached. A mother writing for both parents and professionals stresses:

> The coping process is not a static one with a clear beginning or end. Change and loss will continue to be a part of each of our lives, and we are likely to experience again some of our initial feelings and reactions. . .Acknowledging and accepting the feelings as natural and normal may help each of us understand one another a little better. (Linda Wurzbach, in *Ed/Med*, 1985).

For most parents the range of emotions encompassed by grief work is necessary and adaptive. For example, "shock" may allow the parent emotionally to "take a breath" in preparation for the task ahead. "Denial" serves to protect the parent from overwhelming anguish until he or she has found the internal and external supports necessary to carry on (Moses, 1983).

Parents urge professionals to validate their feelings, to be patient. Grief work occurs within the framework of the parent-professional dialogue. The caregiver who, from his or her own inner strength, is able to say to a depressed or guilty parent, "It must be a rough time for you. Tell me more about how you are feeling. . ." facilitates the formation of alliances that will lead to optimal care; parents are enabled to begin the process of creating dreams that can be fulfilled and realized (Moses, 1983).

Parents continue to refine and reconceptualize their experiences in their private thinking. For example, Paul's mother, a teacher of young professionals, who in her presentations has used the stages of grief listed above, now challenges her own thinking about the concept of resolution:

> As I have changed with Paul, experienced his life and death, I now know that there is no resolution. Maintenance is a more appropriate concept. Maintenance of our life as a family; maintenance of our ongoing struggle to help Paul achieve the best quality of life possible for him; maintenance of our love for our child even in his death. Resolution is a poor term in describing the reality of parents' experiences. It just doesn't ring true.

As parents reflect on their experience of family life with a difference, they, too, encourage professionals to join them in a process of re-evaluating and re-examining overused, often misleading concepts such as "acceptance." Parents are unique individuals at a particular place in their long, personal journey; simplified concepts cannot capture their reality. Mothers of children with special needs, writing for both professionals and parents, stress the ongoing challenge parents face by entitling their booklet *Acceptance is only the first battle.*

Many parents bristle at the term "acceptance" with its implication of an undefined standard to be reached.

> We acknowledge that marriages need renewing; that we must repeat a process of committing and coming to love our partners. Parents, too, go through the necessary work of dealing again and again with sadness for their children. New events, missed milestones, throw the hard facts of life into high relief, often in unexpected ways, making grief work an on-going process for parents.
>
>   If a child dies, will his or her loss ever cease to matter to the bereaved parents? Neither will a disability cease to pain parents whose commitment, understanding, and love of their child is unquestioned. (Laura's mother)

Parents emphasize the need for flexibility in applying a model of grief. Parents are with their child over the "long haul." Sorrow is mixed with joy and pride in their child's accomplishments as grief reverberates over time.

> In order to communicate effectively with parents of children with chronic illnesses and/or disabilities, health care workers must understand a complex grieving process. The grieving process is not a one time event. We, as parents, grieve over and over again as milestones in our children's lives are missed. (Ellen's mother)

* * * *

Being a parent has its ups and down. Being the parent of a special needs child certainly heightens emotional reactions. This is a very important, but very difficult job I am doing. I am human and possess all the wonderful and not so wonderful feelings that go with my humanity. There will be times when I will laugh; when I am angry; when I am sad; when I am happy; and when I just don't care. Please don't overreact or read too much into my normal, human feelings. (Eddie's mother)

* * * *

Respect parents' grief reactions as normal, not pathological, behavior in most instances. (Becky's mother)

Oversimplification results if a model of grief becomes a mere set of timetables and lock step passages. Parents may be inappropriately judged and labeled according to where they fall along a preconceived grief cycle. In summarizing the varied reactions and views of parents whose newborns have had intraventricular bleeding (IVH), a mother urges professionals to suspend judgment and listen carefully and compassionately:

> IVH families respond to their circumstances in vastly different ways.
>
> Those families have a wide range of values and expectations. Some resent doctors who don't supply definite answers; others understand and appreciate the physician's difficulty in making predictions. Some families welcome optimism; others resent a "Pollyanna" attitude. Some families believe in a divine purpose behind their child's injury; others say religion is extraneous. If professionals, friends, and family are to help IVH parents, they must take time to listen and to feel their way gently into each family's needs. (Ronnie Londner, IVH Parents Newsletter)

Caveats

As helpful as a model may be to professionals—and to parents— in promoting understanding of the process of normal grief, caveats are in order:

• A model can never substitute for actively listening to parents: acknowledging, accepting, and affirming their unique realities. Two mothers whose newborns endured difficult, complicated beginnings painfully describe their feelings and memories:

I think it is so hard for my friends and family because there is so little they can actively do as we wait. People want me to feel better, to think positively, not to cry. I don't want to be cheered up. The false reassurances are hollow. The best help for me now is to understand my struggle with a new reality. I have never felt so out of control. Even sleep is a mixed blessing. As I awake, there is a flood of memory: My baby lies in the neonatal intensive care unit. Is he suffering? Will he ever come home to me?

Giving him a bath yesterday drew me closer to him. The neonatal nurses encouraged me, but it was so hard. My tears became part of his bath! In my mind, I must deal with both the best and worst of outcomes. I must be prepared. But can one really ever be prepared? (mother of a seriously ill newborn in the NICU)

* * * *

What I am trying to get at are the things that are so hard to communicate. I can write, "We were devastated." But is that going to tell what happens to you when you are sent home empty-handed while your newborn child is lying tied down under a warming hood, with a respirator tube down her silent throat, her blue face contorting as she tries to cry, mysterious drugs causing convulsions, while monitors spell out how badly she is doing? How you steal a little cloth diaper from the hospital because it smells of her, and try to sleep with it clasped to your chest, with no one to nurse. How you learn that people really do walk in their sleep — when your husband wakes you up and you have been trying to pull his arm out of its socket, because the round ball of his shoulder is just the size and shape of your baby's head and you are trying so very hard to pick up the baby the proper way . . . And how, eight years later, the smell of Hibiclens causes a horrible flashback, all the more dreadful because you had NO idea that it was even something you had noticed at the time; the scent alone brings awful fear sweeping back, the shortness of breath, the lump in the throat. (Laura's mother)

• Despite current knowledge that "grief work" is a normal, if enormously painful process, parents' intense emotions may frighten health care professionals. A thoughtful parent recounts the depth of her despair and how the calming, steady presence of her child's pediatrician helped both her and her husband endure the storm.

I remember the night when Dr. C. told us about Thomas's abnormal brain responses in vision, auditory, and motor areas. He was trying to be as gentle as possible, but I pushed him to be specific. As he spoke, I felt that I was going to drop Thomas who was in my arms. I rushed off to his room and put him in his crib. I turned to see something that will always be etched in my memory—the look of fear and anxiety on my husband's and Dr. C's faces. They feared what I might do.

Within minutes, my feelings toward Thomas had drastically changed: my beautiful baby had become ugly. I saw the change before my eyes. I could not move at first, and then when I could, I wanted to run—run until I could run no longer. During the next few hours, my husband and I talked, and I became aware of what was happening within me. I went from total rejection and let someone else take care of him to I will take him home and care for him.

When I reached that point I wanted to return to Thomas. As I looked at him again, I knew that I still loved him: he was becoming beautiful once again. I knew something about the grief process—that I was experiencing the death of a normal child.

• Parental anger, in particular, has often been viewed in pejorative terms; uneasy, anxious professionals may withdraw from parents. When parental anger is minimized or discounted as "pathological," parents experience increased self-doubt, confusion, and isolation. This mother poignantly remembers:

When my son with severe developmental disabilities was born, I was angry. I was angry at life, myself, everyone and everything. I now can see that as much as I loved my baby I was even angry at him. No one told me that anger was a normal, natural reaction. No one helped me to understand my anger and guilt.

The professionals working with us were afraid of me. Any infraction would send me into a rage. Perhaps, they thought I was angry at them personally. Maybe they even thought that I was a little crazy.

I began to think that I really was going nuts. I went to see a psychiatrist who helped me a great deal with one simple sentence: "You have a right to be angry." Somehow the attitude that I was OK, that my frustration and rage were "normal", allowed me to move on and to gather our troops to work for my child and family within the community. I found that my anger could be a positive force and began to use my energy to achieve specific goals for my child.

My son is still home with us. Each night when I come home

from work, I receive a very special welcome: he is there to greet me. His eyes light up when he sees me. My other boys who are busy with all kinds of activities have grown in compassion and feeling for others. I am very proud of what we have accomplished as a family.

Today when I talk to young professionals, I stress the importance of understanding and accepting parental anger. I know that it can be a real challenge to stay with a parent who watches you like a hawk and cannot tolerate anything less than perfection.

I remember one young therapist who did not run away from me, but openly told me that my anger frightened her. She then allowed me to talk about the many, many frustrations that my son's disability had brought to our lives. She was one of the few people working with my son who encouraged me to talk about my rage—the intense injustice and unfairness that seemed to face me at every turn.

Her patience was rewarded. Helping parents to channel their anger into effective avenues for working for their child can become a source of satisfaction for you. (mother of a teen with multiple disabilities)

• Historically, professionals have focused their attention on the negative impact of "grief work" (Wikler, Wasow, & Hatfield, 1981; Wikler, Wasow, & Hatfield, 1983; Stone, 1989). Parents' discussions of the strengths and benefits they have derived from caring for a child with special needs have often been viewed as evidence of "denial" or reduced to such terms as "overcompensation" (Wikler, Wasow, & Hatfield, 1983). Many of the studies upon which such impressions are based are of poor quality and do not represent the vast majority of parents of children with disabling conditions (Wolfensberger, 1967). Laura's mother challenges the pessimistic views to which she was exposed as both an undergraduate and graduate student in special education:

I read everything as a student, and I continue to read as a parent. A scalding experience, indeed. I am struck by the unrelieved harshness and the repetitive nature of the writings. They all say about the same things, and it's generally all bad.

. . .The generalizations are so commonly repeated as to be unchallenged as fact: Parents deny, they doctor-shop, they reject, they abuse, they obstruct, they resent, they divorce, they emotionally deprive, they upset the child, they fail to this, they fail to that. They fail. . .

As a parent now, and as a parent of a child with multiple

problems, I have a lot more humility. I know *lots* of other parents, much more intimately, and now I see much injustice and outright error in what I was taught to believe about Parents of Children with Difficulties. I wish more professionals in training challenged the "common wisdom," read real research, or at least read books that question the generalities so carefully taught.

When "parent pathology" rather than the potential positive adjustment of families is stressed, a self-fulfilling prophecy may develop. Parents urge those providing services for their children to understand that sensitive, compassionate, realistic care affirms and strengthens them as they reorganize their lives to embrace their children in need. The mother of a young man with multiple disabilities and coordinator of family support services has addressed issues of negative professional perceptions and their effects on parents. She concludes:

> Many of the reactions and problems associated with the birth of a handicapped child are not inevitable and through proper intervention may be preventable. The key to the improvement of intervention with families of the handicapped may be in a complete overhauling of the way society views the parents of these children. If we start from the premise that a positive attitude will be helpful in:
>
> (a) pointing out the strengths and normal aspects of the child,
>
> (b) assuring [parents] that there will always be "someone who cares,"
>
> (c) giving [parents] the support of kind and knowledgeable professionals who make themselves available with assistance,
>
> (d) encouraging the use of support groups. . .,
>
> (e) providing financial supports and entitlements so that [parents] can concentrate on keeping their families together,
>
> (f) providing homemakers and nurses for assisting in the supervision and management of their child,
>
> (g) thinking in terms of a coordinator. . .for every severely handicapped child as someone to whom families can turn in solving their day-to-day problems
>
> —if we give [parents] early interventions, the supports, the programs, and the therapies for their children, only then do

we have the right to analyze their psyches and see if they are
better adjusted. (Stone, 1989, pp.176-177)

Integration: The Dawning of a Feeling of Renewal

Even as the parents have struggled to meet their child's pressing needs—
both those associated with normal aspects of growth and development
and those associated with the medical difficulties—they have struggled to
deal with the reactions and emotions of grieving. Gradually they reach a
more comfortable place in this cycle, integrating the impact of their child's
difficulties.

Integration is only one of many possible terms that describe a feeling of
being released rather than dominated by a hurtful event. Parents find that
they are no longer preoccupied and in constant turmoil, dealing daily with
the painful feelings associated with the impact of a troubling diagnosis.
They are aware of their strengths, able to find joy, and ready for broadened
horizons—both personally and as a family. The potential power locked up
in the process of mourning a tragic event is freed. Ideas have been
reformulated, recast, revised.

Parents describe any or all of these common threads:

New values

A sense of mission

Recognition of one's resources

Different perspective

New relationships

Changed views of one's faith

Regained equilibrium

Deeper appreciation for life's joys

Creative impulses

Changed sense of life's meaning and purpose

Ability to empathize

Growth of humility, tolerance, wisdom

While they will always face times of sadness, of sorrow for their child,
these parents have come to terms with the process of grieving. They
recognize the nature of recycling, and they report that, while it never goes

away, grief is worked through more quickly in subsequent onslaughts of sorrow and hurt. They have gained confidence in their resilience.

For me, having a child who can drive me CRAZY with his slowness is a CLEAR, if frustrating, message about my own inability to live with parts of me that are stuck and parts of me that race around doing ten things half well. I am quite serious - our son is a gift to me in helping me to understand and accept aspects of myself. (mother of a son with developmental disabilities)

* * * *

Our daughter, now 7, is a happy, charming, highly functioning little girl who has proved herself an ambassador for children like her. Her godfather is responsible for writing and passing federal legislation that provides incentives to states to offer early intervention programs to all handicapped children - and all 50 states are now taking advantage of these incentives. She is the light of our lives. Were we happy when she was born? No. Do we now have any regrets? None. Do we expect we'll ever be able to sit back and say our work is finished? Don't be silly. Once a parent, always a parent. (mother of Keough who was born with Down syndrome and many life-threatening complications)

* * * *

We're raised and trained to have things resolved—all of our stories resolve issues or come to conclusions—you're innocent or guilty, happy or miserable, you die or you live. It's black or it's white. That's not the truth, and I didn't want to do that. I especially didn't want to send that kind of a message to the parents of the approximately 10,000 children born with Down syndrome each year in this country. I wanted to tell people not to punish themselves because they couldn't work it out. The fact is there is no way of working this out. It's a very uncomfortable feeling not to have a conclusion, but that's the way it is. I didn't want to give in to a big TV ending of a larger-than-life triumph. The smaller family triumph is more valid. (Emily Kingsley, the mother of a son with Down syndrome and co-writer of the TV movie "Kids Like These", quoted in R. Jacobs, *The New York Times*, 11/8/87, p. 33)

* * * *

Our children have made us real. We have watched them cry in pain, suffer through testing, and still they can brighten our lives with the gentlest smile, the whimsical laugh. They have shown so many people what life truly is - not in the quantity of years, but in the quality of how life must be lived. (Julie Beckett, Comprehensive Care for Medically Vulnerable Infants and Toddlers: A Parent's Perspective, *Equals in this Partnership*, NCCIP, 1985, p. 12)

* * * *

Much of my grief has been for my son. I grieved because my son suffered and because I had no power to end his suffering. I grieved because he was incredibly limited in his ability to enjoy life in any way that I could understand. I grieved over the loss of the companionship I had expected from my son.

I felt pain, knowing that, on top of all of his other problems, my son had to live with such a sad father. I grieved that he was likely to die an early and perhaps painful death. I grieved because my son seemed to have no place in a world too ignorant and weak to cure him, and perhaps too cold and hostile to care. . .

I grieved because my longing to see all of life fit into a meaningful pattern had been frustrated. I grieved because I felt isolated from people and from God.

I grieved because in a time of adversity I proved to be less noble and more vulnerable and needy than I had thought myself to be. I grieved because I could not be a comforter to my wife or to others. I grieved simply because sorrow had entered my life.

Then I made some discoveries. Simple things mostly, but lessons I don't know how I could have learned had I not known sorrow. I learned, for example, that sorrow and joy can be experienced at the same time. They are not mutually exclusive. So, the fact that sorrow had become such a part of my life did not mean that I would always be unbearably miserable, for there could be joy even in the midst of sorrow. That one took a while to learn.

I also began to see that the beating my value system had taken was a necessary preparation for learning how to understand and value my son, how to develop a new vision for his life. It was a process in which I learned in a deeper way to put priority on inward development, rather than outward achievement.

I experienced a needed sense of peace when I began to find sound theological reasons for believing that my son would be in heaven one day, and that heaven would be a place of healing for him.

I discovered that a new sensitivity and ability to assist other people was slowly developing. . .

I discovered the satisfaction of knowing that I grieve over

matters about which all people should grieve. . . (Denny Hoyt, Grief, *ACCH Network*, Volume 8, No. 2, Spring, 1990, p. 5 & 10)

HANDLING THINGS BETTER
Situations to ponder

MISUSE OF A MODEL OF GRIEF

Applying concepts embedded in a model of grief to a particular parent's circumstances must be done with great care *and* with one goal in mind— to assist the parent. Parents have reported that, at times, their legitimate concerns and observations have been brushed aside and labeled as "nonacceptance" of their child's problems, "shopping around," "denial." Such misuse of a model of grief leads to painful scenarios that erode trust. Careful, thoughtful listening to parents' worries will prevent the type of encounter Jerry's mother describes:

> Surprisingly, our most painful experience within the health care system occurred with the center that serves people with developmental disabilities. We had brought Jerry in because of an increase in self-stimulating behaviors. Jerry was about five-years-old at the time. The child psychologist concluded that I had not dealt with Jerry's disability and that it was *my* perception that the negative behaviors were increasing.
>
> Hindsight is 20/20. We have seen Jerry's behaviors improve and regress. He has consistently shown regressive behaviors in inappropriate school situations.

The term "shopping around" has often been used in a pejorative sense to stress a parent's "denial" or inability to accept his or her child's situation. Such views may cloud professional awareness of the reasons behind parents' journey and quest. For many parents, so-called "shopping around" represents a very real search for appropriate diagnosis and treatment of their children. Parents seek professionals who will guide them to services that improve the lives of their children; professionals who like and understand their children and who will act as advocates. A mother speaks of her anger, remembered over 14 years, as she sought help for her child. Her "shopping around" was, in fact, a loving quest to find the help she and her daughter would need to maintain their family.

> I remember the anger I felt towards a particular doctor who told me, "There is nothing more I can do for your child; take her home

and love her." The anger was due in part to the realization that my time and energy had been wasted in keeping this appointment. Also, it was due to the lack of direction from the doctor to seek out other sources of help and support.

. . .I would like to say that over the past 14 years our daughter has benefited greatly from the care and concern of many people in the medical professions as well as family, friends, neighbors, teachers, and support organizations. Initially, the help came through my efforts to educate myself about my child's disability and my good fortune to have enough education, finances, and courage to investigate and use available resources. I shudder to think there may be less fortunate parents of disabled children who get discouraged and give up because of a careless statement made by a medical professional. (mother of a daughter with cerebral palsy)

4 Ongoing Care I: Respecting the Parents

I'm not sure the professionals completely understand what it's like when you get to take your child home—whether it's a diabetic child now "regulated," a child with cancer on a return-for-treatment schedule, or a newborn finally released from the ICU. Although we were relieved and thrilled to have Laura coming home, I was also terrified by the loss of the supports, the dozen people who jumped when her heart monitor sounded the alarm, the equipment and people who knew what they were doing (as I felt I did not!) Even though they told me I could call with questions, I felt cast adrift, as a new mother, as the mother of a child with birth defects, as a traveler facing the unknown. (Laura's mother)

Introduction

Unless the death of a child has occurred, a grief model cannot fully grasp the parents' experience. Although there may be a "symbolic death," their child—warm, needy, loving, lovable, demanding, exasperating, growing—is very much alive. Of critical importance to parents is their child's living. Grief, although intense and painful, is only one aspect of their new lives; parents in reality are every day coping with the very pressing, practical, physical and emotional demands of caring for a child with special needs. The quality of resources, concrete services, and emotional support available to parents will have a major impact on how they see themselves and their child. The mother of Kate, a young woman with multiple challenges, emphasizes:

Today when a family is presented with the knowledge of any disability, all sorts of supporting arms should be available to swoop around the family; arms from physicians, social services agencies, religious institutions and the local communities alike. These attitudes should promote confidence, hope, and a "we'll learn to live constructively together" attitude. This must happen in the first hours, days, months, and years. Service providers must be trained to provide expert consultation and quality care for that child and its family, which will be in a state of shock and then confusion, perhaps for several years. (Addie Comegys, *Massachusetts Department of Mental Retardation Family Support Newsletter*, May, 1988)

There will be a constant flow of new challenges as the child grows, develops, and enters new stages of life. For parents of children with special needs, new doors must be opened, new fears met, new reminders of their child's "difference" confronted just as old barriers have been overcome, just as old battles have been won. Amber's mother explains:

Going from one school to another for a child with handicaps is really stressful, not only for the child but for the parents. We are going to high school next year, and I would rather take a beating, but I guess we will go.

PARENTAL CONCERNS: COMMON THREADS

Schooling is just one example of the many occasions which arise to renew tension and exacerbate the concerns of parents. Broadly, parental concerns seem to contain these common threads: vulnerability, guilt, and isolation.

Vulnerability

Parents fear that their pain will be worsened, their ability to cope impaired, or their adjustment labeled inadequate. Yet they need desperately to receive support for the overwhelming feelings that they at times experience. They express concerns such as this one:

Families of handicapped children feel their lives are out of control for varying periods of time. It is important to understand that this feeling of lack of control can be a recurring experience. I find I am leery of surprises these days as they tend to upset the equilibrium I have worked hard to establish. A professional's job should include guiding parents into actions that will help them regain control of their lives. It has been said many times and will bear repetition again that it is not only a handicapped child that is at risk, it is the child's entire family. (Sue Duffy, *Acceptance is only the first battle*, Montana University Affiliated Program, 1984, p.42)

* * * *

It is very difficult for a parent to turn over a child to caregivers, at least, in my experience. The parent knows how difficult the child is to handle, and how much disruption and difficulty the caregivers will be put through. There is an element of shame—that the parent has in some way failed to handle things—and fear—that the caregiver may not be able to deal with what is coming—and guilt—because the parent needs so desperately to have a small piece of life to call his or her own but at the price of having someone else shoulder the burden temporarily. The parent needs all the help he or she can get from the caregiver to share these feelings and the other deep emotions that go along with living day in, day out with a child who is not like other children. (Bill's mother)

Guilt

For many parents, the burden of irrational guilt does not fade as the acute pain connected with the diagnosis subsides. Ongoing treatment and therapy programs in the home, multiple clinic visits, traumatic hospital stays, evaluations and conferences in the school system, bring continuing demands and strain. Parents are torn among many conflicting responsibilities: the arduous schedule of their child with special needs; the care of siblings; work roles; other family and social obligations; and the desire for the rhythms of normal family life.

Parents ask much of themselves: Are we doing enough for our child? What will happen if he or she misses a therapy session? When will we ever have enough time (or money) to do all that we must do for our child with special needs, our other children who need us, our aging parents, ourselves as a couple? Can we emotionally and/or financially manage yet another referral or treatment program? If we decline, will we permanently impede our child's progress? Keough's mother explains:

Although the arrival of home-based services is generally greeted by parents as a life raft would be greeted by a drowning man, professionals should be aware that the very existence of these services can form the basis for a new kind of guilt. While parents are being told that they will become their child's best teachers and that the programming techniques will help their child progress, the flip side of all this positive thinking is that a parent's failure to teach correctly or work often enough with the child will lead to a lack of progress, if not regression.

From a parent's point of view, that's scary. Not only has the parent produced an imperfect child whose imperfections—as in the case of a child with Down syndrome or cerebral palsy—can never be completely fixed, and not only is the proposed course of action a seemingly endless project without guarantee of success, but the parents are now responsible for progress or the lack of it.

While it may seem unreasonable for a parent to fear this kind of responsibility since parents are normally considered to have the responsibility for raising their children, it is the intensity of the responsibility that is frightening and needs to be understood. If Dad doesn't go out and throw the ball around with his non-handicapped son Billy for a week, Billy isn't going to lose the ability to do it. A handicapped child may not only lose the ability to throw the ball, he may lose the ability to pick it up. (Sue Duffy, *Acceptance is only the first battle*, Montana University Affiliated Program, 1984, p. 41)

Given the gravity of such questions in the lives of families, it is important for professionals to be sensitive to issues of parental guilt as they and parents work together to order priorities and set manageable short- and long-term goals. Barry's mother describes how she and her child's orthopedic surgeon negotiated a course of action following her son's surgery:

My son was in a total body brace 12 to 14 hours each day following his back surgery. Initially, I was told to turn him every two hours. The orthopedic surgeon and I have developed a partnership in which we honestly discuss what is absolutely necessary in Barry's care. As we discussed the reality of my son's care at home, it became clear that negotiation was possible: Barry, in reality, needed to be turned only every four hours.

Isolation

Parents may have few "outsiders"—friends and relatives—who understand what they are experiencing or who are willing to hear the blacker feelings.

Dealing with an ill child is so often a source of frustration—a frustration I felt was on my shoulders alone. Everyone kept a "Pollyanna" attitude and cheered me on. If everything was so wonderful, why did I feel so bad? (mother of Eddie, Janet, Tracy, and Lori)

* * * *

And last, but not least. I am a teacher all day. I want to be a parent, a mommy to my little girl. Not a nurse, physical therapist, etc. You expect so much. All I wanted to do was to have a normal baby and one day have that baby grow up and leave. I was and am not prepared physically, emotionally, or psychologically to take care of someone forever. (mother of a child with spina bifida)

Fathers may be particularly vulnerable as they traditionally focus on the world of work where they receive minimal recognition, appreciation, or support for their crucial role in the care of their children in need. The organizer of many groups for fathers of children with special needs describes such a situation:

I remember two men who came to the first meeting of the Fathers Group and were surprised to find each other at such a gathering. With amazement and some embarrassment, they discovered each had a child with a handicap — amazed because they had worked together for years but had never shared this "secret." I have heard variations on this story almost everywhere I go. What stands out is the *isolation* so many men experience, afraid to share their special world, fearful of being misunderstood, and unwilling to reach out to others for help. (James May, *Focus on Fathers*, Vol. 1, No. 7, May, 1987, p. 1)

Parents experience actual physical isolation. Laura's mother describes her earliest times at home with her infant:

Laura's pediatrician wanted her kept away from everyone with their wintertime germs—"don't take her shopping with you, don't take her near other kids,"—and of course both the season and the presence of a new baby made it harder for me to get out anyhow. I had been used to working closely with adults and teenagers every day—literally having a couple of thousand interactions—and suddenly I was locked up in the house with a very sick newborn and a cat. The telephone helped some, but my physical isolation echoed the isolating effect of Laura's birth defects.

Keeping in mind these stresses, elements of the relationship between parents and professionals emerge which contribute to the optimal ongoing care of children.

BUILDING A CONSTRUCTIVE RELATIONSHIP WITH PARENTS: RESPECT FOR PARENTS

A recurrent theme for all positive, helpful parent-professional encounters is respect. As discussed in previous chapters, respect for parents begins with acknowledgement of the different sorts of experiences they bring to the relationship with the professional. Respect is the foundation upon which parents and professionals build bridges in the ongoing care of children.

Parents as experts, nurturers, learners, advocates, and decision-makers are allies of the professionals whom they meet throughout their long, at times unpredictable, journey; their quest is to chart the best way to help their child. These parental roles reinforce one another and together, when supported and valued by professionals, create a healing environment for children in need.

Parents as Experts: Listening to Parents

Often above all else, parents emphasize their knowledge of their children and ask professionals to value their observations, thoughts, and questions concerning their child. A mother describes her dilemma and poses a crucial question:

> Most of my negative experiences with professionals stemmed from their reluctance to accept my observations as equal to theirs. This would often put us on "opposite" sides and made us both very defensive. After all, if professionals could trust me to administer medication; do CPR; give oxygen; do carotid massage; do seizure management; maintain airways; order supplies for nine pieces of medical equipment; and stabilize during emergencies, WHY wouldn't they accept my observations and ideas? (mother of Eddie, Janet, Tracy, and Lori)

Regardless of the level of sophistication with which parents express their understanding, a sensitive listener and careful enquirer can obtain a depth and breadth of information about the child which would be unmatched from any other source.

Listen! Sometimes parents are wordy, do not use technical terms and are a little "crazy" from their situation. Nonetheless, they know more about their child/children than anyone else Pay attention. Listen. (mother of a child with multiple handicaps)

* * * *

Treat parents—and even their other children—as equals to the professionals in their roles a "observers." Encourage expert observation. Encourage involvement. (mother of a child with developmental disabilities)

* * * *

The people at the National Academy for Child Development put parental observations first and foremost. They treat our input as reliable and valuable. They believe— how refreshing—that we know our son because we live with him 24 hours a day. (Jeannie Murphy, *Acceptance is only the first battle*, MUAP, 1984, p.28)

In an office or therapy setting, professionals cannot count on seeing a truly representative cross-section of behaviors and skills from their young patients. As one father points out, "An hour and a half observation is no way to judge any human being." The professional who extrapolates from a very small sample of behavior in a traumatic setting such as a hospital or clinic will be working from false premises unless he or she asks carefully constructed, open-ended questions and conscientiously gathers thorough details from the child's parents.

Practice active listening to a parent's report of observations. Be as open-minded as possible, solicit details, and ask for clarifications. Try to respect the parents' status as primary caregivers even if their story sounds odd. Parents are reinforced by instinct that is REAL (Becky's mother).

* * * *

Share the wonderful, vast amount of medical knowledge you have with the in-depth knowledge parents have of their children. Pool your information; help each other out. Learn to ask questions and *listen* to the answers. If you work *with* parents, not against them, you will be amazed at the cooperation and understanding parents will have; even if you don't have answers for them. Just *involving* them in problem-solving creates a positive attitude and good working relationship. (Emily's foster mother)

Even with a bright, verbal child who is old enough to answer questions, parents' input can shed further light on responses to treatment.

The idea that a parent is prejudiced and cannot see important things is not always justified. I have said many times, I have a Ph.D. in my son; I have been around him for all his life and while I may have, at times, needed help to share this information in a meaningful manner, or may have needed discussion to see what might be important, what I knew was in many cases very valuable in finding the key to help Bill work things out. (Bill's mother)

The caregiver who is open to the parents' knowledge of their child is in a unique position to help his or her client. A mother explains:

My son had been in and out of hospital tests from age 4 months to 18 months when I changed to Dr. W. He was the first doctor who listened to me, worked with me to put facts and observations together, and helped eliminate the unnecessary testing. My son with chronic diarrhea was suffering from food sensitivities and allergies—not cystic fibrosis, etc.

Only the new physician's willingness to rely on the parents' observations and accounts made it possible to sort through the complex web of symptoms, tests, findings, and diagnostic possibilities that led to the source of the child's problems. In this capacity as "listeners," caregivers are in a position of special potential.

The parents' observations can be linked in significance, given meaning, and used to further the goals of treatment and progress. Respect for parents as experts concerning their child is particularly important when a child presents with difficult diagnostic problems and dilemmas:

My pediatrician did not abandon ship even when the first two neurologists we consulted found nothing wrong with my son. He saw the problem through over a period of years to effective treatment and diagnosis. We needed his unswerving backing and we got it. (Kathy McGlynn, *Acceptance is only the first battle*, Montana University Affiliated Program, 1984, p. 28)

It is crucial for parents, as well as professionals, to appreciate their core role within the health care team and see themselves as "experts" who possess valuable insights and unique observations. Professionals who foster and nurture parents' self-confidence bring a vital dimension to the child's care. Unnecessary trauma to both children and parents can be prevented. A mother reports:

My son's orthopedic surgeon believed in my ability to care for

Barry after surgery. Barry was in a body brace. We were trying to avoid the pain and discomfort of constantly transporting him to the clinic to check routinely for skin breakdown. Barry's surgeon showed confidence in me and my knowledge of Barry: "You're a better judge than any of my residents. Call me if there is a problem." (mother of Barry and Bobby)

In the hospital setting, parental observations offer staff critical, at times life-saving, data as parents "interpret" the child's behavior. A mother of a critically ill boy shares the following vignette:

I could always tell when his condition was going to worsen a half hour before it did - during those times he didn't want me to leave his side (not even to go to the bathroom). He wanted me to hold his hand and touch his head. The way he wanted me to stay, to hold him, I knew he was afraid. It was a fear I had never seen in him before that time or since. He had four life-threatening crises during his illness. I was able to alert the nurses and doctors about the last two crises. Sure enough, his vital signs changed within half an hour after he became so clingy and afraid. (a mother quoted in Saphier, 1984, 13-15)

Parental observations become vital sources of information when the sick child has severe communication difficulties. Parents offer staff a baseline of what "normal" comfortable play is for their child with special needs and help staff to monitor the child's play and behavior. Parental observations and concerns assist caregivers as they follow the hospital course of a child who cannot alone cry out for help. Emily's foster care mother stresses:

I used to get reports from nurses that Emily was active and playing. I would then find her lying quietly, holding a toy. My knowledge of Emily *playing* was that of a child who would roll around in bed, laugh, giggle, throw toys, bang them together.

When caregivers chart "child awake and playing," that statement is interpreted as the child is feeling better and returning to "normal" activity. Emily was not returning to her "normal" self.

When a child with special needs is admitted to the hospital, the hospital staff should carefully document what parents tell them is "normal" behavior and activity for that child. It's too easy to lump all special needs kids into a category.

Parents as experts, teachers, and resources offer professionals intangible, though profound, experiences and images of love and commitment (Leff,

Chan, & Walizer, 1991). Quietly observing a mother comforting a child with severe health impairments may forever alter preconceived values and expectations. Watching an angry, mistrustful parent slowly, almost imperceptibly, over days and weeks become an ally and partner is a lesson never to be forgotten. An intern recounts such an experience, warm and humorous:

> Before I left for vacation, Mrs. Smith, Carol's mother, gave me the perfect gift—panties—three colorful panties which could not have come at a more propitious moment. Savvy Mrs. Smith shrewdly surmised that, as we were spending hours discussing Carol's severe asthma and eczema and future plans for follow-up care, my laundry must be waiting. She made the day smile.
>
> It is almost impossible for me to believe that Mrs. Smith was "once" the angry, distraught parent who desperately guarded Carol's crib and verbally attacked me as I tried to replace Carol's needed IV. Somehow both of us have changed—grown. (Leff, P., excerpt from diary, 1979)

Parents as Learners

Many parents long to understand, to be informed, to make use of what they have observed, to grow in their ability to help their hurt children. When addressing the parents as learners, it is important to convey the assumption that parents are intelligent people seeking to add to their store of knowledge.

> Yes, educate us. If you use a medical term, teach its meaning. We are just beginning on a personal search for our child. You have an opportunity to provide us with accurate information. *Never underestimate our commitment to knowledge.* (Carla Lee Lawson, *Prescription for Participation*, Iowa Pilot Parents, Inc.)
>
> * * * *
>
> *Please* listen to parents and realize we know that child better than anyone. Realize that parents can be intelligent, *can* understand, and want to know what's going on. We can work better with a doctor if we understand the process, the reasons, the dangers, the possible side effects, etc. (Marilyn's mother)

Professionals can play a major positive role in the lives of families when they clearly and thoughtfully give information to parents. It is important to begin from the premise that nothing is inaccessible to parents' understanding if only the information is conveyed with patience and skill.

I remember speaking at a pediatric grand rounds when a resident asked me where I had learned all the medical information. I emphatically responded, "From my doctors!" It is important for young professionals to understand that parents can and will learn the most complicated data as it applies to their children. My sons' doctors have made their knowledge about my children available and accessible to me. (mother of Barry and Bobby)

* * * *

Nancy has severe, poorly controlled migraine headaches. For a seven-year-old child, this is a major handicap. When Nancy develops a headache, she is very ill, usually vomits, and screams out in pain. It is excruciatingly difficult for us to watch our child cry out hysterically.

The caregivers who have responsibility for Nancy have been excellent. We have been very fortunate. Through them we have been able to recognize some early behavior patterns which indicate a headache. We then can intervene at an earlier point. (Nancy's mother)

Parents count the following among their most helpful experiences:

Nurses told me about my library privileges at the hospital, and I was able to get many articles about BPD (bronchopulmonary dysplasia). (Joel's mother)

* * * *

My most helpful encounters with the health care system have been those times when I was offered information written by physicians and nurses for those professionals. . .

Sam's orthopedic surgeon offered to let me borrow journals to review surgical procedures which he recommended for Sam. . .

Physicians have sometimes taken time to explain Sam's seizure disorder, vision impairment, or shunt operation. . . (Sam's mother)

Parents ask professionals to be flexible as they convey information and meet the individual needs of parents at times of great stress. For some parents information presented orally using clear, simple explanations will be effective; others may request additional reading material and more technical language as well. Parents describe various approaches toward gathering and understanding the vital, often painful, information they must assimilate concerning their children's problems. Respect for individual styles of learning is critical:

> Don't leave parents feeling as if they will have to do hours of library research to make informed decisions. Parents under stress need to hear information in simple, jargon-free terms. Anxiety and despair make all of us simple-minded. (Ted's mother)
>
> * * * *
>
> We were sometimes treated as not smart enough to grasp medical terminology, so problems were explained only in layman's terms. We need both—the layman's terms help us understand, but the medical terms allow us to read and research on our own. (Things Some Professionals Did That Drove Us Nuts And Made Us Crazy: Parents Speak to Professionals, *Acceptance is only the first battle*, MUAP, 1984, p. 25)
>
> * * * *
>
> Teach and train parents if they want to know. Teach them words, concepts; train them to become accurate observers or deliverers of treatments. *Use* the positive energies parents have. (Becky's mother)

Parents may independently investigate new approaches or methods for their child. Willingness to accept parents' valid discoveries and ideas both improves care for their child and broadens the professional's knowledge base.

> When Amber was 5, our doctors still had her in long, metal braces with little white shoes that did not come off. After hearing a brace man at one of our parent workshops, we took her 140 miles to see him. He watched Amber walk holding onto bars. Together we decided to see how she would do in knee length plastic braces. With the plastic braces, she flew. When we returned to our hospital, every doctor agreed that there was no reason why Amber should have been held down by those clunkers!
>
> Another young lady I know also had long, metal leg braces. Her mother asked me if I knew where to get decent orthopedic shoes. I said, "Shoes, hell. Why don't you get her some decent braces so she can wear other shoes?" Since then that young lady has lost 50 pounds, has actually needed a new set of braces, looks great, and loves her 20 pairs of shoes! Her mother and father could have killed me, but I was so happy with the way she looks and the pride she takes in herself. . .

Don't be afraid to try something new . . . (Amber's mother)

* * * *

I found out by trial and error that my son was healthier if I gave him more food and water than anyone would have thought a young child could need. With his choreoathetosis, he has a higher caloric need because he moves constantly. . .I later found medical literature reporting that athetoids need 6,000 calories a day. Indeed, when I would bring my son in for his regular checkups, the neurologists appeared to be amazed that my son was growing well and gaining weight. (Ted's mother)

When there are doubts concerning parents' suggestions, parents appreciate open, non-judgmental discussion of why the professional may be skeptical. Parents strive to do the best possible for their children in need; their hope is that they will be able to bring their plans and ideas to caregivers who will thoughtfully and patiently assess the value of such contributions.

We have sometimes offered suggestions or information based on our own reading, observations or thoughts and been rejected as interfering, susceptible to quackery, searching for miracle cures or unaccepting of our children's conditions. We *do* sometimes bring in weird ideas, but the best way to deal with us is to explain why the idea is or is not good for our child, whether it has been proven false or is still being tested, whether it will actually harm our child to try it. We do not need false hope, but we do need hope—and the fields of medicine and early intervention are ever-changing, sometimes from year to year. Few of us have any expectation that our children may someday be "perfect," but we *work* to help them become less imperfect. (Things Some Professionals Did That Drove Us Nuts And Made Us Crazy, *Acceptance is only the first battle*, MUAP, 1984, p.27)

Parents accept that not every question raised can be answered satisfactorily. Bill's mother observes that some professionals may hold "a belief that admitting no one has all the answers will upset a parent." She adds, "I, personally, would have found it refreshing."

Parents as Nurturers

Parents, as active members of the health care team, act as a major resource for other team members in conveying crucial information concerning their child's specific ways of handling painful circumstances and treatments. Parents must be supported, respected, and valued in their roles as "nurturers" as they participate in reducing their child's distress and anguish:

> Hospitals should have policies encouraging parents to be with their kids as much as possible during painful procedures. Parents should be encouraged to support their kids emotionally through the pain. Parents should be encouraged to find ways to be close to their kids so that the kids have a strong sense of their parents' love. I did infant massage with Patty, and I really believe that our closeness and touching helped all three of us through her surgeries and orthodontic work. (mother of an infant with cleft lip and cleft palate)

Children derive invaluable comfort and support from parents who are able to be present with them during painful, invasive procedures. For children exposed to multiple invasive treatments over a prolonged period of time, parental participation fulfills a crucial need. The child's cries and protest occur within the safety of his parents' presence: he has not been abandoned to face his fate alone. The most important people in his world— his parents—are there to help him through the terrifying ordeal; are there to steer him through the physical and psychological aftermath of invasive and frightening procedures (Leff, Chan, & Walizer, 1991).

Parents repeatedly share experiences stressing the positive, soothing effect their "being there" has had for their children in distress and pain. Parental presence during invasive procedures may not be "right" for all parents. Choices for parents and sensitive preparation are crucial. In the vast majority of situations, the fewest possible barriers should stand between parents and their children in treatment rooms, recovery areas, and X-ray departments (Leff, Chan, & Walizer, 1991). A mother of a toddler requiring surgery describes her journey:

> . . . Having been hospitalized as a child, I am aware of the psychological effects of separating children from their parents during hospital stays, and I have always had a strong opinion that I would provide complete support for any of my children should they require hospitalization. . .
>
> After giving my son's history to the anesthesiologist, I told him that I expected to be with my child during induction of anesthesia. He remarked that this is done for "some children and some parents, but that, in this case, it didn't seem to be necessary."
>
> I can only assume that he felt this way because John was so

calm and was cooperating with every hospital procedure. I would like to point out that I believe that John was calm because he trusted that I would be with him and that he wouldn't have to deal with strangers in a stressful situation.

The nurse who would be in the operating room came over to introduce herself to John, evidently with the assumption that such an introduction would alleviate all his fears of separation and the unknown procedures which he would experience. . . Nevertheless, I repeated the fact that I had told John that I would be with him until he was asleep. I intended to keep that promise.

I was then informed that I would need to gown for the operating room. . .

John calmly and peacefully accepted the anesthesia, and I held his hand and stroked his leg until he was asleep. I left the operating room immediately so that the procedure could be done as quickly as possible.

Since I was allowed to be with John throughout his stay, as I had told him I would—including blood work, induction of anesthesia, and immediately upon his return to the recovery room, he has retained his trust in me and has emerged from this procedure emotionally unscathed. His responses to his surgery and his brief hospitalization appear very positive.

One of the factors which made this experience more bearable for me was Dr. M's [John's orthopedic surgeon's] agreement that I could be with John except during the actual surgery. I am very grateful to him for the arrangements he made in order for that to be possible. His acceptance of my belief that it was important for me to be with John was reassuring. I know that he helped to gain such acceptance from others on the team caring for John. . . (mother writing in *Children in Hospitals, Inc.*, Vol. 21, No. 3, Summer, 1990)

Parents may come to caregivers after having endured memorably bad experiences in which their attempts to be with their children have been squelched. Parents may talk about times when they have been viewed as "meddlers" by health care professionals; when they have been denied access to their needy children in recovery rooms, X-ray departments, treatment rooms; when, as consumers, they have had to fight outdated restrictive policies; when, to their despair, promises made to them and their frightened children have been broken. This, too, has been their reality.

It is difficult to learn about such experiences, rife with pain and anger. Parents appreciate professionals who are able to "listen," to understand that the long-term consequences of policies separating parents from their children in need far outweigh any short-term convenience. Parents discuss troubling episodes in their children's care:

> One of my most painful experiences was being told that *my* presence during my son's small bowel biopsy was more upsetting than if I left. I refused to leave. (mother of a child with severe, chronic diarrhea)
>
> * * * *
>
> Reluctantly, I agreed to the feeding tube with one condition: that I be with her when they put it in. . . Within hours, I walked up the hall. I spotted the resident walking toward me and away from Lindsay's room with a tube in her hand. I hoped I was wrong, that they had not gone ahead and put it in without me. . . As soon as I saw her I knew. She was so mad at me, she turned away from me. How could they violate a trust between a mother and her child? (Valerie Constance, describing her relationship with the medical establishment and their treatment of her daughter Lindsay who was hospitalized with complications from leukemia, *Families and Disability Newsletter*, Vol. 2, No. 2, Summer, 1990, p. 8)

Nurture the "nurturers:" adequately prepare them for the procedures their children will endure and regard them as invaluable partners in their children's total care. Sensitivity to the worries and concerns of parents results in improved parent-professional collaboration. Parents and professionals "working together" significantly reduce the child's distress and fear even under the most difficult, trying circumstances (Leff, Chan, & Walizer, 1991). A mother writing in *AboutFace* poignantly describes her family's experience of preparing her young child for surgery and a frightening post-operative period:

> Just over one year ago we were preparing our little girl for surgery. At first, we were having quite a time dealing with this ourselves, but thanks to all the information given to us by our doctor and all the support of the *AboutFace* office and other families, we came to grips with the situation and were able to give positive and compassionate guidance to her.
>
> After explaining the initial surgery itself which was cranial reconstruction and trying to be positive, we discussed what we would do after the surgery and what games and things we could do while her eyes were still swollen shut. Being an avid T.V. watcher, she was not too pleased with the idea of not being able

to see. I think the absence of sight is one of the scariest parts of surgery for young children.

A couple of weeks before the surgery we gathered up her favorite stories, reading them in great length and looking hard at each and every picture.

We explained that when her eyes were swollen shut that if we read the stories and looked at the pictures she would be able to see these pictures in her mind really well. She loved this way of reading and it worked extremely well for us. She felt and de-scribed her little stuffed animals and toys that she was taking with her and felt comfortable in knowing that she could feel them. We took many story tapes, and the family sent tapes from home to her which she enjoyed.

We are happy to share with you that she has had two opera-tions where her eyes were swollen shut for a few days and both times were made easier by using the method described above. She is now fully recovered and doing extremely well. (Elaine R. Abramsom, *AboutFace*, Vol. 4, No. 5, September/October, 1990)

Never underestimate the resourcefulness and creativity of parents who, with the support of professionals, focus their energies on easing their child's fear. The results are positive and rewarding.

Our seven-year-old son, Matthew, was born with bilateral porencephaly and hospitalized frequently in his early years. Although he is quite stable and progressing, there is still a multitude of follow-up medical visits every few months. Mat-thew learned long ago that a doctor's office is unpleasant for him. He hated blood pressure cuffs and little flashlights, and going for a CAT scan of his head was a major ordeal. We have now progressed to the point where none of this bothers him anymore. This is what we did.

About one day prior to an examination, we would "rehearse." We would wrap him in bath towels, "pad" his head with smaller towels to keep it immobile (just like the technicians do in radiol-ogy), and gently talk to him, reassuring him the procedure would not hurt. We would put "floaties" (swim aids for children) on his arm and practice taking blood pressure. Lying flat on the kitchen table to simulate an examination table was also helpful. If he didn't like the game, we stopped and tried again later. Amaz-ingly, he cooperated very well for a procedure that had been rehearsed.

This is simple to try. Don't expect a child's anxiety to disap-

pear overnight, and remember that sometimes there are procedures that DO hurt. However, young children can still learn that
some examinations don't, and it's great when you can calm their
fears. (Margaret Costantino, *AboutFace*, Vol. 4, No. 5, September/
October, 1990)

Parents as Advocates

Parents must often "speak" for their child who is ill and under stress. In the
bureaucratic health care system of changing shifts, multiple personnel,
and inconsistent caregivers, the parents are the child's constant protectors.

> At times, painful things were done to Ron that could have been
> avoided. For example, a young physician started to give my son
> a shot for surgery before Ron's IV had been placed. I suggested
> that the IV be done first and that medication be given through the
> IV. The doctor agreed it was a good idea, but not official orders.
> I got the orders changed. (Ron's mother)

Because parents are so focused on their own child, they often note
activities, behavioral changes, and omissions in care that may have a
profound impact on their child's well-being (Chan & Leff, 1992). A tired,
flustered intern's response to a mother's midnight advocacy:

> One particularly rough night on call, I was forced to manage a
> bed shortage crisis. I was extremely hassled, bedraggled, and
> very tired. I felt that I was juggling beds around rather than
> taking care of sick children. "Is this why I went to medical
> school?," I sullenly mumbled to myself.
>
> My sheer fatigue led me to a solution to the "disappearing bed
> problem" - changing the room of a youngster who had been in the
> same room since his operation to remove a brain tumor.
>
> When his mother learned of the changes, she, bleary-eyed,
> came running over to me and solidly advocated for her son: "Are
> you people serious? It's the middle of the night." She mercifully
> had brought me back to reality and down to planet earth. I then
> was able to focus my energy on her son recuperating from a
> serious operation and his need for a familiar environment and
> consistent care from his primary nurse.
>
> I thanked Bob's mother for talking with me and openly
> apologized to her. A huge burden had been lifted from me now
> that I was a doctor again and not the conductor of musical beds.

With new perspective, the late night staff and I busily worked together until each new patient had been settled down for the night. (Leff, P., excerpt from diary, 1979)

For many parents the role of advocate is fraught with discomfort. A mother describes how she feels some caregivers may perceive her. She uses humor to convey her role as "just Jeremy's mom:"

There have been moments through this experience when I have thought myself perceived as "Hagar the Horrible," stepping out of the elevator on Peds with a broom in hand ready for whatever stumbling blocks are thrown in Jeremy's way. In fact, I'm just Jeremy's mom - his voice and number one advocate. . .

Bear in mind that we, as parents, are the main communication link between our child and the professionals. We know our children as no other person does, and understand their needs like no other. It is important for us to help communicate our children's needs and feelings to the health professionals. We know when they're in pain or if the chemotherapy and/or radiation treatment is mild or severe to them. We know what to do to make them feel better—what works and what doesn't. We know what is normal for them and what isn't. Because everyone is different, . . .doctors and nurses [must] rely on us to communicate our special knowledge to them. . . .We help them help.

There are times, hopefully few and far between, when we simply may have to ruffle some feathers. It is not easy. We, as parents, are under enough stress already without putting ourselves in yet more difficult situations, but if there are some things that need changing or serious incidents needing to be brought to someone's attention, it is important [that we] persevere. . . Someone is always responsible—it is merely finding who it is that has the power to help. [We] try to be firm, yet polite, as sweetness always goes a lot further than vinegar. . .

We are all parents—and in that there are things we will do for our children that we wouldn't do for anyone else on this earth. One of those things is to do whatever we can to make their precious lives easier for them. We are their voice. So, when you see me and you [imagine] me with a broom in my hand, just say, "See, there goes Jeremy's mom." (Susan Mentzer, Advocating for Your Child: A Parental Perspective, *The Candlelighters Childhood Cancer Foundation Newsletter*, Vol. 10, No. 2/3, Spring/Summer, 1986, p. 5)

Parents emphasize that the advocacy role is a difficult, uneasy one. Temperamental issues, fear of confronting authority, fear of "ruffling feathers," fear of alienating those upon whom their child depends all contribute to parental stress and anxiety. Mothers address these sensitive concerns:

> It takes so much out of me to fight these battles over and over. It is agonizing, for I am in reality a shy person and not naturally assertive. An example, I suppose, of how one is forced to grow as a person when learning to parent.
>
> I have had to grow and change, assert and advocate, reach out and initiate. The birth of this child has been the worst and the best thing that has ever happened to me. I would trade every gain of mine for her health and strength—but then that is not an option open to me. (Laura's mother)

* * * *

> Although I am naturally an assertive person, I occasionally shiver at the work we must do to understand our doctors. I feel real concern for parents who do not have the benefit of our education and experience and who are unable or unwilling to force doctors to explain themselves clearly - define their terms or use analogies that make sense to us. (Connie's mother)

* * * *

> For parents, the struggle never ends. They cannot let up for a day if they want the best for their child. (Joel's mother)

Parents urge professionals to understand their inner turmoil and tension when facing intimidating bureaucracies, when confronting authority figures who appear distant and remote. Parents need to be encouraged to assume their vital roles as their children's advocates. Parents need to know that they are valued as the "voices" of their vulnerable children. Parents need to know that they are respected as the trusted "spokespersons" for their children.

Mothers reflect further on what they have had to learn as both "consumers" and advocates as they strive to obtain the best possible services for their children:

> I am careful to recite all of Sam's medical and educational history in the appropriate jargon to "new" residents at Children's Hospital and our local schools and service providing agencies. Because I now make the effort (and with a twelve year history it is an effort) to show my knowledge, those professionals treat me as if I might have a role in choosing procedures and programs for

my child. I resent having to prove my eligibility time and time
again. (Sam's mother)

* * * *

I have learned to deal with the emotional effects of short-sighted
professionals by writing them letters and getting second and
third opinions, if necessary. I also rely on other parents to steer
me to a specialist who is sensitive to people with handicaps. Of
course, once Jeffrey has been mistreated. . . we never return and
pass the word along to others. (Jeffrey's mother)

Parents speak of "growing" into their roles as their children's advocates
after many years of struggle.

I have learned that I can be the best advocate for my child. As an
advocate, I will insist upon certain things—information, a role in
making major decisions concerning my children. I may not easily
say yes or no without questioning the purpose of a test or
procedure. Realize that it is not you as an individual with whom
I am angry or whom I question. (mother of Len and Thomas)

Professionals who assist and accept parents as they grow into their roles
as advocates for their children can prevent years of pain, self-doubt, and
possible substandard care. The mother of a young man with a diagnosis of
autism discusses her past frustrating experiences in light of her current
relationship with her son's physician:

I have had many painful experiences. First, I stuck with a well-
known pediatrician who had a good reputation for 18 years.
When I discussed the concerns about Simon with him the first
time, he made the "crazy sign" to his temple, and told me I had
a problem. For years Simon had no real check-ups. The doctor
would tell me, "How do you expect me to examine him?" I would
go home crying, not knowing where to turn.
   I finally called a highly recommended young doctor and told
him my problem. I said I would pay for as many office calls as it
took him to get a friendly, working relationship with my son. As
it turned out, he examined Simon on the first visit with success
and no new trauma for my son. Now I feel I was abused for 18
years by the "highly successful" doctor.

For years before grasping her new and powerful role as advocate, Simon's
mother was at the mercy of the caregiver's unhelpful conduct and her own
acceptance of the traditional attitude of inequality between professional

and parent. As a partner in health care, as an active decision-maker, she succeeded in obtaining better services for her son.

Parents as Partners, Decision-makers, and Case Managers

Ultimately, the goal for parents is to grow into their roles as partners, decision-makers, and case managers. For professionals, the matching aim is to recognize the partnership and meet the parents half way.

> Assume that the family is capable and can be a part of the team. If you assume that they are incapable, you end up making decisions that should be theirs to make. (mother of Len and Thomas)

Decisions about care—educational placement, residential treatment, therapies, surgery, bracing, medications—must involve the parents at the most basic level of informed consent. Furthermore, any decisions which mandate demanding programs requiring consistent, persisting dedication depend upon the active commitment of parents and families. Parents rely on the integrity of caregivers, those responsible for providing complete information. Underlying that, however, are mutual goals, a shared vision for the child's present and future. As the persons bearing ultimate responsibility, parents need to be "honored," just as they may need to be helped. Becky's mother describes how joint, concerted parent-professional decision-making changed the course of her child's life:

> . . .That summer Becky fed sporadically, seized frequently, developed poorly. In the fall a major change was in order. All of us—parents, metabolic specialists, neurologists, and radiologists— met and agreed to administer ACTH 6 weeks in megadoses. The results were both disastrous and productive: Becky's hypsarrhythmia [severe seizures] faded, leaving some myoclonic seizures; she suffered severe myopathy and neuropathy and Cushingoid syndrome. We intensified the B12 shots. . .
> Becky went slowly from vegetative and comatose to athetoid to spastic quadriplegic to gradually revitalized status. We switched her to valproate, the most benign of anticonvulsants. Becky learned how to use her hands and arms, then her legs, her eyes, her fingers, a tongue and mind!
> At age 13 months she fed herself; at 16 months she stood; 22

months she crawled; 30 months she walked. Her seizures had stopped totally by then. At 44 months, the barest fragments of speech are beginning. She loves solving problems and outwitting her parents and being with friends. Her doctors and parents meet periodically to examine blood levels, readjust or change medications and "micronutrients," and share news. . .

The following stories illustrate the fears and uncertainty that bracket the process of continual decision-making. A mother vividly identifies the many considerations facing her family when five-year-old Jed was diagnosed with leukemia:

In our own case, there were decisions about whether to seek a second opinion or a different treatment center; whether or not to accept the protocol which the computer selected; whether and what to tell our child, his sibling, our families, neighbors and schools; whether to accept the offer of a former NIH researcher and laetrile proponent to give our son injections secretly. These major decisions all had to be made within the first period after diagnosis—the period of shock when one is suddenly confronted with the unthinkable in this day and age— the mortality of one's child.

Later there were other agonizing decisions: what to do about a child who didn't seem able to tolerate the protocol amount of radiation; whether to allow another drug trial; whether to allow completion of a trial which didn't seem to be working; whether and/or when to stop treatment. The decision between living at all and living a quality life may seem obvious. When it is your own weakened, exhausted, shade of a formerly robust child—it is neither obvious nor clear.

There were more minor decisions, but ones which in totality were as crucial: whether to be assertive parents; to press being partners in the decision-making; to insist on accompanying your child through all medical procedures; to question the nurse about what is going into the IV or why something which the doctor mentioned during rounds is not; to request that a doctor honor a promise to forewarn your child about each procedure; to stop an intern who has made five painful and unsuccessful attempts to insert an IV. Even for educated, sophisticated, professional parents, ten years before assertiveness and medical consumerism were so prevalent, these were not easy. . . (Minna Nathanson, Family Roles in Medical Decisions, *The Candlelighters Childhood Cancer Foundation Newsletter*, Vol. 6, No. 1, Winter, 1982, p. 1).

Parents of children with severe disabilities, serious illnesses, and/or multiple needs must sift through a vast array of at times conflicting professional advice and information to find what is most helpful to their child and to their family. This evaluating and weighing of data are crucial to the family's integrity and stability. A mother writes of her early experience:

> There were times when there were too many professionals involved. There was an infant learning specialist, a vision specialist, an occupational therapist, physical therapist, speech therapist, physician, ophthalmologist, and a child development specialist, all evaluating and treating her simultaneously.
>
> Imagine a young, newly wed woman with eight mothers-in-law, and you get the picture. Each specialist had words of advice, sometimes conflicting. At times, I felt this child was not my own, but belonged to the professionals. I felt robbed of "normal" motherhood and even the right to make my own decisions. (Cari's mother)

Parents welcome the aid of trusted professionals:

> . . . We are blessed with a pediatrician who is not only very interested in Connie and her family, but also is willing to assist us in untangling the difficulties of coordinating Connie's medical care. (Connie's mother)

Professionals who reconceptualize and recast their roles to become "consultants," "educators," and "partners" of families begin to explore the sensitive, delicate task of learning when to "step back" as parents make the decisions they must make for their children and families. "Stepping back" involves understanding that, at times, professionals are most helpful and healing when they empower parents; when they create and nurture an environment of trust that allows parents to participate fully in the decision-making process, to experiment, to investigate, to challenge. Hank's father explains:

> Helpful encounters have included support from our pediatrician when we proposed a therapy program for our son that most professionals don't believe would be of any benefit. For us, it reinforced our belief that we are the primary care-givers for our disabled son—a feeling that, although lost through emotional times, is something we feel deeply. We see ourselves as part of a life-supporting continuum in his life. . .

As we get more involved with our son's well-being, and we have more success, two things are happening:

a) it has restored some of our confidence in our ability to help our son;

b) we are more responsive to suggestions from professionals, now that we see our son get better. For instance, I was not prepared to spend time with him to learn to control—never mind start to use—his electric wheelchair because I believe that he will be capable of getting around on his own, and that driving a wheelchair would not be real independence. However, now that he is becoming more mobile on his own, and recognizes that capability, I realize that it is also important for him to learn to use his wheelchair—the idea isn't as threatening to me any more.

"Stepping back" is not withdrawing from the child and family. "Stepping back" does not minimize the professional's expertise, experience, and caring. A "seasoned" mother notes, "A common complaint among experienced parents is that the more competent they become, the less the doctor will do for them." (*A Few Words to Young Professionals*, Sherelyn Campbell) Parents need professional support, knowledge, and sustained involvement. At its best, the professional's role will be to help parents grow into a sense of themselves as partners, countering their feelings of helplessness, rebuilding self-esteem, fortifying them for the long journey. Connie's mother adds:

[Our pediatrician] also trusts us enough to know that we are capable of handling not only the day-to-day matters, but also that our judgments about Connie's treatment are usually correct.

Respectful Conduct

Pediatricians consulted for the long-term care of growing children, specialists who are intermittently involved in treatment of children with chronic conditions, nurses and therapists who care for these children in hospital and office settings, social services professionals with periodic contacts: all must make conscious choices about the ways in which they will relate to the parents who bring their children in for care. Parents are strengthened and encouraged by respectful conduct on the part of professionals.

Viewing the parents as learners, as experts on the subject of their children, and as partners can positively influence professional conduct.

Small, thoughtful acts and basic politeness reap large benefits in terms of enhanced parent-professional communication. Forms of address; physical assistance to parents in clinic settings; conduct of interviews; and behavior on rounds all contribute to ongoing parent-professional partnerships.

FORMS OF ADDRESS: It is common for professionals to introduce themselves by title and surname and then proceed with business, never having established the identity of anyone else except the patient. Parents urge professionals to learn and use their proper names; more familiar forms of address are appropriate only after mutual agreement to relax formalities on both sides. By addressing the parents using appropriate titles, such as Mr. and Mrs., one sends a message of respect and regard for parents and the critical role they play in the lives of their children.

PHYSICAL ASSISTANCE TO PARENTS IN CLINICAL SETTINGS: Parents speak of difficult physical circumstances in which, for example, they have had to carry their children and equipment alone with little or no active help. Elevators may be broken and stairs the only alternative. Many older buildings do not have automatic doors. Professionals who are able to break out of rigid roles and help parents in such stressful situations are greatly appreciated. A human connection is established that will be long-remembered; the guiding principle of respect is held up and renewed.

> I recall our first trip to [a new clinic] where Laura and I were there hours past what I had expected or prepared for; she was exhausted and hungry, and we faced an hour's drive in rush-hour traffic. This was not a baby who handled disruptions to schedule or late mealtimes at all well, and I was feeling desperate. The social worker went up to one of the floors to get some infant formula and crackers to tide us over. (Laura's mother)

The mother of a child with cerebral palsy remembers with frustration a very different kind of experience:

> During office visits, be sensitive to any special needs. Provide privacy and physical help. I once had to carry my 60-lb. daughter up the stairs because the elevator was broken. All the receptionist did was hold the door. If my child had not been ill, I would have left.

Contrast her story with that of Joel's mother:

The most helpful encounters I have had with the health care system have been with *the nurses*. The most pleasant experiences were "people things" - the nurses' commitment to Joel and to his family. During Joel's stay in neonatal, nurses would bring him to the door at least once a month so the kids could see their brother. This was no easy feat, but my nurses were willing to go to a lot of trouble so the kids could see their brother.

Another kind of "assistance" comes in the scheduling of check-ups, procedures, evaluations, and interviews: asking if these should be planned back-to-back or spread over several days. A mother explains:

> I much preferred successive appointments that spared me an over-tired, over-handled baby. I felt that the findings were more valid, too, if Laura was not subjected to more than one evaluation per visit. I always tried to protect her nap-time, but there were clerks who would show a "take-it-or-leave-it" attitude that was completely unsympathetic. I would have to beg.
>
> I often longed for a "customer comes first" attitude within the health care industry; instead, I felt like a captive audience. . .I do think it is important for professionals to monitor the staff behaviors and provide careful training and a good model. (Laura's mother)

CONDUCT OF INTERVIEWS: Parents appreciate the efforts of caregivers to meet them halfway in the conduct of conferences. Parents urge professionals, if at all possible, to have some familiarity with the record before asking parents the kinds of basic questions they may have answered many, many times before. It is common to streamline the review of the records by asking the parents to summarize, but the complexity of many cases, particularly over time, can burden the parents. The tendency is for the professional to try to rush the story; the result is that the parent feels harried and hurried. Moreover, clues in puzzling cases may be missed if an interview is confined to "yes-or-no" questioning.

Thick, complicated charts can be intimidating. However, the effort made to distill basic, pertinent information demonstrates to parents that professionals are trying to learn about their child. Bill's mother shares:

> A small point, but one I found infuriating: the professional's not reading the case before interviewing me. I had gone to the trouble

to keep a diary during Bill's early years, and had digested out all the succinct information on his milestones—when he first sat, crawled, spoke; his immunizations, traumas, etc. I had provided this record for his case record. Almost invariably, the professional interviewing me would ask for the very information that I had already provided; in fact, my own memory was fuzzy without being able to refer to that record, so what that person had in the folder was better than what I could recall on the spot. How many times I wanted to say to the person in front of me, "Please, read the record!"

Sensitive, caring conduct of interviews and meetings with parents entails attention to many details that reflect the caregiver's thoughtfulness and concern. The timing of the meeting; where it will take place; who is present; the time set aside for full discussion; and plans for follow-up are crucial. Parents have stressed the following "Tips for Professionals:"

. . .Remember that you and the parents are part of a team. The atmosphere that you set is crucial, and initial arrangements and remarks set a tone that will affect all future interactions. You have specific knowledge and expertise, but so do the parents. This meeting is a time to share your individual perspectives and insights on behalf of a child.

Let the parents speak. Give them time to talk about their child, to tell you what he does on Saturday mornings or with his grandfather. Let them explain how they are feeling about his progress and what they think a next step should include. . .

Have you made an assumption or reached a decision about the child already? If you have, tell the parents immediately! Is the purpose of the meeting to bring the parents to the same conclusion? Or is it to discuss the child and together reach a decision? Do not pressure the parents to make an immediate decision unless it is absolutely clear that everyone agrees on a course of action. Be prepared to arrange for a later meeting or discussion. . .

Do not overwhelm the family with information and paperwork. When eyes start to glaze over or questions cease, stop the meeting and plan another one.

Thank the parents for their help and their commitment to their child. (Prepared by Polly Arango for New Mexico Parents Reaching Out PRO, 1127 University, NE, Albuquerque, NM)

Displaying Honesty and Accepting Honesty

The basis for communicating with parents *must* be total honesty and openness on the part of professionals...This means dropping the paternalistic notion that families must be protected from the, perhaps, depressing realities. (Minna Nathanson, Family Roles in Medical Decisions, *The Candlelighters Childhood Cancer Foundation Newsletter*, Vol. 6, Winter, 1982, pp. 1 & 3)

Parents and professionals are able to build ongoing, supportive relationships only upon a foundation of mutual trust: parents will rely on one's honesty, even when it pains them.

When we feel that health care professionals and facilities treat us like helpless, ignorant recipients of their services, we're more likely to be distrusting and even hostile. We're also more likely to expect them to be miracle workers, capable of fixing things that can't be fixed.

When there is open sharing of medical information, we feel respected and empowered to ask questions and address concerns as they arise, rather than after they have grown and festered. When we are denied information, or discouraged from seeking it, we resent the paternalistic treatment, and communication between parents and professionals suffers. And then we don't feel like we're on the same team anymore. And how difficult are the jobs of both parents and professionals when it seems as if we're on opposing sides; when all the while we know that our child's welfare depends on a concerted effort by everybody. (Marie Deatherage-Newsom, Have you seen your medical records?, *The Bridge*, Winter, 1988, p. 18)

Honesty may take the form of clarity in language; euphemisms can be less-than-forthright:

I spent almost five years trying to find "developmental disability" in the library. An educator finally took the time to sit with me one afternoon and tell me our son was actually retarded. Big deal! Why didn't someone tell us in the first place? Out of all the conditions listed under "developmental disabilities," we had no idea which one our son fit into.

In all those years of medical reports, the words "mental

retardation" were not mentioned. Maybe, as a health professional, those words might not carry much hope, but, as a parent, I can use those words to connect with other parents as well as with specific information and programs. I now have a "place"— parents and kids with whom I can identify. (Greg's mother)

Accepting honesty is no less vital. Accepting honesty rather than fleeing or minimizing parents' painful feelings sets the tone of all effective parent-professional relationships. Parents understand that this is a difficult, sensitive aspect of one's professional work. Such openness often comforts and heals; it is deeply appreciated by parents under siege:

> If parents seem "overly emotional," be patient. Remember, they live with and care for their child 24 hours a day. The long-term stress this puts on the caretakers is difficult for many professionals to understand. Our families endure much. Be patient. (mother of a child with cerebral palsy)
>
> * * * *
>
> Try to give us a little room when we go crazy. You have bad days, and so do we. You have 8 or 12-hour shifts, days off and paid vacations. We don't. (Keough's mother)
>
> * * * *
>
> Be an effective listener, not only to the words, but also to what is behind the words. At times, I have shared my depressed. . . thoughts with our pediatrician. He listened without panic. His comments were supportive, and I knew that he respected me as a person and a mother. (mother of Len and Thomas)
>
> * * * *
>
> Give parents permission to talk about their feelings, to be extremely tired, to cry. Cry with them if you are truly sad. Don't hide your feelings to protect them. You are in a position of authority and your permission (and modeling) gives their feelings validity. (*Suggestions For Medical Personnel. . .When a Child Dies*, The Compassionate Friends, 1986)

Accepting and Honoring Parental Worry

Every parent can recount anxious calls and office visits which in fact turn out to be baseless. Sensitized by a child's chronic or disabling condition or "at risk" status as the graduate of a neonatal intensive care unit, parents may bring the child in, only to find there is no treatable condition or problem. Parents appreciate gentle handling at such times. Although the acute crisis may have passed, parental worry does not easily fade once a child's welfare, even life, has been profoundly threatened.

Gratefully, if anxiously, taking their vulnerable babies home, parents experience much stress as they watch their children adjust to their new surroundings. Tension and fear may become constant companions of these parents over many months and even years of their children's lives:

> All parents worry about illness and accidents, but parents of formerly hospitalized babies are particularly afraid. Since many babies have been kept on monitors until the day of departure from the hospital, parents are terrified to leave their babies unwatched. A funny cough, a strange gurgle, an unusual color all leave the parents weak with fright, uncertain of the proper action to take...
>
> It can take months before the parents can sleep soundly at night or comfortably leave the baby with another caretaker. Sooner or later the baby, so vulnerable at birth, loses his fragile appearance and begins to look and act more like a normal child. The parents, however, retain their vulnerability and continue to look at their baby with crisis-colored glasses.
>
> Parents and family members of these children are relieved when a baby finally walks at twenty months, only to worry again when the baby is saying only a few words at age two. It seems that one milestone met precedes another one to surmount. Doctors' assurances aside, few parents of formerly vulnerable infants can put aside early fears and face each hurdle with equanimity. For who's to say that the newest hurdle won't present evidence of a heretofore unidentified problem? (Page Talbott Gould & Lenette S. Moses, Mild Developmental Delays From a Parent's Perspective, *Equals in this Partnership*, NCCIP, 1985, p. 15)

For many parents facing such situations, smoldering anxiety and dread remain a part of their lives as they help their children to grow and learn. Even when parents' concerns for their children appear unfounded in professional eyes, caregivers who listen with understanding are able to support and fortify parents, allowing them to acknowledge and discuss their worst fears.

> Eventually, the memories of the horror of early days give way to a feeling of pride that the child survived and the family became whole again. But it's important for those involved with the care of these families to understand that concern and anxiety do not

dissipate when the possibility of a severe disability has been ruled out, particularly if the potential for brain damage was originally raised by the medical staff. Professionals should assume the responsibility of helping the family deal with their ongoing concerns no matter how long they might last or how real they might be. (Page Talbott Gould & Lenette S. Moses, Mild Developmental Delays From a Parent's Perspective, *Equals in this Partnership*, NCCIP, 1985, p. 16-17)

The mother of Joshua and Miriam, premature twins, illustrates how the developmental assessment team helped her to regain confidence:

The follow-up with the developmental assessments for the babies was reassuring. The staff was very supportive of our parenting and willing to listen to our fears and concerns. Sometimes it was just the willingness to listen without judgment or do-it-this-way advice that was helpful.

When parental anxiety is not treated with respect and care, painful conflicts emerge—"the clash of the professionals' perceptions of what's significant with our honest concerns as caring parents." Laura's mother continues:

We have had issues brushed aside when the consultant of the moment considered it irrelevant to his arena. At one point, I asked the thoracic surgeon about the psychological/emotional effects of upcoming surgery on Laura, then 6 1/2 months old. His response: "It doesn't matter because she has to have the surgery anyway."

Parents emphasize that all such things do matter; they matter most of all to those who will be helping their children endure the aftermath of treatments and procedures. In many circumstances there are no answers. Parents also understand that there may be no alternatives. However, their fears and worries must be taken seriously and addressed with compassion and care. Parents and children can be prepared for difficult experiences, and attention to special concerns can enhance healing.

When Conflicts Arise

During times of heightened stress, tensions may often arise between parents and professionals. The mother of a child with many follow-up post-op visits describes such a situation from the parent's perspective and offers an opportunity to consider ways of better handling disturbing conflicts—preventing the anger and hurt that may haunt both parent and professional long after the actual episode has passed:

> After Laura's orthopedic surgery when she was five, she had many follow up visits. During one, the casts were cut off to allow for molds to be made for the new post-op braces and then reapplied. Laura had been a pretty good patient, but she was tired of being "fiddled with" after the frightening noise of the cast saw and the uncomfortable plaster casting of her legs and feet (each one with three healing incisions). When we got back to the clinic floor after the long trip to the orthotics lab, Laura had had enough and began bellowing and kicking as the doctors commenced applying the wraps for the new casts.
>
> Nothing I could do helped; I was tired from the long drive - preceded by elaborate preparations for the care of her baby brother - and hungry, and exasperated myself. Staff members made increasingly frustrated comments - "We can't do this if she keeps kicking," and "You've got to get her to quiet down!" - but I didn't have the nerve to ask them to step out and wait for a minute so that I could talk with Laura. At last a nurse brought in a small paper pad and a green marker and handed them to Laura, who finally quieted and began to doodle while the doctors proceeded. It only took a few minutes for the acrylic wrap to harden, and I said thankfully, "Whew. That was fast." A doctor turned around and snapped, "Yes, once *we* got her distracted!"
>
> He was in effect blaming and punishing me for being ineffective as well as failing to acknowledge how hard I had been trying, how much strain I had been under, and how difficult it can be to calm a child who has "had enough." He was angry at me for failing to make things go smoothly; and I'm still mad at him for unleashing his emotions on me. The situation was hard on all of us. In a better outcome, we could have *both* said, "Whew!"

Few parents will directly talk to professionals about hurtful encounters. Parents may fear reprisals and may feel helpless. However, their anger remains, and tensions may fester. Nonverbal cues, such as tense body language, anxious facial expressions and long silences, may indicate parental distress and a breakdown in communication. At this point, it is crucial for health care professionals to step back, take another look at the painful situation, and honestly ask: "What has been my contribution?" (Leff, Chan, & Walizer, 1991)

Seeking feedback from parents and children is a caring act that demonstrates respect and concern. Such self-examination and openness are difficult and courageous. However, the ultimate rewards of working through this process both enhance professional satisfaction and lead to improved communication with children and families. A mother reflects:

> Of course, it takes courage to look back and really see if you've said or done something that has, in fact, provoked parents' justifiable rage. Parents repeatedly tell us about thoughtless remarks made to them, evasiveness, poor or nonexistent communication with professionals. It takes guts to admit such an error. Real guts. Apologies can go a long way! You will be long remembered as an ally and healer. (mother of a teen with severe developmental disabilities)

The care of children who do not improve places great stress on parent-professional relationships. A mother describes how blame and guilt may erode good care. A solid foundation of open, honest parent-professional communication prevents the painful rifts that only add to parents' despair. A mother explains:

> After a long relationship, it isn't uncommon for resentment and frustration to surface on both sides as earlier expectations are shattered. Unless communication is excellent, as it was with Dr. P., a parting of the ways is inevitable. Treating children who do not live up to a prognosis is difficult—I am sure. But some professionals find it necessary to place blame for the failure or to minimize the impact of the disease or the situation. (mother of Eddie, Janet, Tracy, and Lori)

In high-stress environments, such as intensive care units, a team effort is a necessity in coping with parent-professional conflicts and misunderstandings that may inevitably occur. All concerned—parents, children, and caregivers—cope with severe, moment-to-moment stress. Team support helps to diffuse the unrelenting pressures of the intensive care unit and reduces lapses in parent-professional communication (Green, 1979; Waller, Todres, Cassem, & Anderten, 1979). An experienced social worker emphasizes:

> Some parents with a desperately ill child who is not improving may more easily talk to members of the ICU team not involved with the child's direct medical care. Perhaps, because we are not personally responsible for daily management of the very ill child,

it is easier for us to listen to distraught parents without becoming defensive.

At times, when parent-professional conflicts occur over a poor prognosis, the parents may appear not to hear the grave news and may refuse to speak with medical staff about the devastating prognosis. Nurses and doctors become frustrated with the parents as well as frustrated with their own helplessness; communication breaks down.

When I meet with such parents, many *are* able to talk about both the poor prognosis and their fears. Parents may fear that the medical staff will give their child less than optimal care if they openly acknowledge the horrible news. They fear that the nurses and doctors will not try, will abandon them and their child.

I bring this information from frightened parents back to our team. When we understand that the parents' response is their way of protecting their child, a breakthrough in communication often occurs. Those providing direct care feel less threatened by the parents and approach parents with greater sensitivity and awareness of their terror and despair.

A team approach is crucial. (personal communication: senior social worker)

Commitment to open parent-professional communication; respect for parents' courage and love; and parent-professional collaboration in developing guidelines that clearly describe the role of parents in clinical settings are critical initial steps in resolving and alleviating damaging conflicts and misunderstandings (Brown & Ritchie, 1990; Leff, Chan & Walizer, 1991). Sharing one's concerns with parents often enhances this ongoing process. A mother honestly states:

When you are getting frustrated with my child's care, please convey this to me in direct terms. I am probably feeling the same way and would enjoy the company! I will feel free to share my real feelings with you. The following kinds of statements will help both of us: "I'm not sure what direction to go right now"... "I wish I knew what else to do". . ."I am stumped, but we are in this together, and we will keep on trying." (mother of Eddie, Janet, Tracy, and Lori)

In the face of overwhelming problems, uncertain futures, and unanswered questions, professionals may experience in some degree the limbo in which parents live. Parents greatly value professionals who are able to acknowledge the limits of personal knowledge and ask for help. Professionals who openly seek assistance for both themselves and parents during times of painful uncertainty in a child's treatment convey a powerful message of concern and caring. Parents urge practitioners to view such openness and honesty as a courageous act—not as a sign of incompetence or weakness (Leff, Chan, & Walizer, 1991). A mother of a child who is chronically ill and technology-dependent observes:

> When you are feeling helpless and anxious, you could bring a new face to our appointments—not just for a second opinion, but someone with whom to share your own feelings of frustration. Another doctor, social worker, nurse, or technician would diffuse the overwhelming intensity of our time together and allow me to ask someone else the questions I may have asked you a dozen times or more. (mother of Eddie, Janet, Tracy, and Lori)

In summary, parents grapple with many issues including vulnerability, guilt, and isolation as they care for their children with special needs. Professionals who respect parents' struggles play a vital role in offering support throughout their ongoing journey. Respect for parents as experts, nurturers, learners, advocates, and decision-makers is a core concept. A partnership with parents reinforces and expands the professional's contribution to the care of children with serious problems. Displaying and accepting honesty and honoring parental worry help to alleviate parent-professional conflicts that may arise during times of great stress for children in need, their parents, and the professionals who care for them.

HANDLING THINGS BETTER

Perspectives

PARENTS AS LEARNERS;
REACHING OUT TO VERY SICK PREMATURE INFANTS

Parents deeply appreciate knowledge that extends beyond technical issues and helps them understand their children's emotional reactions and ways of responding. Parents yearn to communicate with their children—lovingly touch their babies. This yearning, this longing for contact, is particularly poignant and acute when the baby is a vulnerable, sick, premature infant who requires life-support technology in an intensive care setting.

Parents of premature babies urge professionals to understand their deep need to nurture their baby. Parents urge professionals to help them learn how to reach out effectively, soothingly to their seriously ill infants. In the following vignettes, mothers discuss ways of improving the emotional care of parents of premature babies; of enhancing the process of bonding; of creating an environment which heals the severed connection between child and parent.

Joshua

Teaching parents what to expect regarding how their children will look, the path of progress, how to touch their babies is so very important.

Joshua was my little fighter. He was the second twin born and was very sick. At one point while sitting by Joshua's bedside, I was touching him gently, stroking him lightly. He began to twist and try to cry. Joshua almost extubated himself. As bleeps and buzzers sounded, the nurse came running over. I felt more like a criminal than a mother.

It was a time of intense despair. I felt reprimanded by the nurse and totally helpless and inadequate. I tried not to cry as she showed me a more effective way of nurturing and touching my son. Had I been taught this approach from day one, a very difficult moment for both Joshua and me could have been avoided.

I now know there are videos that instruct parents how to touch and read the cues of their premature babies. How I wish the staff had presented these tapes to us as a way to understand our babies, to become more knowledgeable, to feel more in control.

Nicholas

Sometime after Nicholas had started nursery school, I saw a grainy, black and white videotape that demonstrated what Dr. Brazelton calls the "irresistible responsiveness" of a premature baby. I almost cried while I watched as a 3 lb. preemie slowly followed a ball with his eyes, looked for the sound of his mother's voice, and with heroic effort, finally turned his head and even reached for her. A nurse practitioner had taught that mother to read the subtle clues that could have drawn me to my son so much earlier. It was a piece of information, a teachable skill, that might have changed the course of our lives. (Ann Oster, *Equals in this Partnership*, National Center for Clinical Infant Programs, 1985, p. 3)

Situations to ponder

PARENTS AS LEARNERS; WHEN PROFESSIONALS
FAIL TO UNDERSTAND WHAT PARENTS SEEK TO LEARN

It is crucial that a professional informing parents is teaching what the parents seek to know; incongruity —a lack of synchronization of the needs of parents with the values of professionals—may lead to deep misunderstandings.

Neil

> Neil's social worker suggested we see a doctor there for *genetic counseling* when Neil was about two months old. We made the appointment and assumed they would tell us how this had happened by studying mine and my husband's chromosomes. When they finally saw us, the doctor and several student doctors came in; they took turns listening to his heart and pointing out all the different signs of Down's that he had. It was like they were picking him apart piece by piece, all the things that were wrong with him.
>
> The doctor then drew a picture for us on the paper that covered the table and told us it was the 21st chromosome that had a little tip on it that caused the signs Ryan has. He asked if there were any other questions, and I finally said shyly, "I thought we were going to go through genetic counseling," thinking they would study mine and [my husband's] chromosomes to see where the problem was; I would finally know *what* or *who* caused this.
>
> The doctor said sternly, "What! What do you think I just talked to you about?" I started crying, embarrassed that I didn't know, that what he had just gone over *was* the genetic counseling! He said to the students, "She's still unaccepting of this situation and is upset; let's go." I was so mad and just too embarrassed to say the reason I was crying was because he made me feel like a *fool* in front of all those students.

Parents came to this appointment expecting a very different sort of experience; the geneticist made an assumption that they understood the nature of genetic counseling for this case. Yet it appears that even the most basic information (of the accidental nature of this chromosomal error) was not effectively communicated to Neil's parents.

Many underlying, deeply painful questions brought the parents to the genetic counseling session. At the heart of their despair is irrational guilt: Are we somehow to blame? Am I to blame? How can I live with this crushing guilt? What are our options concerning future pregnancies? What does this mean for our relationship as a couple?

Given their urgent distress, parents need to hear from "the expert" that they have done nothing wrong, that they have neither "harmed" nor "maimed" their beloved child. Addressing the parents' inner turmoil, eliciting their worries and concerns about the future, and allaying paralyzing guilt are major goals of sensitive genetic counseling for this couple.

The mother's shy question means that the parents' expectations have not been met; the professional has an opportunity to treat the parents as learners, to explain more fully the mechanism of this well-understood birth defect, and to clarify misconceptions. There is potential here for a heartening and sympathetic relationship. The physician, perhaps impatient with this "routine" birth defect, sees no reason to suppress his spontaneous expression of annoyance. The opportunity to recoup, to educate parents and to model constructively for students, is lost when instead of perceiving the mother's hurt and offering a graceful apology, the physician terminates the interview with a judgmental evaluation of this mother's "non-acceptance." Narrowness of vision and lack of manners have separated the learners from a potential teacher.

Professionals who are most comfortable in research or laboratory environments have a responsibility to understand and value the crucial, highly sensitive, healing role of genetic counseling in the lives of distraught parents. Those professionals who by temperament and/or training are unable to counsel the parents of children with genetic defects would serve patients and families by honestly and openly acknowledging their discomfort in the counseling role. Referral to colleagues who can engage parents and speak to their needs is a considerate act.

Contrasts

PARENTS AS NURTURERS; YOUNG CHILDREN UNDERGOING PAINFUL PROCEDURES; PARENTAL PRESENCE; STRESS ON CAREGIVERS

The impact on both parents and health care professionals of a screaming, terrified young child undergoing painful treatments for cancer can never be underestimated. Adults understand that the treatments are absolutely crucial to the child's remission and prayed-for cure. However, the emotional resources and coping mechanisms of young children are fragile. Young children live in a magical world where painful treatments may be viewed as punishment or a massive assault by powerful adult figures. The child is overwhelmed: screaming and fighting become the child's way of assuming some degree of control over the intolerable event. From the child's perspective, fighting may be an adaptive response; a tenuous barrier against passive submission and serious depression. The scenario is set for extreme tension among all involved. Anxiety and dread in such situations are often severe.

In the following vignettes two trainees describe their experiences with young children receiving treatment for acute lymphocytic leukemia (ALL) in the hematology/oncology clinic. Both young health professionals were involved with the parents of the children. In the first narrative, a child life student discusses an episode in Maria's care. In the second account, a pediatric resident shares her memories of Linda.

Maria

Today I encountered somewhat of a contradiction between what I have learned through my readings and work in child life and what I saw practiced in the clinic. A highly trained mental health professional was preparing Maria, a preschooler with ALL, for painful procedures she would experience that day. The mental health professional brought Barbie dolls from her office and asked Maria a series of questions about her treatments. From what I could surmise, she was trying to calm Maria by preparing her for the procedures prior to going into the treatment room.

The "contradiction" arose when Maria began to thrash about in the treatment room. At that time, both Maria's mother and grandmother were in the treatment room with her. Maria's fears and anxieties increased right before the procedure was to start, and she became more and more agitated.

The nurses and mental health professional tried to soothe her, but when their efforts failed, they asked the mother and grandmother to leave the room. I heard them tell Maria that if she didn't calm down, *that* is what would happen from now on.

I do not know the line of treatment that the staff had worked out, but it seemed unfair to threaten Maria, a very young child, with withdrawal of her family at the time of her greatest need. I thought about many possibilities . . .

Perhaps, Maria was quieter and more easily managed when her mother was not around. Still, it seemed unfair *to me* to tell Maria that she had to be a "good girl" in order for her mom to stay with her. What I thought might work were relaxation techniques similar to the ones we saw on the video that Maria and her mom could practice together.

After this "ordeal," Maria's mother spoke with me. She appeared visibly shaken and expressed concern that this *was not* necessarily the best route to go. Since I knew very little about the case, I was only able to listen.

Linda

An incident involving a little girl with ALL has remained with me for many years. Linda was having a great deal of distress during the procedures: spinal taps and bone marrow aspirations. We called in a psychiatrist who could be in the clinic and help Linda and her dad who was always there for his child. The psychiatrist also did medical play therapy with Linda. She told me that Linda took great care with the dolls and was gentle but efficient. A great future doctor or nurse!

One morning I was to do the spinal tap. We had been telling Linda that she could yell and scream all she wanted but that her holding still was really important for everything to go quickly and smoothly. I felt bad when Linda would curse and yell at us, but I knew that she was responding to the stress of the situation: she was coping as best as she could. Five seconds after the procedure was over, she was joking and laughing with us!

That morning was a bad one for me. I tried and tried but couldn't do the procedure. Linda was very cooperative given what she was going through. Her father was gently talking to her and massaging her head. The psychiatrist was encouraging her and her father.

Finally, my attending came to the rescue, and the procedure was done. He was great. There was never any anger from him or suggestion that I was incompetent or a bad doctor. Just-not-my-day. But . . . *I* felt totally inadequate and horrible within myself. I kept saying to Linda, "It's not your fault. It's my fault. It's my fault. I'm so sorry."

The psychiatrist gently turned toward me and quietly stated, "It's nobody's fault. Really - nobody's fault. We're all trying our best."

Linda's father then nodded his head and smiled at me.

Young children may be friendly and cooperative before the painful procedure. However, the invasive nature of the treatment itself may overwhelm the most even-tempered, generally well-coping child. Linda, for example, despite her chemotherapy and its debilitating side effects, was a sweet, affable child who regularly attended school. Maria, despite her blood-curdling screams during treatment, was a friendly, charming preschooler who loved to interact with staff.

Doctors, nurses, and technicians in the outpatient clinic frequently see the child when he or she is in crisis. Learning about and focusing on the child's strengths—life at home and at school; playfulness and friendliness when not in pain—may help besieged professionals endure the child's moments of despair. Clinic staff's hard work and care are crucial elements in maintaining the child as an outpatient. It is important for caregivers to share in the child's and family's accomplishments and value this broader aspect of their work. Screaming and pain are only one aspect of a total picture; clinic staff can take pride in efforts to treat seriously ill children as they learn, play, love, and grow within their homes and communities.

The student caring for Maria shares her confusion. She has learned about the value of parental support from child life philosophy and practice, her supervision, and her readings. However, when the mental health professional felt under extreme pressure to quiet the child, principles vanished. The student is struggling with many issues: to threaten a child with withdrawal of his parents' protection and love in order to control his immediate behavior during a time of great stress may "work" for the moment. What is the ultimate cost to the child, parent, professional, and parent-professional relationship? Parents view such a threat as a grave misuse of power and breach of trust. Parents also must deal with the aftermath of such an extreme situation—an angry, sullen, despairing child who believes that his parents have betrayed him.

What are ways of helping children and parents during painful treatments? What are ways of helping the health care professionals who must endure emotionally exhausting treatment situations? Mutual support is essential. Health care professionals need time to "decompress," unwind, support one another. Health care professionals need time to engage parents as part of the treatment team; as, for example, "coaches" to help their children learn and practice relaxation techniques; as "consultants" who know what has soothed and comforted their child in previous stressful situations.

The role of parents is crucial. Whatever else is happening to the child, his parent is there to comfort him. He has not been abandoned to face his terror alone. Parents able and willing to be with their child throughout the course of the child's treatments offer invaluable support that extends well beyond the limited confines of the treatment room setting.

Despite best attempts at play therapy and relaxation techniques, some children will not be comforted. When all else has failed and the child can only wail inconsolably, his parents remain in the treatment room to massage him, sing to him, be with him, hold him. Parents and children will never forget the strength and compassion of health care professionals who nurtured such moments; allowed such moments to be despite their own inner distress and turmoil.

Health care professionals need time and a safe "space" in which to acknowledge and share their own fear and trembling. The young trainees working with Maria and Linda have briefly stepped into the world of child and parent and have discovered an openness to better ways. Linda's pediatrician has emerged with a new appreciation of her role as physician and healer.

Perspectives

PARENTS AS ADVOCATES

Parents "speak for" their children in many situations—some expected, some unexpected. Advocacy is a never-ending process. Parents will be constantly called upon to bridge gaps for their children; to fight for their children's rights within at times rigid systems and bureaucracies.

It is important for professionals to understand the meaning of these continual "battles"—some small and humorous, others grave and intense—in the lives of families. Parents expend much physical and emotional energy in their struggle to create the most "normal" life possible for their child. They need one's ongoing support and help.

Ellen's mother describes how she changed the atmosphere of Ellen's well-baby visits:

> I used to get so depressed after a well-baby check-up. It took me a while to figure out why. During those visits all I heard was what Ellen *wasn't* doing—not able to hold her head, not able to roll over, and on and on. So I changed that some.
>
> I go in and say, "See how pretty Ellen is. See how well she can smile. See how she follows with her eyes, etc." The professional will usually then comment on something positive. Ellen's inabilities are very visible so there is no need to dwell on them.

Linda's mother describes how she affected the attitudes of Linda's fourth grade classmates:

Never in my wildest thoughts could I have foreseen my role as my daughter's advocate and spokesperson. Mothers do what they have to do.

When Linda returned to school during her chemotherapy treatments, the kids were taunting her because of her hair loss and physical changes. Kids, fearful and ignorant, can be very cruel. But I also had faith in the basic good sense and fairness of most nine-year-olds. The teacher invited me to talk with the class.

I was so proud of Linda. Despite the nausea, pain, and extreme fatigue, she was going to school, working hard, and holding her own. My pride in her accomplishments came through as I spoke to the kids. They asked many questions and learned a great deal about old-fashioned courage—Linda's courage.

You could have heard a pin drop in the class. By the time our discussion ended some kids were crying: others came up to me and apologized. Linda continued to love school and made many friends that year despite her ordeal. (mother of a child with acute lymphocytic leukemia)

Keough's mother presents a humorous experience with health care professionals:

Our "funniest" encounter with medical personnel came when Keough was hospitalized during a period when she was pulling her trach tube out periodically. The medical orders included tying down her hands. Because she couldn't talk with the trach, she had been learning sign language at home and having her hands tied down made that impossible. She became very frustrated.

Of course, the nurses couldn't untie them without a doctor's okay, and the residents wouldn't give it. My husband waited until late that evening when Dr. J got out of surgery and asked for a change in the orders so that Keough would be free to sign.

"Why would she want to sign her name?" asked Dr. J.

"No," said my husband. "She uses sign language! And if she does pull out her trach, there is a whole roomful of people here who know how to put it back in." And Dr. J. laughed and changed the orders.

Amber's mother reports on her battle:

Amber is on catheterization which took us to the Supreme Court of the United States. Now, all children in the United States who need CIC (clean intermittent catheterization) in school can obtain it (even though some schools still say they don't have to do it... YES THEY DO).

The CIC battle was long and hard and still not over. I had the medical. . . advisor to the school as well as one of the medical doctors on the school board pull a lot of dirty tricks, but justice won in the end.

Amber is 12. I started when she was two and a half, and we are still trying to get our attorney fees through the courts. A lot of hard times, crying and a lot of high blood pressure medication.

Contrasts

PARENTS AS DECISION-MAKERS; SECOND OPINIONS

Parents repeatedly and consistently speak of their need for clear, accurate, up-to date information on which to weigh options and make treatment decisions. The stakes for parents are very high. Professionals who understand the limits of personal knowledge and encourage "a second opinion" in difficult situations are acting in the child's and family's best interests. There is strength rather than weakness in knowing when to help parents obtain another point of view or perspective as serious questions arise in a child's care.

Connie's parents recall with bitterness and much anxiety an episode in their child's care in which they struggled alone to seek out a second opinion concerning a critical surgical procedure for their child. Contrast their story with that of Keough's parents.

Connie

Recently, one of our regular doctors, a craniofacial plastic surgeon, gave us some incorrect advice concerning the time when a particular surgery could be performed. In the last month, we sought additional opinions concerning this procedure and were told that not only could the procedure be performed now, but we might be causing Connie's teeth to be significantly damaged if we did not perform it very soon. The reason why our old surgeon could not perform it now was an appropriate concern for adults, they said, but not for small children.

Our anger with the surgeon was exacerbated by the fact that he had actively sought to prevent us from seeking other opinions.

Keough

The comment on second opinions brought back a memory. When Keough was three and trach removal was going nowhere, we decided to get a second opinion. We asked around and got the name of another surgeon and asked our surgeon to send him Keough's records. He agreed and also said that the second doctor was a good surgeon and that he (our first surgeon) had, in fact, trained him. "Tell him that if he can get Keough's trach out, I will personally send him a dozen roses," he said.

Well, we went off to get our second opinion, and the doctor turned out to be a jerk. He told us that it was time to "start living" our own lives and put Keough in her own room (which, at the rate she clogged up at night, was tantamount to a death sentence in our eyes). Needless to say, we returned to our original surgeon with relief and renewed respect.

Contrasts

DISPLAYING HONESTY; WHEN MISTAKES OR IATROGENIC COMPLICATIONS OCCUR

There is no more difficult situation in displaying honesty than under the circumstances of iatrogenic complications. Institutions and human beings are imperfect. Despite efforts to minimize the frequency and severity of mistakes, errors happen. In the following vignettes, parents discuss the role of parent-professional communication (or lack thereof) before, during, and after serious failures in the care of their children.

Laura

Laura's mother describes the silence of many professionals following her daughter's heart surgery and subsequent paralysis that forever altered her child's life:

In our case, one experience—actually a block of time—overrides all others for sheer destructive force. I still have periods of rage, nightmares, and reliving it all, not helped by the discounting and denying from professionals who necessarily hear of some of this. To sum up before I begin: Laura was harmed, and then we were all wronged.

What happened: After medical management had failed, Laura required a second surgery for coarctation of the aorta. . . Since that day, she has been partially paralyzed from the chest down due to inadequate circulation to her spinal cord while the aorta was clamped. A strong possibility is that failure to react to a drop in her blood pressure during the surgery allowed this to happen. Whether or not negligence was indeed a cause, what followed was deliberate, unethical, and unforgivable.

They lied. Not just one doctor, or two, but many, repeatedly, by design. When Laura was released from CCU to the floor, I was horrified to see her. She was in what I now know as a Lumbar 2-3 position; she looked like a frog. While she was waving her arms (this in spite of the huge chest incision), her legs were nearly immobile. She could no longer roll. She did not kick.

I kept saying, "Something is very wrong"—sometimes using my body to block the door so the whirlwind tour of professionals could not escape. . .—only to be told, "You're a mother. You're being hysterical. Ignore it. It will go away." They sent us home with a permanently crippled child without a word.

And—because we continued to question and request appointments—this conspiracy was extended to include the neurologist, the physical therapist I insisted on, etc., etc. When did we learn that Laura had a spinal cord injury and was permanently disabled? When we moved to a distant state six months later.

Didn't we already suspect? Oh, yes, but we *hoped* we'd been told the truth. . .

The cloak of silence surrounding Laura's second surgery raises profound legal, ethical, and moral questions. As growing numbers of seriously ill children undergo intensive, technically complex treatments and procedures, the issues called forth by this family's extreme situation become increasingly pressing and urgent. How will parents be informed of "mistakes?" How will parents be informed of iatrogenic complications that permanently change the course of their child's life? How will professionals react to parents' knowledge of dire complications? What is professional integrity? Laura's mother continues:

Is there any value in going over the reactions we encounter? I have had doctors refuse to put down "spinal ischemia" or similar because they will not accept the idea that this was a catastrophic complication of surgery: they will put down CP or ask if she were evaluated for spina bifida or even put down "diagnosis deferred." I read one chart where the doctor had put that "I realize mother believes this problem is iatrogenic and she is very distrustful and questions everything." I can get a killer headache just thinking about these sorts of incidents: they add to my pain and reopen wounds that I had managed to let heal: it is an additional betrayal that the truth not be acknowledged. . .

No one ever, not once, even hinted they were sorry this had happened to Laura. . .

Contrast the experience of Michael's parents. Honesty and open communication in the face of serious neglect proved to be a powerful deterrent against malpractice litigation as well as parental anguish and bitterness.

Michael

There were several foul-ups in our son's NICU care, the most notable being the time his ventriculostomy tube became clogged and "exploded" in his head. Spinal fluid from my baby's head was dripping on the floor by the time a nurse discovered the problem. The sutures in his head, which had been open too much due to hydrocephalus, were now overriding. He was supposed to be getting one-on-one care, but the NICU was understaffed; we were told they were very sorry. We got differing opinions from the neonatologists whether or not this would cause more brain damage.

Many months later we thought about suing for neglect. We went to the biggest, meanest, nastiest shark of an attorney in Miami. He was willing to take our case, but insisted that we sue everybody—even the obstetrician and pediatrician. Mark and I balked at that. We didn't want to sue them; they had had nothing to do with the ventriculostomy debacle. We also remembered how Michael's main neonatologist would sit with us, twisting his hands, and letting us see the agony in his eyes. He had a young family, too; he related to us; and, therefore, we related to him. We didn't want him to be hurt. We dropped the case before it even got started. The lawyer shook his head over us—he thought we were soft. Maybe so, but we knew we couldn't live with ourselves

if we hurt people who didn't deserve to be hurt. (Ronnie Londner, IVH Parents, May, 1991)

Perspectives

HONORING PARENTAL WORRY

Becky

As wonderful as I'd found the metabolic team to be in communicating to me about [Becky's rare] disorder, I found the neurologists worse than difficult. On hypsarrhythmia [a rare seizure
disorder], they stonewalled me. I found a quiet place on the
ward—a closet—and sobbed. "Poor prognosis. . ."—these words
rang in my ears—"no longitudinal studies. . ., one out of 10 kids
escapes mental retardation. . . severe disorder. . ."
  Wait a minute, I told myself when I wept my eyes to redness.
This is [the tertiary care center]. These people are some of the best
in the world. They can't be blamed if nobody knows more. But at
the same time, someone must know more. So I went back to our
original resident. He was doing rounds on ICUN, but made time
for me. He said, "Becky has a chance. Some metabolic kids have
hypsarrhythmia, and if they get the substrate along with the
anticonvulsant, many do pretty well. Don't go by the neuro
department's statistics. Remember, this is *metabolic*. You keep up
those B12 shots and the nutrients and good feeding, and we'll
work from our end."

In this vignette, the mother of a child with a rare, mysterious disorder
shares both her grief and panic with one of the residents caring for her
daughter. He neither minimizes nor trivializes her anguish but offers the
ray of realistic hope that gives meaning to her struggle. The resident caring
for Becky has enabled her mother to emerge from the "closet on the ward"
and assume once again her vital role in the care of her child.

5 Ongoing Care II: Respecting the Child

Once the worst of the pain was past, Laura was expected to stand using a walker. "She has to start bearing weight," the PT declared. "Start with five minutes." She left. I tried to devise some incentives for Laura—taping a piece of poster board to the locker and having Laura stick stars onto it—but it was difficult to keep her motivated and distracted from the pain. Laura herself set greater goals: "I want to walk to the nurse's station." She was exhausted by the task, but she managed it.

"That's enough for now," I told her, and I lifted her up to take her back to her room. I wondered if Olympic athletes had as much heart. (Laura's mother)

Parents value professionals who unmistakably care about their children. Valuing has been discussed previously, and application of those concepts is important here. Parents appreciate caregivers who strive to understand the child's experience of illness or disability and look beyond diagnostic labels; the importance of respect for a child is a consistent theme.

Understanding the Child's Perspective

When children enter the frightening hospital or clinic environment, they experience major disruptions in their normal routines and activities. Important aspects of their lives are taken out of their control, a devastating experience at any age (Pendleton, 1980; Leff, Chan, & Walizer, 1991). Intrusions by large numbers of strangers, however well-intentioned, are common. Parents understand the necessity for hospital routines: however, basic courtesy and thoughtfulness soften the impact of the many disruptions they and their children must endure. Victoria's parents describe frequent, frustrating experiences:

Our daughter's defects have required surgery for correction. A quite annoying and hurtful experience has been when health care professionals come into the room without introducing themselves or even asking if it were an OK time for them to look at Victoria. . .

Some staff members would come into Victoria's room in the middle of the night, turn on the light, drop the bed rail down, and then wonder why my husband and I weren't very friendly or why the baby was scared to death!

Sensitive professionals on the front lines of care can play a major role in helping children to develop ways of coping with the unrelenting, unforgiving loneliness and terror of illness and hospitalizations (Kunzman, 1972; Koocher & Berman, 1983; Patterson & Geber, 1991; Leff, Chan, & Walizer, 1991). An understanding of developmental needs and tasks guides caregivers as they interact with frightened, at times confused, young patients and try to clarify misconceptions and quell fears. Parents observe:

It is stressful, even for a small child, to feel that you have no control over what is happening to you and no idea what is wrong. I think it is extremely important to help children understand and deal with what they are experiencing. Children can, even at a young age, learn to be active in their own care if they are prepared ahead of time and given information on a continuing basis. (Stan's mother)

* * * *

Some young doctors fail to introduce themselves to the kids or fail to explain what it is that they're doing. It is also important that the doctor ask for a response. Sometimes my children reveal misconceptions or fears in the questions they ask doctors, if they have been given the opportunity to do so. (mother of Mickey and Todd, children with a severe neuromuscular disorder)

Children undergoing treatment will worry about missing friends and favorite activities, separation from their family, pain, reasons for actions and events, and the security of their hospital room. Gently asking a child about his or her concerns, fears, and hopes often opens the door to understanding. A teen who has had multiple hospitalizations emphasizes:

When patients are in the hospital, they wonder what's going to happen next. What tests will be done? What medicines do I have to take? Who's going to take out my blood? Will he get my vein? How many times will he stick me? Will I be able to sleep? What will I be able to eat? Will I get an IV? Do I have to stay in bed? I feel afraid, confused, upset, in pain, and sometimes mad. But I still have to live with it. But, please doctor, can you please be more of a partner, more like a friend? And I know it will make it easier. (personal communication: a teen with chronic kidney disease)

It is critical to listen to young patients and learn about their concerns and lives outside of clinical settings. A young girl "...who has just discovered that she's 'different'" speaks to professionals:

> My name is Tracy. I'm 12. . .I have epilepsy. . .I will try to explain what epilepsy is. You get dizzy, headaches, and light-headed and see things and people disappear. I feel dumb sometimes. I don't think I will ever get the lead part in ballet because I have epilepsy. I'm afraid of having a seizure because I'm embarrassed that someone will see me.
>
> I always wonder if I'll be able to drive. I sometimes wonder if my children will be born with epilepsy. . .One girl in my school has epilepsy and is in a mental hospital now. I don't want to be like her. I wish something could make school easier so I wouldn't feel different. Sometimes I think the teachers are lying about my grades to make me feel better. I'm afraid my friends will find out about my grades. . .
>
> I would like help from my doctors or anybody who knows how I feel.

The young child with a chronic illness who requires repeated invasive treatments presents health care professionals with intense emotional and physical challenges. The cries and screams of young children who cognitively and developmentally cannot help but see doctors and nurses as threatening, intrusive figures may arouse much anxiety in their caregivers. One's own discomfort may lead to underestimating the vulnerability of children who have endured multiple invasive procedures. There is often an assumption that these children are "prepared" for the procedure. Children may appear open and cooperative until the time of the actual procedure when they react negatively—screaming, kicking, cursing. Other children may withdraw, quietly suffering within themselves (Kunzman, 1972; Leff, Chan, & Walizer, 1991).

A child life intern discusses her feelings as she tries to understand what painful, invasive treatments and tests mean in the lives of young children:

> Since the clinic was quiet, Ned was called almost immediately to the finger-sticking room. What followed really came as a shock.

I heard voices first . . . that was common enough. Then the pitch rose sharply: it was Ned. He was screeching and hollering about the procedure. Loud quarreling and physical restraint by his mother followed. Eventually, he was screaming and crying and fighting with more force than any other patient I had ever heard in the clinic. Two children in the play area were both startled by this and stopped what they were doing. Quietly, I walked over to the door way and said I was going to give them some privacy by shutting the door. I closed it.

The receptionists behind the desks called me over and said they couldn't believe that Ned still responded that way. [Staff] thought that since he had been receiving treatments for a long time, he would be used to it. Why did he carry on the way he did?

Immediately, a dozen thoughts ran through my mind. Did I do the right thing by closing the door? . . . Isn't it OK that he is still fighting? . . . I mean some kids do seem to get used to it, but maybe they do not show their discomfort . . . Perhaps, Ned needs to scream and protest to get by . . . Perhaps, it is that fight that helps him take control of the situation he is in. I was not able to answer the question that was asked of me . . . (child life intern: journal entry)

While parents are totally committed to making the child's treatment possible, they ask professionals to understand the adaptiveness of a child's "fighting" response. They ask that the child's feelings be recognized as valid. "Please see children as whole people with feelings and reasons for crying," says Marilyn's mother.

Children are entitled to have parents as active helpers in their care. As discussed under "Parents as Nurturers," respect for children must acknowledge their profound need for parental support during times of fear and pain. Stan's mother shares the thoughts of many parents who have offered support and comfort to their children in strange and threatening medical situations:

Parents need to have access to their children in every area of the hospital; they can provide information and reassurance which will help the child cope.

Ellen's mother speaks to the needs of children with severe communication difficulties:

It is absolutely mandatory that parents be with their children during hospital stays. Often you are trying to treat an emotionally unstable, previously traumatized, non-verbal person with no means of communicating fear or discomfort. So many times our children are unable to cope with these situations alone.

Laura's mother poignantly recalls:

Sometimes I wondered if I was really of help to Laura in her moments of extreme fear or anguish. One unforgettable, touching moment gave me my answer.

Laura's legs were in casts from toes to knees after the surgery; the doctors had allowed room in the casts for swelling, but Laura's feet and legs, despite being elevated, began to swell far more than expected. The pain woke her out of her morphine sleep; she began to whimper and then to scream. The puffy toes peeping out of the cotton began to turn bluish. The nurse ran for the phone. When the breathless resident rushed in, she took one look and muttered, "I wish they had told me to bring a cast saw," and hurried out to find one.

(The minutes of waiting were endless. I had never seen Laura in such overwhelming pain. The screams were literally ripped out of her as the pressure increased; she was so in the grip of pain that it was as if she had been transported beyond my reach. I tried to encircle her with my arms, saying over and over, "Mommy's here; mommy's here. The doctor is hurrying." She seemed not to hear me.)

Now, cast saws were chief among Laura's true hates; the noise had always frightened her out of her wits, and no amount of demonstrating had ever assured her that she would not be hurt by the blade. I braced myself for a grim scene as the resident plugged in the saw. I brought my face in front of Laura's and told her, "Honey, the doctor must cut the casts to give your legs room and stop the squeezing and bad hurting. You *absolutely must* hold still, but you can scream as much as you need to, and you can hold my hands as tight as you want to, as long as you don't move your legs."

White and sweating, Laura took my hands and gasped, "Thanks; it's good to have a friend like you." (Laura's mother)

Parents report experiences in which professionals have tried to comfort children with security objects in lieu of parents. While security objects can be helpful to a child, there will be times—the most important times—when a beloved doll, stuffed toy, or blanket is not of help; when the child cries out for a parent. Laura's mother discusses both the value and limitations of security objects as parents and children face great terror and distress:

> . . .Not all children form strong attachments to items as "comfort"
> objects. For every Linus inextricably attached to his blanket, there
> is an independent, bold child who sallies forth unencumbered by
> extra baggage. My daughter was such a child. When she was ill
> or threatened and afraid (as she always was when we visited the
> doctor), she wanted one thing: her mother. My shy son was often
> helped by his fuzzy coverlet, but when he had really been hurt,
> he wanted and needed the comfort of real arms: he wanted his
> mother.
>
> I often felt that the professionals wanted the security object
> more than my child: they wished to feel that they were meeting
> psychological needs. I could sympathize with their feelings:
> when the moment came that my child was wheeled away into
> surgery, I was grateful to think that she was not completely alone;
> that bear was my stand-in. It probably comforted me more than
> it did Laura that she took it in with her. . .Maybe the grown-ups
> need the security objects, the talismans, as much as the children.
> After the surgery, during her days of great pain, Laura never
> asked once for the bear. She wanted only her parents, touching
> her, comforting her, never out of sight.

An understanding and awareness of the child's developmental and cognitive abilities will help caregivers to be flexible as they reach out to the child. Approaches that may be appropriate for older children and teens may simply terrify very young children. Engaging young children in strange and frightening situations calls forth one's creativity, sense of humor, and ability to try new ways. Laura's mother remembers:

> At my first encounter with one agency, the social worker led us
> to her office and sat down behind her big desk. Laura was always
> alert for danger signals that meant "doctor," and she freaked. I
> tried to tell the social worker what was upsetting Laura, and
> suggested that she use the other chair near me, but I don't believe
> she took me seriously. Laura was only 14 months old; I certainly
> couldn't explain to *her*. I think the professional needed to do the
> adjusting. We could have just as easily had our interview in a
> playroom, or sitting on the floor, or even in the hall.

Recognition of developmental and cognitive issues not only improves communication with the child but also spares the family unnecessary blame and guilt. Stan's mother reflects upon her past experiences:

My son has mild cerebral palsy, a profound learning disability, and. . .emotional and behavioral problems. He also must cope with a very low tolerance for pain. The greatest problem we have had with medical personnel is getting them to understand that he perceives his world in a different way. This has been a particular problem with mental health professionals. Stan started receiving counseling when he was six years old; the major problem was finding a counselor who understood learning disabilities and how a neurological condition can cause emotional fragility. I so resent the implication that if they could just fix what is wrong with our family that Stan would be all right.

Professionals as Nurturers

Attention to subtle aspects of treatment and care enhances the healer's own identity: How does the child understand what is happening to her? Have we listened to her worries and possible misconceptions? Are we aware of her pain or discomfort? Have we considered the importance of the timing of the procedure? Will she be embarrassed—her privacy invaded? Has she been offered some degree of control? (Leff, Chan, & Walizer, 1991; Patterson & Geber, 1991)

Parents can help caregivers develop creative, individualized approaches. A child's "lifestyle" issues may thus influence treatment decisions. Laura's mother explains how her daughter's potential isolation was avoided when the youngster's point of view was given weight and respected. Responding to this mother's advocacy, professionals caring for Laura adopted a more flexible planning stance for the timing of her surgery. Through his alliance with Laura's mother, the surgeon came to understand the child's priorities and the value of peer support:

When an orthopedist initially suggested that Laura would have to have surgery, he told us, "Of course, we'll do it during the summer so she won't miss school."

I was thinking, though, of a friend who had told me that the worst thing about having polio was that every summer she had surgery, and by the time she was recovered, the summer was over and she had missed all the fun. Laura was only in Kindergarten; how much could missing some school matter?

The more I thought about it, the more reasons I could see for doing the surgery during the school year. Laura's teachers included a little unit about doctors and hospitals in their curriculum. When Laura entered the hospital, her class drew pictures and wrote her letters. Her teacher paid her a special visit. The second week was a school holiday period anyway, so Laura in reality missed only five days of school When she returned, she wasn't a victim, she was a heroine. By summertime, her casts were off and she was in new braces, ready to swim and dig in the sand like all the other kids.

Health care professionals greatly reduce anguish and fear when they appreciate children's helplessness and powerlessness and provide their young patients or clients with some measure of choice over treatment. Parents tell with deep gratitude:

> Before one of Amber's eye operations, the anesthesiologist remembered that Amber had hated the mask and had been terrified by it. He decided to use another method. We appreciated his concern for our daughter's feelings. (Amber's mother)
>
> * * * *
>
> Two weeks ago my four year old had an IV done *in* the office for dehydration. Trauma was reduced for *all* of us in a familiar setting. (Marilyn's mother)
>
> * * * *
>
> Getting Laura to the recreation room was a task for Hercules. Acquiring a bed cart, assembling pillows, moving Laura with her IV, maneuvering down the hall and onto the elevator, managing the swinging doors. . .and then Laura, flat on her back with her legs up on the piles of pillows, announced she wanted to paint, of all things. I was daunted by the logistics, but the child life workers arranged a way to let her paint. No one even tried to talk her into something more easily managed. My hat was off to them! Laura could only interest herself for a few minutes before she was too tired and uncomfortable to keep on; and no one tried to keep her at it. I appreciated the space they gave her. . . (Laura's mother)

Preparing the child for painful procedures; gently easing his or her distress with calm, comforting words; giving the child as much control as possible over the terrifying experience; and encouraging the child to practice very simple relaxation techniques open paths of caring and healing. Health care professionals illustrate such a process:

> Nina looked very frightened while she waiting for the fingerstick. I told Nina that she could hold my hand and even squeeze it tight while the technician was taking the blood. We practiced

"holding and squeezing." I also told Nina that if she both squeezed my hand and talked to me maybe the testing wouldn't make her so upset.

When it was time for Nina to go into the treatment room, we made our plans together. Nina and I then put our plan into action. It was a success. (child life intern: journal entry)

* * * *

Julie, 11 years old, very much wanted to participate in her own care. She would tell me which arm was best for finding a vein, cut strips of tape, carefully cleanse the area, and ask many questions. She was truly my helper, and I tried to let her know what a good job she was doing. However, when the actual puncture occurred she wanted to turn away and be comforted by her mother. Julie's mother and I tried to work out a schedule where she could be with Julie during these procedures. Involving Julie in her own care helped to reduce anxiety for everyone. (personal communication: pediatric intern)

Parents add gentle "touch" to this list of positive interactions with young patients:

> Touching is a privilege some physicians [and other health care professionals] under-utilize. It can be very healing. Many chronically ill children are handled medically, but rarely touched. (Sherelyn Campbell, *A Few Words to Young Health Professionals*)

* * * *

> . . .One nurse in Michael's NICU often "wore" him next to the watch pinned to her blouse; she went about her business with Michael like a boutonniere on her lapel, caressing him with her hands and her voice. Debbie was a perfect example of how health care professionals can communicate their affection for their patients. . . (Ronnie Londner, IVH Parents, *Address Delivered to the North Central Neonatology Issues Confab*, Koehler, Wisconsin, May, 1991)

Time with the child is well spent (Brunnquell & Hall, 1982). The child and professional share nurturing moments that resonate throughout the child's health care experience. The dividends in both patient and professional satisfaction and well-being help to counter the stress inherent in treating devastating childhood illnesses and/or disabilities (Leff, Chan, & Walizer, 1991).

Children with mental handicaps are particularly vulnerable to a brusque, hurried approach. Calm words, gentle touch, eye contact with the child, time to explore medical instruments, and simple explanations of what the child will experience go a long way in engaging children who may be unable to express their intense worries and fears verbally.

It is crucial for caregivers to appreciate and value their attempts to "meet" the child at his or her level of understanding. Such efforts forge a positive bond between child and professional. Parents of children with severe communication difficulties and/or multiple handicaps realize that their children will require more attention, more skill, perhaps more time, and more true use of the art and science of taking care of children. Parents rarely forget a professional who has treated their special child with care and respect.

> If you treat people with handicaps, you have to be willing to take extra time and put forth extra effort. Don't take shortcuts. Handicapped people cannot afford them. Show them the medical tools. Explain what you are going to do.
>
> Most importantly, show a caring attitude. If you cannot do these things, don't traumatize our children by rushing, restraining or drugging them. Refer them to professionals who have a positive attitude toward the handicapped. Parents will never feel abused if they see you are treating their loved ones with care and understanding. (Simon's mother)
>
> * * * *
>
> Don't be (or act) afraid to touch the child or adult in an appropriate manner. It is easy to be turned off by people who, for instance, drool. Always acknowledge the child or client even though he or she may [be unable to] acknowledge you. Think of how you feel when you're ignored. Believe me—our children comprehend eye contact. (parents of a daughter with cerebral palsy)
>
> * * * *
>
> I would like young health and family care professionals to understand that members of our families with disabilities and chronic illnesses are first and foremost—human beings. Even though thoughts and feelings may not be expressed easily by a person with a disability, it certainly does not mean that those thoughts and feelings do not exist.
>
> When Jill is placed in a situation that she does not understand, she feels fear. When someone takes the time to talk to her and explain the procedures involved, the fear subsides. What a person can or cannot do should not be the measure of how much respect he or she receives. (Jill's mother)

Seeing Beyond the Diagnosis

Children with multiple problems and disabilities are children first. The mother of a preschooler with spina bifida stresses:

> Caregivers working with chronically ill children constantly need to remember that there is a child within the body. Extra care must be taken not to cripple the spirit of the child (or the spirit of his parents!)

As important as diagnostic categories are in developing treatment and remediation programs for a child, they cannot encompass the reality of the child's world. Larry's mother, a pediatric social worker, explains:

> I am the mother of a "low incidence neurologically impaired" five-year-old boy, Larry. Other labels include: mild learning disability, attention deficit disorder, receptive language disorder, mild hearing impairment, sensory integration impairment. A more human description of my son is that of a child of normal intelligence who is creative, has a great imagination, talks up a storm, and loves to be with people. Larry needs a great deal of adult help in thinking through solutions to problems, following directions, and working with other kids. As in my son's situation, a simple diagnostic category rarely captures the reality of complex children with unique strengths and weaknesses.

Professionals focusing on a child's complicated technical needs may, at times, lose sight of the fact that all of this complexity is wrapped up in a very real child, generally more like any other child than he is different. Ben's mother recounts:

> When Ben was 7 years old, he was admitted to the hospital for a hernia operation. Staff encouraged me to go home in the evening to rest. Shortly after my arrival home, a nurse phoned. She was very upset because Ben was standing up in bed, and staff didn't know what to do. I asked her if she had told him to sit or lie down. She replied, "No, of course not. He's retarded, isn't he?" I suggested she go back to his room and tell him to lie down and behave. When I called back later, Ben, indeed, was lying down and sound asleep.

Ellen's mother contrasts two contacts:

An orthopedic doctor evaluated and examined Ellen without touching her once. Needless to say, we never went back again. When a professional touches and holds a baby, he or she shows acceptance and caring.

[Another] doctor, upon seeing my daughter for the first time in an emergency situation, treated her as a *child* first. He talked to Ellen knowing full well she could not answer him. He was the first professional to attempt to communicate directly with Ellen. Although she is nonverbal, he continues to address questions to Ellen, and I'll answer if necessary. Ellen doesn't fuss with him.

Jill's mother echoes those words:

The most helpful encounters within the health care system have been those where professionals have dealt with the issues at hand as they would with any so-called normal patient. [Those] who have taken the time to talk to Jill and explain the reason for the visit and the procedure have accorded her the respect and dignity that is the right of any human being.

When a child's essential individuality is denied and he or she is seen only in terms of a diagnostic category, "overattribution" may become a serious problem. In this troubling situation, caregivers perceive every difficulty or temperamental trait the child may display or develop as a manifestation of his or her underlying illness, disability, or other condition. Not only may health care providers lose sight of the child, they may risk misdiagnosis or fail to give optimal care as well. Parents count "overattribution" among their most negative experiences with professionals. In the following quotation from a letter (never answered), Jeffrey's mother describes such an episode:

Looking back to Jeffrey's appointment. . .with you and comparing it to the appointments with the other two doctors, I now know why I felt so uncomfortable with your opinion. When you first walked into the examining room that day, you questioned me as to whether Jeffrey did, indeed, have Down Syndrome. When I replied yes, you murmured something to the effect that that answered a lot of questions. When I asked you what you meant by that, you said you wondered why his X-ray showed such small bone stature for a six and one-half year old boy.

At that point, I feel you formed an opinion of Jeffrey's problem based solely on the fact that he had Down Syndrome. I don't believe you listened to anything else I said. You treated Jeffrey as a Down Syndrome boy who had a limping problem. The other two doctors viewed him as a boy who had a limping problem who happened to also have Down Syndrome. They treated him and me with the sensitivity needed, and unfortunately not always found in the medical field, for a person who has a medical problem and who also happens to be otherwise handicapped. . .

In my heart, as the child's mother, I found it hard to believe that there wasn't a physiological reason for the limping and that there wasn't anything I could do to help Jeffrey. . . Surely you realize that people with Down Syndrome are just that; people who happen to have Down Syndrome. To treat them otherwise is insensitive and could be, as with this case, a dangerous thing to do.

In fact, Jeffrey did not have lax ligaments; he was suffering from Perthes disease. The doctor to whom Jeffrey's mother was writing was unable to see beyond the diagnosis of Down syndrome. Unlike the other two physicians Jeffrey's mother would consult, his judgment had been clouded by assumptions about "children like this."

Jeffrey's mother speaks of her long quest to discover the reason behind her son's pain and discomfort. Anxiety and worry were ever-present:

This was one of the most traumatic emotional experiences I had to go through with Jeffrey aside from the initial diagnosis of Down Syndrome. I'm just thankful that the proper diagnosis and treatment were found, and that the damage and long-term effects are minimal. I'll never forget that gnawing feeling I had in my stomach for 15 months wondering what was the real problem. Even harder was watching him go through what had to be painful limping episodes, all the while denying he was in any pain.

Building Long-term Bonds

The dream of many parents of children with special needs is that they find professionals who are stable caregivers over time and who show themselves willing to learn and to grow. An educated and objective professional, delivering services over a continuous period, is in a position to develop a relationship which is uniquely caring. Parents realize that no one outside the family circle can know their child as intimately and thoroughly as they do, but they welcome the special alliance of long-term bonds. Parents are alert for signs that a caregiver is willing to plan for the

long haul, to give the benefit of a doubt, to wait and see, to learn and even
to change.

> . . .My OB told me to put Neil in an *institution*, because I was
> young and this was just a freak thing, so I could go on and have
> normal children. *I cried. I couldn't believe he was saying this.* Five
> years later after getting an update every year from me on Neil,
> and Neil coming in to hear the heartbeat of his two brothers, my
> OB apologized. He said he told me to institutionalize Neil so I
> would have an out if everyone else was telling me to keep him
> home. He wanted me to know it was OK not to keep him home
> if we didn't feel we could. I didn't see that at the time. I
> thought he. . . didn't realize how much these kids could do.
>
> We really love our family practitioner and feel very close to
> him. We've been with the same OB all these years, too. We feel
> pretty lucky to have had them.

Neil's family is, indeed, lucky. They have had the healing experience of
seeing a doctor learn, grow, and ask their pardon. Many families would
have left the practice after the crushing blow of the obstetrician's suggestion; the doctor might have gone on to repeat this hurtful advice. Instead,
he has acknowledged to himself and to others that he needed to change; the
long-term relationship allowed this to happen. Clearly, Neil's mother
values the bond that the years have built.

Many societal trends impede the establishment of all-important long-
term bonds. A mobile society in which people move frequently as well as
uncertain financial commitments for human services are among such
impediments. Although parents hope for the ideal, they greatly value
those professionals who are able to prepare them for unexpected possibilities. Keough's mother describes her relationship with her daughter's
home trainer:

> One of the first things Jan, our home trainer, told us was that her
> goal was not only to show us how to teach our daughter specific
> skills, but to teach us *how* to teach her so that if we ever found
> ourselves without services we would still know how to facilitate
> progress. After three and one-half years of working with Jan and
> my daughter, I know I would hate to see Jan go—she has become
> a good friend as well as someone whose professional abilities I
> respect tremendously—but she has come close enough to her
> goal that if we were suddenly shoved out of the nest to fly on our
> own, I think we could. In these times of uncertain and shrinking
> funding for human services, it's a real comfort to know we've

learned well. (Sue Duffy, Parents, Professionals and Conflict, *Acceptance is only the first battle*, MUAP, 1984, p. 42)

In summary, professionals convey respect for children by embracing attitudes, behaviors, and policies that further humanistic and creative solutions to the problems of providing services to complex clients. By recognizing children's needs for dignity, support, and developmentally-appropriate choice and control over their lives, professionals make the necessity of ongoing care less burdensome. Through their continuing relationships with children, professionals derive enhanced satisfaction from their difficult work.

HANDLING THINGS BETTER

Perspectives

UNDERSTANDING YOUNG CHILDREN'S FEARS: DEVELOPMENTAL ISSUES

Health care professionals in training speak of their fear of causing pain and fear in their young patients. A child life intern currently in medical school expresses his anxiety as he observes children's responses. The distress and panic in the eyes of his very young patients elicit many questions and concerns. Writing in his journal, he discusses his dilemma:

Timmy

I was somewhat surprised today to see the negative reaction of a patient to a doctor. I was playing with Timmy in the playroom when a doctor, wearing street clothes, walked in. At first, Timmy became a little apprehensive, but when the doctor walked over and checked his neck glands, he became agitated and tried to push the doctor away. I understand that the child considers that doctor a threat, but before [my experiences this summer,] I never realized to what extent these feelings pervade his mind.

Influenced by my own knowledge, I thought that even though the child might not like the procedures performed by the doctor, he or she would know, down deep, that the doctor was ultimately a positive force. Timmy's actions, however, made it quite clear to me that no such understanding is present. In fact, Timmy further showed his fear as we walked back from the playroom; as we moved past the "treatment" room he stopped, pointed, and said, "This is the room that makes me cry."

...Is there anything [doctors and nurses] can do to improve the situation, or are they doomed by circumstance to be the object of hatred? These questions have made me re-think my position: am I a trusted friend as long as I am no more than a "play partner," or does my status change if I am present when a child goes through discomfort?

Young children are developmentally unable to distinguish a "healing" hurt, the result of a test or procedure, from pain inflicted maliciously. To very young children—toddlers, preschoolers, and primary-grade children—bodily intrusions by adult figures, no matter how benign or well-intentioned, are profoundly threatening. In the young child's magical world, illness and treatment may be perceived as punishment for bad thoughts or deeds—real or imagined. Many young children must be reassured that they have done nothing "wrong," that they have not caused the illness. Very young sick children must be constantly reminded that they are "good," that they are loved.

Knowledge of cognitive and developmental issues can help professionals to realize that a young child's anger and protest are not a personal attack. As professionals and parents navigate the stormy seas of a young child's panic, despair, and terror in health care settings, an understanding of developmental issues provides perspective on the long journey. Gentle touch, communication with the child, open, positive regard for the child, and humor help adults, both parents and professionals, to endure, survive the years of inevitable panic and dread. There is light at the end of the tunnel: over the long haul, supportive caregivers develop warm, meaningful relationships with children.

Laura's mother and Thomas's mother address the concerns of Timmy's child life intern and present experiences that have helped them and their children. The steadfastness, gentle humor, and unflappable good will of caring professionals during their children's early years laid a foundation of trust and hope for the positive relationships that would eventually come.

Laura

During Laura's early years, she was terrified of doctors. This was not surprising, but it was very difficult to handle. I clung to my faith that eventually my calm, my reassurances, my comforting—and Laura's own increasing ability to mediate her behavior by verbal reasoning as she grew older—would all bear fruit. But it was a long road, and I could understand the exasperation that some professionals demonstrated even as I winced to witness it.

Occasionally, my sagging spirits would receive a tremendous boost. After our cross-country move, Laura developed some sort of rash on her scalp, and I took her in to see our new pediatrician. Laura clung frantically to me, screaming; you could not have gotten a piece of paper between us, so tightly was she pressed against me in her attempt to escape the examining hands. I will never forget Dr. Z's imperturbable good humor. He prescribed this shampoo, that lotion, and took his leave, lightheartedly exclaiming, "This just wasn't my day with Laura."

How much that meant to me! Not only did he accept with good cheer her disproportionate fear and loud protest of his completely uninvasive examination; he implied his faith that better days with Laura would come. And they did.

Shortly after Laura's fifth birthday, her orthopedist reluctantly concluded that surgery could no longer be deferred. All of our plans were made and Laura remained healthy despite the wintry weather, as her Sunday admission neared. On Friday, I gave in to a wish that I felt was a little irrational: I took her in to see Dr. Z, her pediatrician. He confirmed that she was in great shape for her surgery, and he spent a little time chatting with her about going to stay in the hospital in the city. As I look back, I think what I wanted, actually, was the reassurance of contact with this understanding and special caregiver; in other cultures, it would have been known as seeking a blessing, a "laying on of hands." I wanted to focus on the gentleness we would experience again, once we returned from a place where Laura was to face great pain.

Thomas

Interact on a personal basis with your patient. Dr. C talks with my children, answers their questions, sometimes acts funny to relieve their tension, and will ask them for their assistance. It took almost three years, but Thomas no longer starts crying and trying to escape when he sees Dr. C.

On one visit, Dr. C was making funny faces at Thomas trying

to calm him down, and it worked. On the way home, my daughter Debra said to me, "I didn't know that doctors could be funny."

Perspectives

ENTERING THE CHILD'S WORLD

Parents value caregivers who appreciate the struggles of children in need and see themselves as allies of their young patients or clients. Children strive for dignity and self-respect as they endure illness and treatment. A mother stresses:

> Your patients are children first. Their wisdom and maturity often seem to stretch beyond their years, but don't be fooled. Their spirits are very young and tender... (Sherelyn Campbell, *A Few Words to Young Professionals*)

The process of entering the child's world is not an easy one. Shock, pain, and sadness for the child coexist with respect and regard for the child's hopes, dreams, and courage. A child life intern shares a young patient's story with her supervisor and searches for understanding and meaning:

> The children in the clinic are forced to deal with experiences many adults will never have to face. Take, for instance, the conversation that started right in front of me:
>
> Debbie: (She pulls at her smock and points at her band-aid many times.) I have a boo-boo.
>
> Me: How does it feel?
>
> Debbie: It hurts me. I cried when they did it. It doesn't hurt as much now.
>
> Pat: (Looks up from what she is drawing.) That is O.K., Debbie. I am older than you and I still cry. It hurts me, too. It always hurts more when they first do it. You learn to get used to it.
>
> I facilitate the conversation for a little while longer though I can't remember what I said. After we were all done talking, Debbie got up from the table to get her blood pressure taken. I was amazed at what happened next!
>
> Pat turned to me and said, "She sure is cute. It is always hard in the beginning. I know how she feels. I like her." Immediately I was struck by her maturity and her almost nurturing eyes. She is only eight years old. These two children talked of transfusions and needles; the mere thought of which makes some adults

queasy and terrified. When Pat turned to me, she spoke to me as no other eight year old had. I did not see her age: I saw a very strong human being.

Later in the morning, I wandered back into the treatment room. Pat was lying in the bed, encased by the sheets; her body looked frail. Pat's eyes were closed, and she was resting soundly. What a different image I saw before me. Many of the children do not look outwardly as if they are sick. Pat did. She looked very young, and there was an odd expression on her face. I don't want to project my own feelings, but it looked like an expression of pain. I had to pinch myself to remind myself that this was the same child with whom I had spoken before.

I left the hospital with a lingering feeling that I do not yet understand. I am hoping to discover what it is—maybe with your help or maybe on my own. (child life intern: journal entry)

Situations to ponder

THE USE OF LANGUAGE TO DESCRIBE A CHILD

To parents, the language used to describe their child is a sensitive barometer of a professional's respect for them and their child. Anxious, frightened professionals may grope for words to say to embattled parents. Professionals under stress may unintentionally blurt out comments and statements that deeply hurt parents. Silence or simple expressions of concern and hope offer an alternative when there are no "right" words to say. Parents present the following vignettes with the goal of helping student caregivers to develop better ways of handling anxieties and feelings of despair.

> The radiation oncology doctor told us the treatments "might make her stupid." I'm still reeling from the shock of that statement. The saddest thing that could happen to Wendy would be for her to lose her exceptional intellectual ability. To use the slang word—"stupid"—was, to me, grossly offensive. (Wendy's mother)
>
> * * * *
>
> Miriam was a surprising 4 lbs and a relatively "healthy" premie. She had trouble with heat maintenance, jaundice, and keeping weight on. At her lowest point, she dropped to 3 lbs 6 oz. A nurse referred to her as "a good-sized chicken." As Miriam's mother, this gratuitous, off-the-cuff comment made me feel extremely bad and utterly inadequate. I was given a visually painful,

uncomfortable image of my daughter.

Parents are trying so hard to be hopeful and to bond with a sick baby in the frightening, hi-tech NICU environment. Health care professionals who stress the baby's spirit, strength, and similarities to the parents help parents to rebuild shattered self-esteem. (mother of Joshua and Miriam)

* * * *

Certain random statements made to us during times of intense stress have been extremely painful. At a point three years ago, it appeared that Mickey, then less than one, was not going to survive. A couple of doctors had tried gently to prepare us for that probability. A nurse in the PICU tried to console me by saying, "We know these kids don't live very long anyway." I was outraged that this comment was made to me. It seemed more appropriately stated about a pet goldfish! This comment still haunts me.

An otherwise sensitive neurosurgeon once said to me that my husband and I made a mistake by not being certain about our genetics before we married. When we learned that our second child, then an infant, could have this condition, an educator said, "Well, it's not that bad. At least you have the experience of dealing with Todd." I realize that these statements and others like them were made with the best of intentions, but silence would have been a better alternative. (mother of Mickey and Todd)

Silence, however, that is both cold and indifferent and signals disregard for the child can be extremely painful to parents. A mother discusses the reactions of her obstetrician who is unable to acknowledge the existence of her son. There are no questions about her son; no expressions of concern; no awareness of his role in her life.

With some professionals, I feel there is no hope of understanding, so why try to talk about feelings. My ob/gyn is a man of science, of technique. I don't think he understands my feelings about prenatal testing. I go to him for his skill, but I wish I could have his understanding as well. When I went in for my post-partum check-up after Thomas was born, he never asked me about Thomas. Thomas was not perfect, and he only delivers "perfect babies." I realize that he probably was uncomfortable and did not know what to say, but his silence hurt.

Sincere compliments and words of praise for a child's effort and courage mean a great deal to parents. Here, as in all communication with parents, honesty and caring are core concerns. Parents easily spot "compliments" that are patronizing or condescending. Thomas's mother shares:

> Choose words that are meant to compliment a child with care. Be honest. I vividly remember Thomas' therapists' first comments about him: "Oh, how cute." Thomas may have been cute to me at that time, but I don't think that a baby with a tube in his stomach, a hole in his mouth, and a bad case of cradle cap would be cute to someone else. Recently, a professional said to me, "I like Thomas because he has spirit. He knows what he wants." I thought—how nice of her to say that. And I felt good.

Perspectives

ENTERING THE CHILD'S WORLD; WHEN POLICIES SEPARATE PARENTS FROM THEIR CHILDREN IN NEED

Health care providers cannot assume that all children and families have access to institutions that actualize the most basic tenets of family-centered care: unlimited visiting by parents. In the following story, a child psychiatry fellow working in a large, general public hospital attempts to enter the world of a young child whose mother was forced to leave him at the time of his greatest need—late at night as he lay alone in his hospital bed.

Although this child is fictional, the story is based on actual observations of a child. He represents many children whose struggle against despair and isolation is a cry for help and change. Severe staff shortages and inadequate security in poorly structured health care settings may lead to policies that separate parents from their children most in need of comfort and support. It is crucial to rethink such blanket policies and support parents as they care for their children.

Sammy, are the stars still shining?

> Sammy, are you scared? It's so dark and lonely. I hear the little babies crying in the next room. The nurses are busy. Will they check my IV soon?
>
> My arm feels like it's burning. Am I on fire? Is there smoke coming out of me?
>
> I want to cry, Sammy. But everyone tells me to be a big boy. I'm almost 7 years old. I'm not supposed to cry like a yucchy baby. Sammy, can I tell you a secret? Don't you tell anyone! Promise? Sometimes, just sometimes, I wish I could yell and cry like a baby.

I wish Mommy would pick me up and hug me and rock me like a little baby. Mommy would kiss my tears away.

Mommy had to leave tonight. The guard came and said, "It's 9 o'clock. Visiting time is over." She hugged me goodnight. I didn't want her to worry. I was a good boy. I didn't scream for her to come back. I didn't want the guard to be angry at her and put her in jail. But I miss her so much.

Sammy, do you see that gray blob over in the corner? A monster! What should I do? Oh—I guess it's—just a shadow. But he looks scary to me. Do you see him passing over Bill's bed?

Sammy, please help me close my eyes. Tell me a story. Remember all the stories we used to make up together? We were in a rocket ship all by ourselves—just you and me. The countdown was so exciting—10, 9, 8, 7...We put on our big, shiny space suits. Up, up, and away! We landed back on earth just in time for our favorite lunch. Mommy even made a pretend peanut butter and jelly sandwich for you.

Sammy, why do people get sick? Do they do bad things? Curious George ate a piece of puzzle. That's how he got sick. He was pretty dumb! Everyone knows that puzzle pieces aren't candy.

I must have done something very bad. Help me find my thinking cap so I can figure out what I did. Is my thinking cap under the bed?

One day last week I didn't take my vitamins. Vitamins make you strong, you know. Last week I got angry at my little brother Joey. Maybe I shouldn't have pulled my toy away from him. He cried and cried. Mommy told me to be a good big brother. I'm sorry, Joey. Can you hear me, Joey? I miss you.

I sure wish Joey were here now. He needs me. I make him laugh better than anyone else in the whole wide world. When he's crying, I put on my clown face and dance around, and he's all better. He's not so smart. But I love him anyway. And I'm teaching him how to walk.

Are the stars still shining, Sammy? Do you remember how we used to sit by the window and try to count them? Maybe you can put on your wings and fly away and tell me about them. I can't see the window from my bed. I try to move, but it's so hard.

I know that Mommy is worried. She tries to smile and make silly jokes with me, but sometimes she just sits and stares at the wall. The smile goes away, and her eyes get red and sad.

She and Daddy don't talk to each other the way they used to talk. They used to laugh and tell funny grown up stories to each other. I would giggle, too, because I was so happy to watch them play. Now when Mommy and Daddy think I'm fast asleep, they whisper and cry. I hide my head in the pillow. I don't want them to know that I'm listening. My ears start to hurt. Sometimes they don't talk to each other at all. Is it because of me, Sammy?

Grandma once was sick and went to the hospital. An ambulance with a loud siren came to our house. Strong men put her on a stretcher. Everyone worked quickly and quietly. Daddy was very busy.

Grandma's hand was cold, very cold. She grabbed my fingers tightly before she had to say goodbye. She didn't want to let go. She didn't want to leave me. She cried a lot, Sammy. Her tears fell onto me, and I touched them as they fell.

Grandma never came home from the hospital. Mommy told me that Grandma died and went to heaven. Is heaven a nice place, Sammy? Why do people cry when you go to heaven? Can you show me heaven and Grandma's new house?

Sammy, let me tell you something very interesting. I figured it out all by myself. When I grow up and have kids, Mommy will be their grandma. Isn't that funny? Mommy thought it was funny when I told her. She laughed and hugged me.

Sammy, will I ever leave the hospital? Will I grow up to be a big man like Daddy and have my own little boys? I have lots and lots of questions. I am dizzy with questions. Sometimes all the questions make me cry.

Will I die and go to heaven? Will I see grandma there? Is she still sick and sad in heaven? Mommy tells me that she's happy now. Do people get well in heaven? Will Grandma bake me chocolate chip cookies? Can Mommy and Daddy come, too? I don"t want to go anywhere without Mommy, Daddy, and Joey. We're a family, you know.

You're my imaginary friend, Sammy. I-m-gi-na-ry. You and I used to play together everyday. Now I have lots of real friends, too. Mikie and I whizz our trains over bridges and highways, through tunnels, past forests and cities. You can play along with us. I'm a good "sharer". I'll teach you all the names of the stops on our line.

Look, Sammy! The sun is beginning to smile. A tiny rainbow is tickling the wall next to me. Do you see the colors shiver and sparkle? Mommy will come soon.

Our brains have done a lot of hard thinking. My eyes are tired. Are you yawning, too? Come lie next to me, Sammy. There's a soft place right here on my pillow. I'll make room. Let me hug you goodnight and give you a big, mushy kiss. I'm still lonely. Don't go away. Stay with me in my dreams. (Leff, P., *Newsletter of the Thanatology Program*, Brooklyn College, 1985, 4, pp. 4-5)

6 Ongoing Care III: Respecting the Family Unit

What is it like being the father of a disabled child? What does it mean to a man to have a child who must sit and watch from the window as other children play outside? What stresses do fathers feel when thinking about their child never attending regular school classes? How does a father deal with the reality that his child will never compete for first chair in the band's flute section? And what goes on inside a dad when he sees his 15-year-old child still making a one year old's disaster out of the kitchen at meal time?. . . (David Cornell, D.A.D.S., Family Support Project, Focus Report, Fathers of Special Children, Fall, 1989)

The chain linking many of the thoughts and observations expressed by parents throughout this book is respect for the families caring for children with special needs. Respect for the family, with its nurturing structure of love and trust, is a core, organizing concept as one reaches out to parents and children.

The Child in the Family

While each child should be seen as a unique and valued individual, the best care also recognizes that each child (ideally) has a place as a member of a family and participates in the life of this larger body. Mothers of children with multiple special needs emphasize:

Many professionals seem to forget sometimes that Laura is not only a little girl with Turner Syndrome or congenital heart disease or malformed kidneys or complications of surgery or multiple orthopedic problems. . . she is also a horse lover, a fish breeder, a Girl Scout, a student of the viola, a reader of great books, a sister who comforts a crying brother, a daughter who sweeps the kitchen, a granddaughter who crafts homemade Valentines, a niece who tickles a cousin—all of the things that are more important about her than the string of diagnoses that we can choose from. (Laura's mother)

* * * *

We have been fortunate in that almost everyone in the family rallied around from the beginning. Those who were too upset to deal with the idea of Keough at first (the grandfathers) came around quickly when they actually met her. Keough's cousins have been taught by their parents to be proud of her, to applaud her successes and to help her when she needs it. They look forward to her visits. Friends and acquaintances have amazed us with their interest and several we thought we knew well before Keough's birth have confided since then that a brother, sister-in-law, or cousin has Down syndrome. . . (Keough's mother)

Parents face a formidable job: to integrate their child's "unwished for difference" into family life; to create a "healthy" family in the midst of chronic illness and disability. This is a lifelong task. A mother of a medically fragile child emphasizes:

I am her mom. I am responsible for how she is, who she will become . . . even for the most part, whether she will live or die. The responsibility is awesome, and it frightens me to be so account-able for something over which I have so little control. Each time I resuscitate her, the pain becomes unbearable. She is only eight, and when she asks, "Will I ever be nine?" or "Why did God let me have this?", again my pain is unbearable.

The dreams I had for her, for us, before she became ill are surrounded by tears. Yet, each milestone passed causes me to grab at those dreams and run towards our goals. Each crisis causes me to slow down and take my eyes off the path momen-tarily. I do my best at maintaining our family "status" and keeping us in touch with the realities of life. (mother of Eddie, Janet, Tracy, and Lori)

The nature of many professional interactions, and the systems by which services are delivered, are such that the life of the family may be hidden from view. This lack of awareness may impede good care. Just as sensitive professionals take a child's lifestyle into account in planning treatment, so caregivers must acknowledge a family's need to design its collective life.

The Life of the Family

The recommendations and actions of professionals reach in and affect the way a family's members live and interact. There is no perfect solution to the perplexities this phenomenon introduces; wise professionals learn to tread carefully, to negotiate rather than to pronounce, to honor preferences without judging, and to keep commitments with integrity. For some families, these issues are a constant aspect of daily life. The mother of two children who are medically fragile emphasizes:

> One of the most helpful experiences we've had with the health care system has been with our home nurses. Our best nurses are like family members with special insights into the workings of the medical community. They help us in many ways to live a relatively normal life. On the other hand, having a nurse in our small house 24 hours a day is a constant intrusion. Our best nurses have learned to deal with episodes of intense family stress; others, unfortunately, haven't.

Public Law 99-457 is an attempt to ensure that families are considered in planning: professionals and parents working toward good care must include the family unit in assessing needs and setting priorities. Implementation of early intervention policies and of P.L. 99-457 brings a legal dimension to the total care of the very young child "at medical and/or developmental risk" within the family unit (DeGraw, Edell, Ellers, Hillemeier, Liebman, Perry, & Palfrey, 1988).

Families struggle with complex needs. Good care of children honors the role of the family and makes every effort to strengthen and energize its members in the roles they choose. When the family's needs and choices are not understood, poor communication results; the parent-professional alliance is placed in jeopardy.

> We're not all one type of parent. We care and are concerned in many different ways. For example, my husband is self-employed and is the person who frequently takes our son to the clinic. I work outside of the home. People at the clinic judge me as a mother. I feel as if I'm under a microscope when I am able to go to the clinic with my child. Our doctor knows about our family's situation, and he and I frequently discuss my son's care over the phone. However, the information about our family has not been given to the clinic staff. I feel extremely uncomfortable with the nurses and social worker. (mother of a child with kidney disease who herself has cerebral palsy)

Greg's mother describes a very different kind of experience and reaffirms parents' appreciation of professionals who value and support the family's unique way of life:

> Some health care professionals recognize that we are a family *first* and a family with a member who is disabled *second.* This was brought to light after years of juggling various speech, behavior, fine motor, gross motor, and repositioning programs all to be implemented in the home. A social worker intervened by reminding us that we were still a family. She helped us to discover approaches that would weave the demands of Greg's care into our family life in ways that would allow our family to function as a healthy unit. The social worker made us aware of various support services and then offered us the opportunity to decide for ourselves which, if any, we would utilize.

Assessment of family needs and strengths calls for great care and sensitivity to the family's dignity and pride. Parents speak of situations in which they have not applied for services to which they and their children were entitled for fear of intrusive and humiliating intake procedures. The parents of three children with special needs describe their experience:

> We postponed our involvement with human services for many years. . .The dehumanization and invasion of our privacy interfered with our submitting applications for assistance. We finally decided that we were denying our children access to programs because we were not applying for available resources. It is very difficult for some parents to ask for help. . .

Families manage staggering, often overwhelming, practical demands as they strive to nurture "ordinary" ties of love and protection—the profoundly significant goals of family life. Parents urge caregivers to understand that there are many "right" ways to cope with the tasks and responsibilities of special parenting. A mother sketches her family's demanding life and a couple shares their family's vision:

> Please remember that you see our family in only one dimension . . . the medical. We have husbands and wives, other children, grandparents, friends and neighbors, jobs, school, mortgage payments, chicken pox and a dozen other things to juggle every day. We do the best we can on too little sleep and under a great deal of stress. And some of us have been doing it for many years.

If we seem distracted at times, forgive us. (*A Few Words to Young Professionals*, Sherelyn Campbell).

* * * *

One of our dreams is that we will not have to be concerned about meeting the enormous financial obligations related to Nathen's medical needs. Currently, our insurance policy carries a one million dollar cap, but this amount is about to be exceeded, and sources of future financial assistance are at best uncertain. Our dream, both for our family now, and for Nathen in the future, is that we will not have to live on welfare.

For ourselves, we dream of somehow receiving the emotional and social support we ourselves need. Because most people do not even realize the all but overwhelming challenges we face day in and day out, we do not find much in the way of emotional and social support in our small community. Those who are aware of our family situation often see us as successful copers who are coping so well that we don't need any extra support. . .

A dream for our entire family is one of "normalcy." (Bill and Christy Boyce, *Families and Disability Newsletter*, 1990, p. 8)

The mother of a young woman with multiple handicaps discusses the physical and emotional needs of her daughter as family members and professionals work together to maintain Kate in her home.

I have often been asked, "What are the services that families require on an ongoing basis?" Kate needs partial assistance and partial independence in every phase of her life—dressing, toilet schedule, washing, eating, leisure activities, positioning, stairs, and nonverbal communications. (She does not need assistance to either give or receive love!) This takes careful planning on the part of her caregivers. It requires physical stamina, knowledge, creativity, dedication, determination, and the ability to drum up a positive outlook each and every day. Every family with a disabled family member has extraordinary daily tasks to perform. (Addie Comegys, *Massachusetts Department of Mental Retardation, Family Support Newsletter*, May, 1988, p. 5)

Respite care, often difficult to obtain or afford, becomes a vital issue in the lives of families caring for children with serious chronic conditions. Kate's mother explains both her need for respite care and problems associated with many current systems.

Respite care is a term I dislike. In many states it is hard to get. It is bureaucratic and often unreliable. I do not plan my frantic moments. When I feel exhausted, I must know that I can anticipate relief tomorrow at 10 AM... (Addie Comegys, *Massachusetts Department of Mental Retardation, Family Support Newsletter*, May, 1988, p. 6)

The mother of a young child who is technology-dependent adds:

Plan for some type of relief for the parents. They will never forget totally their responsibility for that child they brought home, but give them an opportunity to get away for a while to be who they are. With a medically vulnerable child your life revolves around [her] care. I wear my watch on Iowa time so I know where Katie is every minute. As long as the players I have put together for her do their job, she'll be fine. But I still need the time to get away to be Julie Beckett, not just Katie Beckett's mother, even though that role has given me the greatest pleasure in my life. (Julianne Beckett, Comprehensive Care for Medically Vulnerable Infants and Toddlers: A Parent's Perspective, *Equals in this Partnership*, NCCIP, 1985, p. 12)

Families of children or young adults who must be cared for outside of the home are deeply affected by how they are regarded by staff responsible for their loved ones. Wherever they reside, children remain in the lives, thoughts, and hearts of their parents and siblings. Support for the family continues to be an important goal as children leave the home; the vulnerability of parents never fades. Bill's mother has maintained a deep and supportive friendship with Toby's mother since the days both their children attended a therapeutic nursery school; here she describes such a situation:

Even though my son is out of the system—as I write this he is planning his trip to London—I am constantly reminded of the daily pain by my contact with Mary and her son Toby. Toby bit Mary recently, necessitating painful shots. In general, he is not doing well. He's 22 and he's not cute anymore, and the cutbacks in funding. . . make it less and less likely that he will receive appropriate care.

　　Toby will never live independently. There is Mary's never-ending frustration at not being able to advocate for Toby, not being considered seriously, watching him be over-medicated, coming back to her for visits with unexplained wounds (self-inflicted? put there by staff? other patients? She'll never know), and in general being definitely an outsider in his care—she would give virtually anything to deal with someone who would try to see her side of things, indeed, even try to see Toby's side of things.

Support for one's choices can be hard to come by; families often find that extended family relationships and friendships are altered by the presence of serious illness or disability.

> Of course, it hasn't been all roses. Before Keough's birth, we had asked another friend to be a godmother, but after the birth she withdrew from us. For awhile I felt very bitter about this, but our relationship eventually smoothed out. Still, our friendship will never be as strong as it was. Many parents of children with handicaps find their other relationships shifting after the handicap is discovered, making a difficult time even worse. . . (Sue Duffy, Surviving The First Three Years: One Parent's Perspective, *Acceptance is only the first battle*, MUAP, 1984, 34)
>
> * * * *
>
> Inspiring new friendships will be made. Some old ones will go by the wayside, unable to understand your new priorities and time restraints. I recall a small dinner party when our friends who opposed a group home on their street moved to the other side of the living room for the rest of the evening when they learned we were proponents. It is difficult. (Addie Comegys, *Massachusetts Department of Mental Retardation, Family Support Newsletter*, p.7)

Under the pressing, often conflicting demands and responsibilities of family life, parents struggle to balance many aspects of their relationships: their life as a couple; their life as members of their community. They describe difficult problems and creative solutions.

> Marital relations reflect the stresses and joys of the family situation. If one has come to the marriage ill-equipped to handle any major adversity, life will be stormy. . . (Addie Comegys, *Massachusetts Department of Mental Retardation, Family Support Newsletter*, p. 7)
>
> * * * *
>
> Family relationships can be strained. Raising children with special needs is very demanding, time-consuming, and hard on a marriage. My husband and I share responsibilities. In our case, we need to make appointments with each other to find time to

make love. We have also tried to put aside one or two weekends a year just for ourselves. We spend these weekends in our local hotel where we enjoy being alone together—free from the constant responsibilities of caring for three children with special needs. (mother of Lisa, Norm, and Nancy)

Families reach toward health and balance. In their daily lives, families assess the impact of the directives of professionals, the tyranny of chronic illness, or the physical demands of dealing with disability. While the logistics for, say, a camping trip can be staggering, the act of enjoying aspects of "normal" family life has a therapeutic effect.

We have been strong advocates of total community integration. When Lisa was born, we decided to continue with life, giving the children as much stimulation and normal experiences as possible. We, the entire family with Lisa on the monitor, went camping in a tent to the Black Hills for two weeks. We had great fun. We did everything including going through caves, train rides, etc. The monitor would periodically go off, and people would look at us as if we were nuts. But who cared! (mother of Lisa, Norm, and Nancy)

* * * *

. . .We even managed to have some fun in all that mess. We took the boys to lots of baseball games, going to batting practice, etc. (They and my husband caught 7 balls last season!) And we went to a Beach Boys concert, took some short trips, and had a season's membership to a swim club. . .enough to break up the difficult times, anyway.

I wish there was a way for us to call a big TIME OUT, like they do in baseball, but it doesn't seem to be likely. We manage home and health, our business, school (I'm teaching Jesse at home; Doug goes to parochial school), and are happy enough. I guess you can't ask for more than that. . . (mother of two children who are medically fragile)

* * * *

Our entire family went to Disneyland. Brent was with us. He was happy, I should say, *elated* to be with us. Although he cannot speak, there was a wonderful glint in his eyes. I carried him around. I've often thought that I should have my own special T-shirt: *This Mom Carried Her Twelve-Year-Old Boy Around Disneyland.* When you're in the sea, you roll with it. Brent is and will always be part of our family's love. (Brent's mother)

All families prepare for the future—through childhood and beyond. Families of children with special needs, too, look to a time when their children will leave the home. They anxiously look toward a society that will provide appropriate care, support, and appreciation of their children and young adults with long-term special needs. They envision a future in which their children will be offered opportunities to live the fullest lives possible.

> My hope for the future is that my children, as well as all individuals with special needs, will remain in their communities living in homes of their own with attendants to help support them. . .I hope our communities will listen and learn not to be afraid of people with disabilities. I hope we will all realize that people with disabilities have the same rights as people without disabilities. Children and adults with special needs have feelings that are no different from our own; they want to be valued and respected for themselves. (mother of Lisa, Norm, and Nancy)
>
> * * * *
>
> Peace of mind for the family is an integral part of the dream—peace that results from knowing that Mindie's future is secure, that there are several interested, caring individuals that are invested in Mindie and her future, and that there is a family-friendly, flexible, responsive system that will support the efforts of Mindie, my family, and her friends. (Diane Crutcher, mother of Mindie who has Down syndrome, *Families and Disability Newsletter*, Beach Center on Families and Disability, University of Kansas, Vol. 2, No. 1, Spring, 1990)

Cycles of Stress and Grieving

Families will grow through periods of strain and distress. The family bond—the love that ties individuals together—is in a sense to blame for the grief. Yet the loving relationships within the family may also provide the solace which enables them to ride out the storms. The mother of a seriously ill newborn explains:

> . . . I remember wishing desperately not to care, not to be so completely involved; it would have saved me the devastation (and also made me a lesser person, but that's another point). The bond made the pain possible, even inevitable. Love given and received helped me heal, and so did the support I got for myself personally. . .

Here the professional's role may be that of sounding board offering family members the opportunity to share and verbalize their pain. In providing a listening ear, the caregiver offers support and care during times of great stress when little can be done to spare the child and family. Reverence for the family's struggle is a powerful comforter. Vanessa's mother describes her intense emotions as she, Vanessa, her husband, and her family face one of Vanessa's multiple surgeries for facial reconstruction:

> . . . Several emotions take hold of me as I see my daughter for the first time after surgery. I see the bruising already setting in. I see swelling throughout her face and head. I see blood drenched bandages covering incisions, stitches, and staples. I see a different face on my little girl.
>
> As I recognize her discomfort and her fear of what is happening to her, I become paralyzed with fear myself. My entire body aches for her. How can I comfort her? Why did we have to go through this? Will she ever understand why? Will I ever understand why? I feel guilty, and I wish she could tell me she loves me, and it is going to be all right.
>
> Finally, at night when she is asleep, and all the family has returned home, I begin to relax somewhat. Suddenly, without much warning, I start to cry. I cry so intensely I feel every part of me crying too. So much sadness overwhelms me. It feels as if someone has literally ripped my heart from my chest. It hurts so much! I love her so much. I want to make her all better. I wish things would get back to normal.
>
> She looks worse before she looks better. The swelling increases until her eyes are swollen shut and her skin appears shiny. Because of the lack of vision, her fears and her irritability increase. My husband's and my inner strength must increase as well to better care for and comfort her. She feels miserable and is unable to rest well. Therefore, another toll is taken on us; we are unable to rest well. Emotions tend to run quite high It is not uncommon for my husband and me to be quite irritable. We try to take turns resting and caring for Vanessa.
>
> Within a few days, things do begin to get better. . .I leave the hospital with unrealistic expectations. I think that when we get home *everything* will be better. Again, it gets worse before it gets better. However, we are glad to be home. We begin to relax in familiar surroundings; then fatigue sets in. For me, more depression and sadness accompany the fatigue. We have all been through so much in the past week! And we know it isn't even over yet. . . (Colette Lau, *Facial Expressions Newsletter*, November, 1988, p. 2)

After the crises have passed, parents must reestablish ways of coping with new (or renewed) family routines and expectations. This coming to terms with changes in the carrying on with family life can be extremely stressful. Keough's mother describes her family's needs after a long-term problem was successfully resolved:

> Keough's trach stoma was sewn shut a year ago, and we still find ourselves readjusting to a so-called normal life. One thing we've done is taken up marriage counseling in large part because the coping strategies that served us well when Keough had the trach now impede our growth.

Empowerment

Professionals best serve families by defining their roles in a sensitive and nonintrusive fashion. Their greatest impact—most far-reaching and helpful—may be in the form of empowerment. Families feel powerful when they make choices, affect decisions, and work together with caregivers. Professionals may actively foster parents' sturdy functioning.

> When I take Ellen in, her pediatrician always listens to what I have to say about what is going on with her. If there are options in the method of treatment, he'll discuss them, and we mutually agree on what is best for Ellen. I guess what I'm saying is that the doctor communicates well. I feel that we are working together as a team for the welfare of Ellen.
>
> * * * *
>
> You can encourage autonomy among your patients' parents by sharing basic assessment and treatment skills with them. As their confidence and discernment develops, they will need to turn to you much less often and only for the more serious problems they encounter. (Sherelyn Campbell, *A Few Words to Young Health Professionals*)
>
> * * * *
>
> Our home trainer let us know right away that Keough's handicap is secondary to her being, and that she likes Keough. She knows when it's time to dump the day's program and talk over coffee. She knows when one more medical referral or new program will be too much for us. She knows what she is doing and how to explain it to us. She has made us feel important. (Sue Duffy, Plaudits for Professionals, *Acceptance is only the first battle*, MUAP, 1984, p. 30)

Care must be taken not to undercut (even unintentionally) parents' roles as partners. A mother explains how parental expertise and input are crucial in preventing such an unwanted outcome:

> Parents developing literature or programs containing medical or educational information must turn to professionals for guidance. Professionals developing services for families must draw on the special expertise of families. A few years ago, I saw an intensive care nursery parents' booklet developed by nursing staff. The project had been undertaken generously as a service to parents, and the booklet contained good information, but it began with a list of prohibitions and its terminology "allowed" visiting, rather than encouraging it. Exactly contrary to its purpose, it subtly reinforced the powerlessness of parents. (Ann Oster, *Equals in this Partnership*, NCCIP, 1985, p.32)

Although individual professionals may solidly support parents' roles and enthusiastically welcome parents, it is crucial that families have a voice in planning for the facilities that will actualize family-centered goals and practices. Empowerment includes inviting and encouraging parents to participate actively in designing areas of the hospital or clinic they must use in order to be close to their children in need. Failure to include the parents' perspectives and needs in creating "family friendly" environments may undermine parents' vital role. For example, policies that do not fully include the expertise of families in planning for facilities such as intensive care units may lead to the following frustrating situation for parents:

> Mickey has only been hospitalized four times in the past two years, which is a low frequency for kids with the kind of problems he has. We admit him directly to the PICU in a nearby teaching hospital. Mickey requires intensive care always, and this is the only place where such a unit exists locally.
>
> Recently, the unit was renovated without any consideration being made for the families of the children in the unit. Naturally, an adult family member is expected to be with the child as much as possible. In our case, Mickey gets upset when I'm not nearby. It's also necessary for me to answer questions asked by medical personnel and to serve as Mickey's advocate during his stays there. But no provision has been made for sleeping or eating!
>
> We are not allowed to sleep next to our children. Parents compete for the couple of couches available in the waiting area for desperately needed naps. Eating is not allowed in the unit or

in the waiting area. If it's possible, we run down to the cafeteria for a bite during the few hours that food is served. I almost always come home from a hospital stay slightly dehydrated because of the inconvenience of drinking while Mickey's there. . . (mother of Mickey and Todd)

Traveling the long road of ongoing care, parents continue to emphasize the value of support from parents in similar circumstances. The gains are many: understanding; an end to isolation; practical advice; modeling; influence on the wider world.

When I'm depressed everyone knows it. I look the part. I dress the part. Today was the first day I actually wore a dress and heels to work in months. I even wore makeup. I attended my first Parent to Parent meeting last night, and I feel better than I have felt in a very long time.

My son has Attention Deficit Disorder with Hyperactivity. He has been expelled from a number of preschools. Babysitters have changed their names and gotten unlisted phone numbers. I was always torn between those who told me that he was normal and I was overreacting and those who simply stopped calling us because they didn't want to be around him. . .

When I got to the meeting I was a little nervous, but not for long. Everyone was so supportive and open that I felt I had known them all before. These people have been there. . .and back. Listening to them and knowing that they'd listen to me, took a great weight off my shoulders. For once I could speak about my feelings without being judged. My son has special needs, and it's not because I'm a bad mother. These needs won't go away, no matter how good a mother I am. You cannot say that in the outside world. But you can comfortably say them at a Parent to Parent support group, and everyone will agree with you because they've felt the same way. . . (a mother writing in *Cues for Special Parents*, Vol. 4, No. 1, Oct.-Dec. 1989)

* * * *

The treatment team should have a parent on it. Parents will talk openly to another parent and confide their confusion over what health care professionals have said to them or are proposing to do to their child. A knowledgeable parent helps to clarify and interpret medical information. (Amber's mother)

* * * *

Our boy has undergone surgery and recuperated. I cannot imagine how. . .unprepared we would have been without what we learned at Heart-to-Heart. Nor can I imagine getting through surgery without the friends and support we got from Heart-to-Heart.

We discovered that everyone else at Heart-to-Heart was just like us—regular people thrust into extraordinary circumstances. Having a child with a heart problem didn't make them different from other people. It is a common experience which draws us together, but doesn't brand us so that we can be picked out in a crowd. We found that instead of people sitting around telling sad stories, Heart-to-Heart meetings were full of useful information served up with Mrs. Field's cookies!

We have only missed a couple of meetings since that first one, and we've encouraged others to attend because of the positive effect they have had on us.

Regarding surgery—we learned from other Heart-to-Heart members what would happen in pre-op; what ICU would be like; which parent's shower worked best and the best hours to get hot water; when and what to eat at the grill; what to bring to the hospital and what to wear. We met Zack's surgeon, learned about the heart-lung machine, met the chaplain, and became familiar with the hospital because of Heart-to-Heart. (Karen Walker, *Heart-to-Heart Newsletter*, April, 1990, p. 3)

Critical Role: The Special Needs of Fathers

Fathers play an irreplaceable role in the lives of their children with special needs. The active participation of fathers in the care of their children in need brings benefits to the whole family. Physical and emotional stress and tension decrease for all family members; a healthy rebalancing of family life occurs (Frey, Fewell, Vadasy, & Greenberg, 1989; May, 1991). Over time, fathers set the tone of how the child is viewed by the family; when fathers come to derive pleasure and a well-deserved sense of accomplishment from their nurturing roles, families are strengthened (Frey, Greenberg, & Fewell, 1989).

Far too often the feelings, needs, and resources of fathers have been ignored by health care professionals.

The parents of a child with cystic fibrosis talked about their struggles to cope with the stresses, the fear of the future, and their own evolving relationship. The father said, "My biggest complaint as a father is that many professionals act as if I am not in the room, that I don't exist."

He wondered aloud as to why this was so. Were the professionals threatened by him? Did they assume he knew little or nothing about his child's condition? Had they bought into the assumption that dads are just not effective caretakers? Why wasn't more effort being made to help him understand the health needs of his child? (James May, What About Fathers?, *ACCH Network*, Vol. 8, No. 1, Winter 1990)

Growing awareness and appreciation of the importance of fathers in the lives of their special children and families are beginning to alter such attitudes. A father who has organized groups across the country for dads of children with special needs questions old myths and describes the power of peer support in helping men to redefine, to discover what fatherhood has meant in their own lives:

The old male models—being self-sufficient, capable of handling all problems without asking for help—die slowly. To finally openly talk about one's child, to know we all have the same fears, angers, frustrations as well as the joys of personal accomplishment, is an incredibly powerful experience. I routinely ask men why they come to the meetings. Most often the answer is, "My wife wanted me to," or "I came because I was asked to." When I ask them again at the end of the first session, the simple answer is, "Now I know why I came—to share my experiences and feelings with other men of similar backgrounds." The isolation begins to slip away and the commonalities become evident
. . .I would be remiss not to comment about the laughter, the good humor and enjoyment the men bring to discussions regarding their children. The child's first steps at age five; the father's success at a feeding session or a diaper change; the joy in taking a son swimming on a Saturday afternoon; the relief of making it through a child's heart surgery; and the chance to take a daughter on a camping trip— these are the stories that make our times together such a joy. The playful kidding with each other, the earthiness of discussing who had the last vasectomy, the exchanging of cigars with the birth of a child, and the preparation of a spaghetti dinner for the wives—all are done with great zest. Never have I left a session feeling down or overwhelmed by sadness.
For special needs dads, success comes in such different ways— slow and measured, hopeful after all had seemed so hopeless. The child becomes a "gift of love." (James May, *Focus on Fathers*, Vol. 1, No. 7, May, 1987)

New programs which reflect changing attitudes are increasingly becoming part of good care: "pops 'n tots" classes; speaking to fathers when calling homes; planning important meetings when fathers can attend; scheduling "family" events such as picnics and suppers; peer support for fathers; maintaining contact with divorced fathers (Meyer, Vadasy, Fewell, & Schell, 1985). A parent stresses:

> . . .Essential elements of the program. . .include a picnic held twice a year. . .The picnics usually bring out many of the fathers. Often only one parent will accompany a child to clinic or for treatments; this is a chance for the whole family to be together. . .For many fathers it's a chance to relax and share some of their frustrations and fears with other men in the same situation. . .(Anna Barrantes quoted in Brent Novick, "Parent Volunteers: Breaking Down Barriers," *UCLA Cancer Center Bulletin*, Fall 1985)

Throughout these pages fathers and mothers have spoken openly and directly about their lives with a child with special needs. Several issues particularly relevant to fathers emerge from their thoughts, observations, and experiences.

- **Women and men may grieve differently.**

> I have noted in my conversations with other parents that men and women have distinctly different reactions when they have a child with a disability. Many women need to talk it through, many times, as I am now eight years later. Many men seem to want to get on with their life, return to work soon after the birth, and focus on other aspects of their lives. Many times this creates a chasm in their relationship. . . (Cari's mother)

- **Fathers are deeply involved in the lives of their children; sorrow may be mixed with love and joy.** A father shares:

> My eleven-year-old daughter, Mandy, is severely mentally delayed. . .Pragmatically speaking she will probably not be significantly different at 22. However, she does show definite signs of progress in very specific areas which is encouraging.
> The past eleven years have been a journey that I have at times completely detested and at other times thoroughly enjoyed. . .My love for Mandy is unquestionable. . .I have spent many days and

nights in emergency rooms and doctor offices, on therapists' floors, and at Mandy's hospital bedside. Our home has many modifications. . .all for her safety. Her mother and I have successfully fought through Due Process action with a school administration on her behalf. And possibly institutionalizing her will not only break up our family, but my heart as well.

Yet, I still find it hard at times to accept her habits of licking windows wherever she goes, slobbering uncontrollably, and being incontinent. . .

The treadmill stops when I put my competitiveness in proper perspective. After acknowledging for the ump-teenth time that it has come between Mandy and me, I am able to back off and give Mandy more space. By allowing her the freedom to not have to function in my space at levels I demand of myself, . . .I am able to like her for who she is. (David Cornell, D.A.D.S., Family Support Project, Focus Report, Fathers of Special Children, Oklahoma State Department of Health, MCH/Pediatric Division, Fall, 1989)

- **Fathers derive pleasure from the accomplishments, hard work, and courage of their children with special needs.**

My husband and I try to give our children as many normal experiences as possible. . .We are proud of their accomplishments, and know how hard they try. . . (mother of three children, Lisa, Norm, and Nancy, with special needs)

- **Fathers benefit from peer support, understanding, and appreciation of their crucial roles within the lives of their families.** A father speaks:

It's so hard to express how alone I felt after the birth of Robby, my son with Down syndrome. All the dreams I had had for Robby and me were crushed. I didn't know if I could ever feel close to him. I didn't know if I could be strong for my wife.

The Dads' group was the beginning of my healing. I listened to other men's experiences, learned of their heartache and pain, learned of their love and joy in their kids. During some of our meetings, I was able to play with the older kids. I remember one little guy who tapped me on the back, giggled, and shyly asked me to play frisbee with him. As I laughed with him, I began to develop new dreams for my own baby. Robby and I grew closer and closer. (Robby's father)

- **Fathers need professionals to understand and respond to both their pain and sources of strength.**

> I very much appreciated a male nurse in the NICU who came over to me and asked me what I wanted to know about Joshua's care. I guess he understood it was hard for me to approach him. I had never felt so out of control—guilty and powerless. My mind and heart were spinning. His support and his understanding that I needed to be a part of Joshua's care meant a great deal to me. (father of Joshua and Miriam)

The father of a 31-year-old man with Down syndrome writes of his life with Mark:

> For 31 years, Mark has been a central fact of our family life, knitting us together, trying our patience, helping us laugh, probably making us better people than we would have been without him. . .
>
> Indefatigable, Mark has handsawed his way through storm-toppled tree trunks without resting, mowed lawns, backstopped me on cement-laying jobs. I repay him with prodigious hero sandwiches, which he seldom fails to praise.
>
> At 31, he still cannot read, but he does guess at numbers, at times embarrassingly well. When, here lately, he began to put a cash value on his toil and asked for pay, I offered him a dollar. He looked at me with a knowing grin and said, quite clearly despite his usual speech problems, "Five bucks, Dad, *five* bucks." I gave him five ones.
>
> For signs like this that the manchild is coming of age, I am grateful. And for something else: I can't say we feel he's ready for Congress, but he has given us hope. Unlike the night he was born, in part because of Mark, I am no longer afraid of the dark. (James C. G. Conniff, About Men: Manchild Coming of Age, *The New York Times Magazine*, August, 18, 1985, p. 62)

Siblings

Health care professionals and institutions all too often have disregarded the complex feelings and needs of siblings. The worry and pain of siblings may be "forgotten" or not seen at all during hospital or clinic visits. A mother shares her children's story:

Marc had taken his place on his potty after supper one night, his usual ritual. However, because I was busy, I asked his seven year old brother, Nicolas, to watch over him for me.

Suddenly I heard crying and wailing coming from the bathroom. As I burst in, expecting to find all kinds of horrendous problems, I discovered Nicolas sobbing his heart out, saying he wished Marc wasn't blind and how it wasn't fair. . .Meanwhile, Marc was as happy as could be and thought all this noise was great entertainment.

I gently took Nicolas into the family room and hugged him close to me. My heart was breaking, and I found it difficult to speak coherently over the huge lump that had formed in my throat. I told Nicolas how lucky Marc was to have a caring and sensitive brother who loved him so much, and also lucky to have parents like us who give him enough love to challenge and guide him through life. Not forgetting how lucky we were because Marc had given us strength and compassion.

Nicolas pondered over these profound words for a few minutes and then promptly asked for cookies and milk!

What wonderful innocence! What a great leveller! Cookies and milk should be the answer to all our problems. The proverbial placebo. (Linda M. Jeffery, *Participating Families*, Vol. 1, No. 6, October, 1988)

Siblings of children with serious problems experience a broad range of painful feelings. There may be fear—"Will I, too, become so sick?" There may be guilt—"Did I do or say something bad to make my brother need a wheelchair?" There may be anger—"How come Mommy spends so much time with my brother? She's never home with me. But what can I do?" There may be sadness: "Watching my sister struggle makes me cry. I want her to play with me and laugh with me. No one tells me this, but I think she might die."

Parents explain:

Siblings, as much as parents, need compassion, understanding, and concern for their worries and fears. They should not be ignored; even young children can feel devastated, scared, lost, angry, or guilty. (the mother of a son whose death was due to trauma)

* * * *

My children are all special to me and play active roles in our family life. The illness of any child in the family has an enormous ripple effect; too often caregivers underestimate the resulting trauma placed on siblings. (mother of Eddie, Janet, Tracy, and Lori)

* * * *

There is a *no sibling policy* which means that not only is Mickey barred from seeing his brother, but his worried brother is barred from seeing Mickey and his mother. I have been unable to locate the person responsible for these policies. (mother of Mickey and Todd)

Siblings, speaking about their family's experience, describe their own worries, panic, and fear. Lori, for example, ". . .struggles every day to find and maintain her family position:"

My name is Lori. . .I am nine years old. My brother is four years old, and he has epilepsy and apnea. That means he stops breathing. My sister, who is 12 years old, has epilepsy. My six-year-old sister has severe apnea, and her heart goes too fast. This bothers me because our house is like a hospital. Sometimes this doesn't seem fair because my brother and sister come first. I wish I could spend more time with my mom.

The saddest time in my life was when my little sister stopped breathing, and I had to go shake her. I thought she would die. The happiest time in my life was when my little brother and sister have gone to the doctor, and he said they would be OK. The thing I most worry about is the kids dying. It bothers me at school because I am gone eight-and-a-half hours. One night my little brother quit breathing so now I sleep with him because I don't want him to die. I remember when we had a nurse. I wish we had one now. Mom and I could go out to eat.

Lori's twelve-year-old sister Tracy continues with her perspective on her own struggle and the struggle of her family:

. . .I'm afraid my little brother and sister will die while I'm not near them. It's not fair. I wish my little sister could run and jump like a normal kid. I wish she didn't have to be on a monitor or oxygen. The saddest time in my life was when I sat and watched my little brother almost die while my mom did mouth to mouth on him. It scared me a whole bunch. The happiest time of my life is when I see my little sister run just a little bit. I wish we could get a nurse to come to the house so we could get away. I'm afraid they'll die while I'm gone. When I watch them play, I think they probably won't live very long so I try to make it the happiest part of their lives.

Sibling support groups encourage children to identify feelings of guilt, embarrassment, and loneliness. They provide guidance, information, and support to well or non-disabled children coping with many confusing and ambivalent feelings toward sick or handicapped brothers or sisters (Powell & Ogle, 1985). A young member of such a group expresses his worries:

Sometimes I feel bad when we go out to eat, and my brother starts walking around and bugging everyone. Other times, I feel like letting him walk around and see the people. Even though he sometimes bugs me, I still care a lot about him. (Written by a fourteen-year-old male whose brother has Down syndrome, in Daubenspeck-Ulrich, B. Family Support Project, Focus Report, Siblings of Special Children, Oklahoma State Department of Health, Winter, 1990)

Family-oriented policies that acknowledge the concerns of siblings are needed to help children coping with many emotions— sadness, anger, fear, love (Meyer, Vadasy, & Fewell, 1985; Adams & Deveau, 1987). Charlie's mother illustrates such practices:

Our hospital was very good about letting our other children visit anytime. The staff treated Charlie, and, at the same time, treated us. The hospital was very family-oriented, and that is the way it should be.

Sharing Victories, Bestowing Credit

Parents of children who had suffered IVH episodes were asked, "Was anything particularly kind said?" One parent responded, "Those who said they respect us, and think we're great parents." This positive statement offered encouragement and hope. Other parents appreciated doctors who "celebrated with us as the bleed resolved and all traces of it disappeared." (IVH Parents Newsletter)

While celebration after a complete recovery, a happy ending, is natural, parents value professionals who are able to join them as they rejoice in the family's victories when a total cure is not possible. The mother of a child with severe communication problems explains:

The same doctor [who always talks with Ellen] told me that I was doing a good job with Ellen and patted me on the back. I really appreciated his regard and respect, and I guess he sensed my need.

A "seasoned" mother emphasizes:

> Parents appreciate some recognition. . .for all they do, and for all they have become, under the difficult circumstances of a child's illness. A timely word of praise, a compassionate remark, a hug, or an unexpected phone call/note will render you truly unforgettable as a caring professional. (*A Few Words to Young Professionals*, Sherelyn Campbell).

Parents ask those caring for their children to see, value, and support the positive aspects of their family's life—what brings joy and happiness despite the stress and pain of chronic illness.

> In my family's situation, we are at our most vulnerable when it comes to the illness of the kids. While my family is remarkably happy at most times, we are often left feeling somehow defeated after a visit to a doctor. I think this is because it is typical to discuss only problems, the negative aspects of our lives, with doctors. Some of our doctors find a way to bring in more positive issues in their discussion. My children are bright and respond well to jokes and other things. I enjoy talking about medical issues not specific to my kids. A couple of sensitive doctors talk with me about [my profession]. This deviation from the down side of our lives is most helpful. (mother of Mickey and Todd)

In the face of incomplete recovery, permanent disability, and chronic conditions, parents and their professional allies are able to find strength and satisfaction in the child's and family's growth and hard-won triumphs. The recognition of caregivers is underscored in importance because the society at large may not understand such achievement:

> I wouldn't even bother telling the guys at work about Toni; they just wouldn't understand. If I told them that Toni finally started to walk at two-and-a-half, I'd probably get a strange look. If I tell the dads at the class, they'd say "Hooray! Great!" because they know how hard we've been working at it. (Meyer, Vadasy, Fewell & Schell, 1985)

Professionals can make victories all the sweeter by sharing in the pleasure of a child's achievements. Parents see this as a validation of their youngster's progress and their pride. Parents appreciate honest praise of their child's efforts and hard work.

Bestowing credit can be a sensitive issue:

> During much of Nick's early life, the successes in coping with his problems belonged to professionals. Only the failures were mine. I hadn't had a healthy baby, couldn't seem to get him healthy, couldn't comfort him and, most painful, didn't feel connected to him. I believed that I wasn't capable of doing him any good. (Ann Oster, *Equals in this Partnership*, NCCIP, 1985, p. 30)

In view of such feelings, by no means rare, it can be particularly important to recognize what parents and their children achieve as progress does begin. Professionals who understand the family's accomplishments—the child's cooperation; the parent's faithful struggle to keep appointments, to follow up on a program at home, and to challenge the child in his daily activities—participate in the life of the family in a caring, special way. When caregivers (people in a position to know) recognize that credit is due, they touch parents deeply.

> Our son is now 21. Since he was 4, he has been served by the same pediatrician. I can think of several instances when I was thankful to have such a "friend." One instance that comes to mind is when he told me that I was doing a fine job as a mother of a handicapped child. In all my years of motherhood (30), no one had ever taken time to tell me that—especially where Ben, our son who is mentally retarded, is concerned. (Ben's mother)

Beyond Care

There are children and parents whose circumstances are so compelling and moving to an individual professional that he or she may go "beyond the call of duty" and reach out in extraordinary ways. Care that stretches beyond limits of time and place is valued and remembered throughout the family's life. Such situations offer professionals moments of renewal, "refreshment," enhanced personal gratification in their work. Time clocks and schedules give way to caring—pure, unfettered.

In the following vignettes, parents discuss events in their children's lives that elicited unusually warm, giving responses from those caring for their children. Parents realize that such "nurturing" goes beyond standards of basic good care. Professionals must have their own lives, hours away from their work, relief from thinking about their work. However, in those cases, where the professional can "go the extra mile," revitalization and renewed professional pride are one's rewards.

> The labor and delivery nurse, although her shift was over at the time, rode in the ambulance with our daughter to the medical center. I can't tell you how much that meant to my husband and me. (Victoria's mother)

* * * *

> I remember Dr. C stopping in Thomas's room before leaving for home. He would sit in the rocking chair and listen to our concerns and, in a quiet, gentle way, be supportive. He never then, nor now, seemed to be in a rush to get away from us and on to the next case. (mother of Len and Thomas)

* * * *

> There were two nurses. . ., one in the NICU and one in the nursery, who particularly helped us. They signed on as Keough's primary nurses and got to know us as well. In time they opened their homes to us, putting us up in spare beds when we came to town, loaning us their cars when we arrived by plane and visiting us on their vacations. As Keough's situation dragged on for years, they knew that the only "vacation" we got from her care was the time she spent in the hospital, and they helped us to feel less guilt about enjoying it.
>
> One of the best encounters we had with the medical system came out of one of the worst when these two nurses came across town to visit my daughter, who had been hospitalized elsewhere for a surgery that required collaboration with an additional surgeon. When my daughter's trach tube clogged up and she began turning blue, that hospital's staff just stood around looking, so our nursing friends jumped in and dealt with it - even though it wasn't their "place" to do so. More power to them! (Keough's mother)

* * * *

> I value the physicians and nurses who have treated us with compassion. I'll never forget one doctor who phoned from Mexico on his honeymoon to check on the status of my daughter. That same doctor once put his arm around me when he sensed I needed a little support. Such gestures mean a lot. (Cari's mother)

* * * *

> He got to know us. He got to know our family, and he got to know me. I think it helped. It was a comfort to my parents to know that the professionals cared about their son. We actually got bills that said PAID. The doctor had paid our bill. (David Oberhart, who

lost his sight as a result of congenital glaucoma, reflecting on his family's relationship with his ophthalmologist when he was a child, *Families and Disability Newsletter*, Vol. 2, No. 2, Summer, 1990, p. 8)

* * * *

Summer's the worst time in the world to have a medically fragile child. Everybody's on vacation except you. You watch your kid's seizures worsen, know the anticonvulsant has reached tolerance or toxicity (or *both!*) or is just plain not touching the seizures, and there's no one around. But our resident left his vacation phone numbers in two states 1000 miles away and said, "Call me with a report. No," he revised, "I'll call you. You use these for any emergency." He also gave me the home phone number of the metabolic supervisor, who was off on a professional leave to write. Through the summer the phone would ring, and I'd pick it up to hear a gentle voice, "How's the baby?" (Becky's mother)

In summary, a community-based system of care relies heavily on the functioning and well-being of families. At a time of great stress on family life, how can professionals contribute to family strength and integrity? Recognition of the vital role of fathers in nurturing children in need; acknowledgment of families' choices and unique styles of caring; empowerment of families; and appreciation of the daily struggles and victories of families lay the foundation for positive parent-professional collaboration.

HANDLING THINGS BETTER

Situations to ponder

RESPECTING THE FAMILY; CYCLES OF STRESS AND GRIEVING

Families of children with chronic illnesses and/or disabilities will experience times of stress and devastating uncertainty. Professionals who are able to listen to parents and refrain from snap judgments help parents to regain some control over their family's life. Offering parents one's concern and respect without the burden of unsolicited advice enables parents to gather their strength and make the difficult decisions they alone must make.

The mother of a medically fragile child recalls a time of crisis in the care of her child. As she confided her distress, a professional's intrusive advice caused much pain. However well-meaning, the professional's judgments led to a breakdown in trust and care. Parents repeatedly emphasize that a restrained, nonjudgmental "listening ear"—the presence of someone who cares—often provides the greatest help as they face emotional, physical, and ethical conundrums.

Janet

One of my most painful experiences was when a doctor, feeling that I had probably reached my limit in handling crises, recommended that we remove our daughter, then two, from her apnea monitor. She felt we should let "nature take its course" so our family could get back to normal. Since Janet was still having numerous, uncontrolled apneic episodes with severe bradycardia, I asked the doctor if Janet would die. The doctor sighed and said, "Whatever—anyway your family would be back to normal." Her blase attitude cut into me like a knife, and I was at that point turned into a sobbing, shaking, distraught parent.

I felt so vulnerable and distrustful of the entire medical community. I was very much afraid to let my true feelings and emotions out, as I thought they might be interpreted as my not being able to handle the situation. I feared that if anyone suspected that I couldn't handle the stress, the hospital might take the monitor away against my wishes—whether Janet was well enough or not.

I kept imagining that all of the medical staff felt that our family would be better off if Janet were to die. I was frantic trying to think of ways to prove we could handle ANYTHING and that Janet was a very important part of our lives. Thankfully, I later told a hospital social worker what had happened. I was reassured that the monitor would stay as our only defense against the apnea, and the doctor was dismissed from our case. Still, I will never forget the vulnerability and lack of control I felt that day.

Perspectives

CRITICAL ROLE, SPECIAL NEEDS OF FATHERS: A DIVORCED FATHER SEEKS HELP FROM HEALTH CARE PROFESSIONALS

Institutions and caregivers are often unprepared to deal with current family realities—divorce and the needs of "noncustodial" parents. An intern recounts her confrontation with a child's "night visitor," his father, who struggled for information and a place in his son's care.

Danny

"Doctor, what is wrong with my son? I'm his father. . .I have rights. . .I have. . .," Mr. Clark's despair called after me as bedtime rounds came to a frenetic end. His face was red with pain and frustration. Furrows, etched deep with worry and fatigue, framed his flushed eyes as he struggled to hold back tears.

Bedtime. Lights off! The busy hum of the ward would know no rest. No lights off to crises sharply blinding the night. Visions of sick children struggling to breathe, children wildly thrashing and seizing from high fever and deadly infections, children bleeding. . .potential disasters of all kinds. . .raced through my mind.

I felt intensely alone—bedraggled. The beginning of a long on-call. The junior resident and I must stay one step ahead - always one step ahead.

Mr. Clark, more and more insistent, flagged me down. His hand waved forcefully struggling to capture a look, a glance, an acknowledgement.

At 8:30 P.M. I must be firm, tough, in control—able to avoid a lengthy, complicated discussion with a distraught parent. So much for me to do. So much for me to fear.

"Mr. Clark," I coldly stated, "I'm the only intern here now. The attendings and specialists have all spoken in great detail to Dan's mother today. It's really impossible. . .Why don't you speak to your wife?"

My words landed with a thud. A father's tenuous grip over his world faltered, and his tears shimmered against the bleak hospital night. "My wife, my former wife and I can't talk. We can't. . ."

Mr. Clark's honesty and pain swept over me: irritability and brusqueness suddenly were gone. "I'm sorry, Mr. Clark. I didn't understand. I didn't know. Let's talk. Let's find somewhere to talk."

As we walked toward an office, Mr. Clark, embarrassed, proud, quickly brushed his tears aside, hiding them precariously in the sleeve of his work jacket. A father's tears - the tears of the night visitor who stroked his little boy's ghosts and demons away.

"I never thought things would be this way," he softly whispered. "I've lost so much already. Dan's leg. Just a little kid's falls and bumps. So I thought. Now he can't walk, and I've heard words like cancer. . .like cancer. Yes, my wife and I are divorced. But Dan is still my son, my boy."

Mr. Clark slowly arched his arm toward his eyes and reached for a tear. As he turned toward the window and quietly regained his composure and dignity, I pictured six-year-old Danny - freckles, laughter, and a tattered, very special baseball cap. Danny wore his cap everywhere—day and night—through X-rays, through baths, through scary blood tests. His little boy's fist grasped his worn prize as if it were life itself. A cherished present from Dad? A loving reminder of their "first game" together?

Mr. Clark once again turned toward me. He did not want sympathy. He did not want pity. He wanted facts. Hard facts. An intern's facts - garnered from daily rounds, incomplete, a beginning - broke the silence. "Danny has been examined by several doctors—orthopedic surgeons, radiologists, pediatricians—and has had many blood tests, x-rays, tomograms, bone scans. Yes, cancer was. . .was a great fear, a great fear. But the latest information is encouraging. More tests are needed. . .Danny's tumor may not be malignant."

Mr. Clark's eyes would not let me go. He would hold me captive until his quest and journey were finally over. "Please," I pleaded, hectically thumbing through pages of my notebook, "call the attendings. Track them down until you get the details and facts you must have. Here are some numbers. It won't be easy. . .I'll tell them about our meeting tonight."

A father relaxed. Had he found a strange, unexpected ally? Had he found hope? After a hesitant "thank you," he carefully wrote down several phone and beeper numbers and returned to Danny's side.

I gathered up my equipment and splashed cold water on my face. For a moment, the harsh fluorescent light faded, and bitter-sweet memory emerged. For a moment, an image of my father's tears—the first time I had seen him cry—pierced through the night. For a moment, my father—gently, warmly— joined me as I walked back to the ward, back to our long vigil. (Leff, P., excerpts from diary, 1979)

7 Ongoing Care IV: Special Concerns

For any wheel to turn, it has to be balanced, just as a family needs the balance of love, trust, understanding, and strength—with the knowledge of never thinking what could have been, only working on what can be! (Beach Center on Families and Disability, University of Kansas)

Evaluations

Families are proud of their children with special needs and deeply value hard-won accomplishments. They come to judge their children's efforts and achievements according to standards appropriate to their children's individual needs and personal goals. A mother explains:

> ...Problems are measured in contrast to a norm, and you must tell me how my child is not "normal," but also remember to view my child in terms of what progress he or she has made.
>
> For example, my child is a year behind in most areas of development: by comparison with the norms, he is "developmentally delayed." We can live with this problem more easily, however, if we also judge how much more self-sufficient he is now than he was a year ago. On his first birthday, he was struggling to learn to sit up. This year, on his second birthday, he sits up as if this action had never been a problem. Now he struggles with walking. Realizing that progress gives me great hope, a commodity that I need every day. (Alexander & Tompkins-McGill, 1987, p. 361)

Current standardized tests may be unable to demonstrate or measure what a child's abilities are; a child's severe motor impairments may impede accurate testing. Ted's mother describes her frustration—and pain—in such a situation:

...This brings me to a discussion of Ted's mental retardation. At the neurology clinic, it was termed psychomotor retardation. Professionals advised me that due to Ted's serious motor problems they could tell me little about Ted's future intelligence. Of course, I have learned from the literature that athetoids are often thought to be intelligent but unable to demonstrate their abilities because of the type of motor problems they have. So—I have lived for years wondering if he is as retarded as his tests would show or as smart as most people who work with him begin to suspect he is. The bottom line is that it functionally makes so little difference; it seems that none of us really knows how to reach past his bodily problems to the mental ability he may have.

The manner in which evaluations are conducted will deeply affect parents. Sensitivity to the child's and family's individual strengths and needs greatly soften the impact of painful assessments. Parents appreciate professionals who make the effort "to get to know" their child as a child first: a more accurate picture of the child can thus emerge. Greg's mother contrasts two kinds of experiences with evaluations:

> ...Some of the most painful experiences have occurred during what my husband refers to as "blitz" evaluations. "Blitz" evaluations are those times when an entire day is spent with assessments and evaluations being performed by people who have never met our son in the past and have taken no time to get to know him. These people will make the diagnoses that will result in long-term health, home, and educational planning. Of course, the numbers of persons involved is overwhelming—to say the least.
>
> ...One of the most helpful encounters our family has experienced within the health care system centers around health professionals taking time to get to know our son as a young boy and *then* as a young boy coping with particular challenges or handicaps. This happened during an inpatient stay in which the health care personnel familiarized themselves with our son during the first few days. The remaining days were then spent in formalized evaluation and testing. This process provided health professionals, educators, as well as our family, with probably the clearest overall picture of our son's abilities.

The time surrounding evaluations in which children are assessed according to "standard norms" can be particularly painful to parents who derive pleasure from their children's "personal best" and value their children's courage and determination.

Even when a child has been involved with early-intervention services for some time, the periodic evaluations of the child's progress are hard on parents. No matter that the parents have seen even great progress in their child, developmental tests are normed on regular kids and the handicapped child is always going to be behind in comparison. Parents may be able to ignore these comparisons in their daily routine, but the day that test results are discussed is almost always a tough one, and professionals need to be aware of this. When one is working with many families and children, it can be easy to be insensitive to individual pain.

A double-bind in which parents can be caught when it comes to evaluations is the conflict of wanting their child to do well while knowing that evidence of real progress may cut the family off from the very services they need. SSI payments, for instance, depend on a child's doing relatively poorly. No matter what the results of testing are in such a situation, there may be little cause for rejoicing. If the child is doing well in comparison to non-handicapped children, the family will be ineligible for SSI payments they may really need. If the child is not doing well in comparison, that difference is once more thrown into harsh relief and all the money in the world will not make the parents feel better.

There is little a professional can actually do about this other than be there for the family, understand and accept their emotions, and be a friend. That's quite a lot, when you think about it. (Sue Duffy, Parents, Professionals, and Conflict, *Acceptance is only the first battle*, MUAP, 1984, p. 40)

Medical Records

On a broad scale, policies differ from state to state and from institution to institution regarding access to medical records. Very little is mandated, however, in the private medical records arena between professional and patient/family. In fact, giving parents access to records—actively encouraging review of records—can have several benefits. Parents reviewing records may prevent errors; their very intense involvement insures a careful check of accuracy. Their questions about entries, lab results, and recommendations allow a professional to monitor their understanding and clarify mistakes in comprehension (Stevens, Stagg, & McKay, 1977).

Given such potential benefits, it is difficult for parents to understand why access to their children's medical records has been discouraged by some professionals. Blaine's mother, struggling to help her baby with spina bifida, chronicles her journey from "wimp" to Blaine's advocate. Fighting for access to her son's medical records was the starting point:

. . .Then a funny thing happened. I became a mother. And suddenly I discovered that although I was inclined to let all manner of things happen to myself, I wouldn't begin to imagine tolerating them for my offspring. I who refused to struggle on my own behalf would challenge a mama grizzly bear for my son.

Mind you, I didn't instantly become completely wimpless. But there were early clues that I might be dancing to the beat of a different drummer. And those first signs involved Blaine's medical records.

When Blaine was but a few days old and still hospitalized, Michael and I were sitting reading through his medical chart when a nurse came by and said, "You know, you're not supposed to be reading that."

We were stunned. See, we were just beginning to get a dim picture of what we were facing, and it was abundantly clear to us that before we could really even begin to face up to our challenge, we needed as much information as we could lay our hands on. A logical place to begin laying our hands on seemed to be our own child's ever-thickening medical chart. Sometimes the information we were given verbally hadn't sunk in; sometimes it sounded contradictory and left us confused; and almost always we couldn't even remember how to pronounce the words we were hearing.

As we sat reading through the chart, so many of our questions were answered ("So that's what he said. . .") and confusions cleared up ("So that's what they meant. . ."). By this time, of course, we had heard that given the prognosis we were dealing with, some families felt so overwhelmed by the task they chose not to undertake it. That being the case, we expected that the medical community's attitude would universally be: "Since this is such a challenge, we are going to do anything and everything to support you as you need it. Now how can we best do that?"

So imagine our surprise when, as we were looking through Blaine's chart and so much light was being shone on so many dark and scary places, we were told we were breaking the rules.

Our response was decidedly not wimpy. Although we had some very strong allies and advocates within the medical community along the way as we worked to see and obtain copies of Blaine's medical records, we met with disappointing and surprising resistance. . . (Marie Deatherage-Newsom, Have You Seen Your Medical Records?, *The Bridge*, Winter, 1988, p. 16-17)

Discussions around a child's medical records may elicit additional questions or private fears that can be addressed in a comforting, caring way. This openness, this encouragement of involved parents, this extra step in caregiving, all communicate powerfully the professional's respect for parents as learners and partners. Keough's mother emphasizes:

Neither Keough's surgeon nor the pediatrician we switched to when she was 6 months old have ever pretended to know something they didn't. If I expressed concerns about her, they believed there was reason to check it out. Their egos are strong enough and knowledge vast enough that they have no problem with consulting specialists in other fields. They have treated me and my husband as rational, intelligent people. They have involved us in the medical process and have always made medical records available to us. They *like* our child. (Sue Duffy, Plaudits for Professionals, *Acceptance is only the first battle*, MUAP, 1984, p. 30)

In a climate of consumerism and growing access to medical records, professionals do well to assume that parents will, at some time, read their child's charts and files. Comments concerning the parents' situation must have clear goals—to be helpful, supportive, and lead to appropriate services. Offhand, gratuitous judgments about parents have no place in the child's permanent record and may cause a painful disruption in the vital parent-professional relationship. Parents may feel that they cannot speak openly with those caring for their children. A mother explains:

Our vulnerability of having our emotional level on medical records discourages honesty and promotes distrust. It encourages a "Supposed-to-be-in-Control" Syndrome which obstructs communication. (Carla Lee Lawson, *Prescription for Participation*, Iowa Pilot Parents, Inc.)

Medical and Diagnostic Testing

Parents urge professionals to explain and clarify medical testing: What information is needed? How will this information contribute to the total care of the child? What test or procedure will provide the required data with the least discomfort to the child?

Amber's mother discusses her experiences around diagnostic testing:

> When a test is given, I don't want to know only what the doctors feel like telling me; I want to know everything. I am a well-informed parent, and I have the final decision in Amber's care... not the health professionals. They may be the ones who do the work, but my husband and I are the ones who are responsible for the care of our child, both medically and at home. . .
>
> Sometimes health care professionals feel that the parents should not know, that they don't have the knowledge to make a decision. They are wrong. We are the ones who, if anything goes wrong, have to live with that decision and feel the remorse and guilt. It is usually not the professional. . .
>
> I would say, don't do a test for the test's sake. Amber has had IVP's, and it would take 10 times to find the vein. I finally got disgusted and insisted that they try to find the vein before they start poking. Now sonograms are done which are so much easier on all of us. Try to find the test that will show you what you want to know without making life more hell on earth for these kids. They go through enough. . .

Understanding the meaning of diagnostic tests to parents is extremely important. When a child presents with a complex picture of confusing symptoms that do not easily point to a clear diagnosis, an abnormal test result may become "the clue" that parents desperately seek. Parents want and hope for answers from the testing process, for results, for direction, for identification of a treatable condition. With children whose conditions defy straightforward diagnosis and treatment, parents cling to the hope that an abnormal test result will open doors to care.

> I am afraid that many professionals don't fully understand what a "test" means to the parent of an ill child. It took me many years to realize that an abnormal test doesn't always transfer into an easy diagnosis or treatment. I have very often hoped that a test would come back abnormal in the hope that someone would then treat the problem and "make it go away."
>
> I think students should know that they can expect this in

parents, especially if the diagnosis has been complicated by a complex array of symptoms. When dealing with uncertainties, an abnormal test seems like a certainty; a foundation [for possible treatment].

After all, many parents don't think you would do a test for something you can't treat. I don't want my child to have some terrible disease or syndrome, and I am not a neurotic parent who thrives on medical attention. I would only like to see some abnormal test to be the puzzle piece we have all been waiting for. I would just like the testing to stop and an actual treatment for cure to begin. I know this probably isn't possible; but it is my fantasy. (mother of Eddie, Janet, Tracy, and Lori)

Excessively long waiting periods for test results add to the confusion parents experience. Parents discuss the emotional costs of weeks or even months of waiting. The mother of an infant with chronic diarrhea describes the tension and anxiety surrounding her son's diagnostic tests:

I would be told that it was imperative to do a test. I would get charged up and nervous, and the test would be scheduled for two or three weeks later. The results wouldn't be in for two or three weeks after that! One and a half months is a long time for a parent to wait for results of an important test—especially when you're dealing with an infant who can't eat anything but meat-base formula, and you're struggling to understand why.

A mother of two medically fragile children emphasizes:

Anxieties multiply faster than e. coli while waiting for results from tests or procedures. Don't keep parents waiting any longer than is absolutely necessary. If you cannot deliver the results personally, or if a delay is anticipated, parents will appreciate your sending word to that effect with someone else. (*A Few Words to Young Professionals*, Sherelyn Campbell)

For children, long periods of waiting prior to tests in lab areas, X-ray departments, or clinics add to their distress and pain. Children need to be prepared for what they will experience and tests performed as quickly as possible. A child life intern records her experiences with a child undergoing long, anxiety-provoking waiting periods:

Joanie had finished with the finger-stick. She thought she was all through and was thrown off by the fact that she had to endure further blood tests.

Joanie sat with her grandmother, and the grandmother tried to comfort her. She continued to cry and truly appeared tormented. Besides the crying, she was biting her nails and shaking a bit. . .I think the worst part of the situation was the waiting. There was no one else in the clinic, yet Joanie was not taken in the back for about 15 minutes. The more she waited, the more anxious she appeared. (child life intern: journal entry)

Paperwork

Parents are dependent on professionals for the vast and endless paper trail that leads to equipment, services, financial assistance, and program admission. The bewildering array and complexity of forms, letters, and evaluations are absolute requirements that unlock doors for children and families in need. Parents sympathize with professionals' impatience with bureaucratic requirements, yet they cannot lessen their need.

> It has reached the point that Laura needs to have an Individual-ized Education Plan for some of the related services in the school district. In order for the district to proceed with the evaluation, we had to obtain a doctor's letter stating that she has a handicap.
>
> On our next visit to the orthopedist, I gave him the address and requested that he send a letter out. I felt like I had to apologize for asking this highly trained physician to use his time in this way; three moderately-bright five-year-olds could look at Laura and conclude that she has trouble walking.
>
> We are fortunate in our doctor; he is always kind about these requests, and he always dictates the letters within a day. He takes an enormous burden from my shoulders by being so cooperative and understanding. I have had so many contrasting experiences that I am able to appreciate him properly.
>
> From time to time, I have needed to discuss the specific diagnosis he puts down. Some programs so narrowly define their qualifying conditions that a particular label placed on Laura could exclude her. In Laura's case, we have so many diagnostic categories to choose from that it's ridiculous. At times, I have asked that a particular diagnosis *not* be used because ill-informed recipients might be upset by it.

At times, "paperwork" may offer the opportunity to explore new ways of healing and enhancing a child's self-image. A child psychiatrist, who admits to abhorring paperwork, describes a special encounter:

> Whenever possible, I like parents to participate with me in writing important letters to other agencies or institutions. We discuss the goals of the letter—whether we want to put the child's best face forward or emphasize problems.
>
> During one such session, Kay's mother and I decided to involve Kay in the process. Kay and Mrs. M were moving out of state and required many letters of introduction. Kay was a young teen with a seizure disorder compounded by severe learning disabilities, panic attacks, and very low self-esteem. Mrs. M and I felt that Kay's help in framing a letter stressing her strengths and abilities would be of great value to her. We used our last meeting together "to write" this letter.
>
> Initially, there were long silences and pauses as Kay struggled to find positives about herself. Slowly, hesitantly with help from her mother, Kay began to identify and believe in her strengths: "Yeah, I do like to swim. . .I *am* a good swimmer; "Yes, my friends like me. . .I'm a good friend; Mommy's right. . .I am a member of the school chorus. . ." As Kay began to enumerate her many fine qualities, a broad smile lit up her face.
>
> "Dreaded paperwork" had led to a healing moment. (PTL)

The Difficult Parent

Professionals cannot expect to like or feel comfortable with all parents; problematic situations will arise (Groves, 1978). Temperamental and personality differences; stages of training or clinical experience; parental despair; parents' unmet expectations; and parents' disappointments with other professionals may all contribute to difficult matches. Young professionals are often unprepared for such encounters.

Negative or even angry feelings toward parents may lead to guilt or blame: "How can I be angry with someone I should be helping?" "This is an impossible, demanding parent who will never be satisfied no matter what I do." Both guilt and blame drive deep wedges between parents and professionals (Moses, 1983). An early intervention specialist shares:

> After several years of work, I've grown more confident as a therapist and have seen children make strides. For the most part, I have good relationships with parents. They bring questions and problems to me, and we try to work things out. I've learned that some of my home exercises, combined with everything else

asked of them, would have kept families going until the wee hours of the morning. I've learned to listen and work with parents.

So—when Rosie's parents came along, I was thrown for a loop. They watched everything I did with hypercritical eyes. They challenged me constantly; no matter what I said or did it would never do. Either I was too rigid and demanding or not doing enough for Rosie. Their constant disapproval and hypervigilance really scared me. I felt as if they were preparing a legal case.

I was beginning to feel very guilty; the parents' attitudes were beginning to tarnish my work with Rosie. I began to dread our sessions. Others on the team had similar feelings but simply tried to avoid contact with the parents. If I didn't know in my heart that I could develop good working relationships with parents, I would have felt crushed.

One day after months of tension, my honest feelings just had to come out. I openly told Rosie's parents that I was very uncomfortable with them and that *our* relationship was affecting my work with their child. I was very surprised at their response. These parents, who felt so out of control of their lives since Rosie was born, could not believe that they were actually having any effect on the professionals responsible for their child. They felt so alone and vulnerable. True, we're far from perfect, but, at least, we're talking to one another. Things are better. (personal communication: early intervention specialist)

Attempts to focus on solutions to the problems at hand—what can be done; how parent and professional can pool their energy and skill—may help to build a working relationship and move beyond the boundaries of dislike. Locking horns with parents is of little value. Honestly accepting the parent's distress and trying to understand his or her pain may open gates to improved communication. Straightforward, reality-based statements of concern often defuse the conflict. For example, one might say to a parent, "Given the frightening situation for you and Stevie, it is understandable that you are angry and upset. It would be unusual if you weren't feeling frustrated and overwhelmed. How can we work together to do our best for Stevie during this hospital stay? Let's make a list of the problems and do some brainstorming."

A veteran mother offers her perspective on the dilemma of parents who, at stressful points along their child's journey, may be viewed as "difficult." These parents strive for some degree of control and influence over a desperate reality. Their intense struggle mirrors the helplessness and vulnerability of their situation.

Anybody who does not work in a NICU will feel out of control in an environment full of strange machines and unwelcome sounds. You feel you've walked into a high-tech torture chamber: victims are tied down; wires and tubes protrude from their most private places; strangers bustle in and out to puncture the victims; and rest is impossible. And the victim is your helpless, raw baby whom you can't protect.

This lack of control can make parents panicky and angry. The lack of voice in their child's treatment can provoke some parents to terror and misery, while others withdraw emotionally. Those who withdraw themselves are likely to be easier for NICU staff to "deal with." They are quieter and don't confront the [health care professionals]. They are overwhelmed, and, at least for now, they've given up their parental duties. . .

But the "difficult" parents—the ones who ask questions and challenge the wisdom of surgeries or procedures—these parents are still trying to *be* parents. They may be harder to cope with and take up more of your time, but they stand a better chance to help their child achieve and grow, because they haven't given over. (Ronnie Londner, IVH Parents, May, 1991)

A team approach may ease tensions and increase understanding of the parents' perspective, of the parents' underlying fear and dread. Support from colleagues is crucial. Non-judgmental team meetings to discuss complex, draining encounters with parents provide caregivers with a safe "home base." From this home base, they are better able to observe threatening interactions clearly and take steps toward positive change. A resident recalls:

A parent was constantly hounding me about every detail of his child's care—day and night. There was no peace. In order to avoid him, I would literally change course and march in the opposite direction.

For the first time in a team meeting, I vented my feelings of frustration concerning the child's illness and the father's struggle. I asked for help. We talked about the child's continuing poor condition. We talked about the father's vulnerability and despair. In reality, he had so very little control over the devastating illness that had gripped his child.

We developed a plan. The senior resident and I met with the father and stressed our commitment to his child's care and our desire to work with him. Each day at a set time, barring emergencies, we would meet with the father to discuss his concerns. This new routine has helped all of us. (personal communication: pediatric intern)

Professionals who try "to step into the parents' shoes," reflect upon the parents' pain and distress, and understand parental reactions without taking such reactions as personal attacks open doors to good care. There are no easy answers, and resolution is not always to be had. An intern describes her relationship with a "difficult" mother and the barriers that separated them:

> "That woman - she never leaves me alone," I mutter to my friend as we dash to the cafeteria. "Every lab value. Every pulmonary treatment. Every IV. Every insulin injection. Every bowel movement. . ." My buddy nods knowingly. All of the interns have served time with Mrs. Davis, Christy's mother.
>
> As we whizz past the clock, I turn my head for a second. Mrs. Davis is flying after me and quickly gaining ground. I shiver: Patty, won't you ever learn to muzzle your mouth? "That woman" has probably heard a good 90% of the nasty things you've said about her.
>
> "Dr. Leff, I thought we were going to see the radiologist *together*," she attacks.
>
> "Mrs. Davis, we will. Let me grab lunch first; you could take a break too. Then we'll go straight to radiology. There really is no hurry," I plead, I implore; I'm hungry, I'm exhausted.
>
> She senses the earnestness in my voice and begrudgingly nods approval. On some level she probably knows that we both need a rest.
>
> As I wolf down my sandwich, I look toward her table. Her lonely "break" consists of black coffee and cigarettes. I imagine going to her table and inviting myself to join her. Fear stops me cold. Would a discussion with Mrs. Davis be anything more than an onslaught of complaints?
>
> Yes, we both are afraid. The calm, knowledgeable senior attending, our expert on the care of children with cystic fibrosis, is on a two week vacation, *and* Christy, 11 years old, once again needs hospitalization. Mrs. Davis has watched Christy's days outside of the hospital dwindle in both number and quality. Pulmonary infections, diabetes, GI complications, heart complications. For months, there has been no peace. Is Christy becoming the hospital's child; each day a struggle for life?
>
> Agitated puffs of smoke surround Mrs. Davis as we begin the short walk to the radiology department. There is a wedge of

silence between us. How can I tell you, Mrs. Davis, that I'm on your side; on Christy's side - that I, too, feel panic? Christy's rapid deterioration over the past year has sent shock waves through me. We've all tried to manage Christy's care as best as we can. Will your bright, pretty "fighter" shrivel to a shell of herself? Will Christy die while I'm still an intern?

Holding up the film, the radiologist points out signs of improvement. For the moment, Mrs. Davis, hovering on the edge of time, relaxes. In a sane moment for both of us, my eyes reach out toward hers: a reprieve. Christy's painful, embarrassing enemas will no longer be necessary. A reprieve.

There is less tension as we walk back to the ward and even some light conversation about spring and Christy's upcoming birthday. Mrs. Davis returns to her daughter, and I return to my work. We hesitantly smile at each other as our paths part. Mrs. Davis, you have a right to be crazy, impossible, unbearable. We see only a tiny fraction of what you do bear. But there is so much more I wish I could say to you. So much more.

Mrs. Davis, the social worker and the hospital's psychiatrist have offered to talk with Christy about her feelings about being sick, missing her friends, missing school. Nothing scary—just a chance for her to share her worries and concerns. They've offered to talk with you and your family— your healthy son and husband. Your response has consistently been a forceful "NO:" "No one is going to talk with my child about dying! I am still her mother. Have you people just given up on her?"

I understand how frightened. . .No—I cannot possibly understand the depth of your fear; the years of hope and disappointment; the bitter helplessness; the hellish nightmare that has become your reality—arbitrary, menacing. Have you survived by not "talking?" Will "forbidden" words cast a hideous spell over Christy?

I cannot know your pain and terror. You are Christy's caring, loving mother, and we have no right to interfere. But may I share my own story? It may help; it may harm. During the final months of my father's life, secrets and half-truths wreaked havoc on our family. However well-intentioned, secrets and half-truths "protected" no one. The pretense only intensified our grief and longing. We could not cry openly together; say "good-bye"; wrap each other in warm, painful, final, tender hugs.

Christy knows she is very sick. You have seen her try to hide her bloated tummy; massage her stick-like arms; cough, gasp, and cry through each respiratory treatment. Mrs. Davis, I have

watched you watch her - the despair in your eyes. . .
A nurse gently taps me on the shoulder. "Mrs. Davis wants to ask you about. . ." Inwardly I cringe. (Leff, 1989, p. 402)

Larry's mother, a health care professional, comments on both of her roles:

I have *been* a difficult parent especially at the beginning—the anxiety—the fear of the future—the focus on your child, his symptoms, every nuance of progress and care.

I, too, have been a professional trying to communicate with difficult parents. I think professionals find this aspect of their work the most trying and frustrating. I have been exasperated with some parents and have made mistakes. I still do, but hopefully I can be open and continue to learn.

Negotiating for Compliance with the Treatment Program

In the care and treatment of ill or disabled children, compliance is identified as a serious issue. As a source of provider stress, it can lead to feelings of frustration, deteriorating interactions, and ultimate withdrawal from responsibility for giving care. Many professionals see friction between themselves and the patient, or patient's family, as a result of the patient's or family's non-complying behaviors/actions. A more productive view, however, is seeing noncompliance as a result of friction, whether the strains in the relationship are identified and acknowledged or not. Non-complying behaviors follow when the patient- or parent-professional relationship has broken down. Failed communication has interfered with cooperation (Zisook & Gammon, 1981; Vining & Freeman, 1985).

Patients or parents may not fully understand or articulate the reasons for their failure to meet the expectations of a professional's regimen. Through reestablishing a helping role—problem-solving to discover the unmet needs and hindrances—the professional can maintain the vital parent-professional relationship and work with the family to achieve realistic cooperation.

Families of patients are expected to meet a wide range of responsibilities. Multiple appointments must be scheduled and kept. Referrals are made by professionals, but the follow-up is expected of the parents. Medications must be obtained and administered while side effects are monitored. Physical therapy home programs leading to mastery of new skills involve setting aside regular exercise time. Occupational therapy recommendations may mean obtaining equipment, changing habits, and adapting to new, time-consuming self-care routines. Diet changes often call for extra shopping and lengthier meal preparations. Restrictions on activities demand extra parental supervision and may create conflict between parent and child. Post-op care can be tedious and unnerving. Casts and braces need maintenance, refitting, and proper care. Even so "small" a need as eye-patching presents a family with a demand for time, adjustment, and potential intrafamilial friction.

Families experience the *cumulative* effect of complying with the many requests, recommendations, and absolute decrees of professionals who have at heart their child's progress. A mother describes the complexities involved:

> . . .Most efforts to alleviate a child's problem will succeed only if you can elicit support from the important people in a child's life. These people may include family members, extended family, friends, or even the other experts trying to help the child. If, for example, you want my child to wear leg braces during all his waking hours for the next six months, explain to me in detail why they are important, how they will help my child's problem, and how the braces should be worn. Then talk to me about other family members' attitudes toward the braces. Will my spouse be sure that our child is wearing them properly? Will the people at the day care center where the child goes do the same? Perhaps you could talk to a spouse who is not convinced and give me the suggestions for making wearing the braces at the day care center easier for the child and the caretakers. (Alexander & Tompkins-McGill,1987, p. 362)

In the following vignettes, a "senior" mother (Blaine's mother) responds to the mother of a baby with spina bifida, Torey. Torey's mother is struggling with the many pressures surrounding his exercises and care:

> . . .I'm sure I'm not alone in feeling that if I did all the exercises and hooked Torey up to all the devices, we'd be working at it from sunup to sunset. But, if I don't do everything I feel guilty from sunup to sunset. I know that we need to decide what is best for Torey, but when you're new at this you really don't know what is best! I'm hoping that we'll hear from enough parents that have already gone through this and know how some of these things worked or haven't worked. Maybe we'll hear of something we haven't thought of. Hopefully we will then have enough information to make some decisions of our own. . . (Jamie Hett, writing in *The Bridge*, Autumn, 1988, p. 4-5)

Blaine's mother replies:

> . . .And did you ever describe our feelings so very well about either "working" on something every waking moment (and even sleeping moments with those night splints!), or feeling guilty for slacking off! I remember when I was presented the list of all the things we should be working on at home, I asked, "So when do we go to the zoo? When do we just play?" I think relaxing and having fun and just plain being Blaine's mother have been far more beneficial to him (and me) in the long run than any particular therapy.
>
> We need balance in our lives so badly, and I can tell from your letter that you too are seeking it, and you will find it. The information sometimes comes in slowly, but you're doing the very best that you can do. That's enough. . . (Marie Deatherage-Newsom, *The Bridge*, Autumn, 1988, p. 5)

Because so much, at times, may be asked of patients, parents, and/or families as a whole, it is essential to emphasize the importance of the parent-professional relationship, the professional's communication skills, and the professional's willingness to comprehensively address issues related to compliance. Parents offer the following guidelines:

- **Explain fully what is necessary in clear, precise language free of jargon and medical-ese.** The reasoning behind the recommendation is an important part of this explanation.

- **Respect the family's right to self-determination.** Discussing possible alternatives is crucial to the decision-making process. A mutual commitment to a course of action is more likely to lead to compliance with a plan.

- **Anticipate difficulties and assist the family in identifying further possible problems.** (This might take the form of introducing and consulting with veteran parents.) Addressing these roadblocks prepares the family and demonstrates the professional's awareness of the difficulties involved.

- **Be prepared for ambivalence.** As patients and families follow a new program, protocol, or procedure, they may change; enthusiasm may give way to disillusionment. The family and/or patient may come to feel that what is asked is "too much"—that the demand for change is too far-reaching, that too much must be given up, that the cost of complying is too high in terms of the quality of the whole family's life, compared to the benefits to one member of the family.

"Noncompliance" is not without expense. Parents wrestle with guilt and question if they might have helped a child gain more. Balanced against those painful thoughts are the reduction in stress between parents and child and the more "normal" life allowed the family if the problematic plan is dropped.

The continuing support and involvement of a professional may keep the spirits of family members high enough to maintain commitment to a "costly" regimen. Rochelle's mother stresses:

> The most successful times I have had with professionals have been with those who are willing to listen and give positive feedback. Tell the mother or father that she or he is doing a good job. Such encouragement gave me great strength.

- **Be willing to change plans.** When difficulties arise, when a family has "had enough," all-or-nothing thinking on the part of professionals is to be avoided. Such conceptualization is a barrier both to the child's care and to the parent-professional relationship. Compliance, like a treatment plan, can be renegotiated. Once again, clear communication, mutual decision-making, and anticipation of difficulties will play a major role working toward these new goals.

WHEN A CHILD DIES

The Parents

Parents have written moving and compelling accounts of the life and death of a child. It is hoped that this outline will encourage professionals to read these books and to incorporate grieving parents' feelings and perspectives into professional thinking and practice. Whether the child is a newborn whose life is measured in terms of hours or a teen who has struggled with a chronic, debilitating illness for many years, the death of a child sends shock waves throughout a parent's being. There is no comparable pain. For parents, the natural order and flow of life and death is sharply and cruelly disrupted. In modern, twenty-first century societies, children are expected to live and to thrive; the death of a child destroys parents' deepest dreams and hopes.

No one can dispel or take away the crushing agony and pain that may remain a part of parents' lives for many years. However, parents stress that the manner in which caregivers handle events surrounding the death can greatly affect parents' views of themselves, the child they have lost, and their relationships with their living children. Health care professionals have the opportunity to help parents and families endure this most devastating of crises. Through their concern and caring, health professionals have the opportunity to help parents carry on with productive, loving lives.

> There is little anyone can say or do to help ease the pain of losing a child.
> It is a time no parent ever forgets, a time of unbearable anguish and sorrow. And yet, experience has shown that what happens in the hospital while a child is dying can have lifelong repercussions. It can affect the severity and length of parental grieving as well as the ability of parents to resume a normal life. (*Suggestions For Medical Personnel. . .When A Child Dies* The Compassionate Friends, 1986)

Parents of children with life-threatening illnesses repeatedly speak of their need to maintain vital, active parenting roles. As the the child's life comes to an end and the gravity of the loss confronts parents, these issues assume a poignant, pressing reality. Parents need to remain close to their child and participate as fully as possible in the care of their child. Truthful information from caregivers is critical and forms the foundation upon which parents must make agonizing decisions. The parents of a critically ill premature newborn who would die after weeks of care in an NICU explain:

> Give parents some control over what you do to their child. Instead of telling them what you are going to do, give them the facts and let them participate in making the decisions. After all, they are the parents of this child, not you. Some parents may not want to have this level of responsibility, but most will if appropriately informed. During so much of Pammy's life, we felt as if she weren't our child at all.

During these most painful hours, days, and weeks of a child's life, parents need to talk about their feelings, talk about the child's condition, cry, and be heard. Pammy's parents continue:

> I would like young doctors, nurses, and social workers to understand that parents desperately need to know that you care. Getting close to parents who are hurting, whose child is dying in

front of them, must be rough for you. Please, don't run away.

Parents of critically ill children anticipate "the worst" as they simultaneously pray and hope for "the best." They speak of riding an emotional rollercoaster that is totally out of their control. There is little in life to prepare them for this level of inescapable stress, anxiety, and fatigue. Parents urge caregivers to be patient, to understand the magnitude of their anguish and despair:

> Some parents may not be able to accept bad news and may cope by denying it. DO be patient with parents as denial is a form of emotional protection which will disappear when an individual is ready. Everyone is on a different timetable. (*Suggestions For Medical Personnel. . .When A Child Dies*, The Compassionate Friends, 1986)

Parent-professional communication assumes heightened importance. Parents need to know that everything possible is being done for their child. Parents need to know that they and their child have neither been abandoned nor their concerns trivialized. Emily's foster mother describes her ongoing pain, the result of a breakdown in parent-professional communication during Emily's final hospitalization. Caregivers were unable to listen, to hear her distress.

> I think part of the reason I still struggle so with Emily's loss is because I feel like I spent so much time and energy trying to get people to see what was happening to Emily and never really knowing whether people could really see her deterioration or if they were just unable to communicate with us—that our concerns and fears were real, but people just didn't know what to do to turn things around.

Parents greatly appreciate professionals who are sensitive to the needs of their other children during this period of great anxiety and tension. Carl's mother writes:

> I feel siblings should be included in the care. They should be encouraged to know their brother or sister—no matter what the expected outcome.

As the time of death approaches, every effort must be made to honor the parents' wish to be with their child; to hold and to comfort their child at the moment of death. Some professionals see their role as "protecting" parents

from this experience. However well-meaning, such views fail to understand that nothing can alleviate the pain. To parents, the final moments of
their child's life represent an opportunity—the opportunity to parent in
the fullest sense, to ease the child's transition, to demonstrate unending
love, to say good-bye to their child, to say good-bye to a part of themselves.
There is loving, bittersweet closure. Emily's foster mother, writing to
hospital personnel, describes her haunting wish to have had such an
opportunity for herself, for her husband, for Emily.

> The senior resident. . .was suddenly and physically taking my
> husband and me by the arm, leading us to the door, and telling
> us that we had to leave because "there was no time to waste."
> Emily watched us leave; all we wanted to do was to give her a
> kiss. I still question, "Why the sudden urgency and concern?"
> Time was up. Three months had passed since the surgery; it was
> too late now to do anything.
>
> That was the last time we saw Emily alive. In our grief and my
> relief that people finally realized she was as sick as I had been
> saying, I allowed you to try to save her. I regret that decision.
> What Emily deserved and we needed was to hold her and allow
> her to die peacefully in the arms of the people who loved her. . .

Professional attitudes, behaviors, and values that lay the foundation of
compassionate, honest parent-professional communication assume critical importance immediately following the death of a child. Parents repeatedly share how caring professionals can make a difference, can comfort,
can promote healing:

> As a leader for a local chapter of The Compassionate Friends, I
> often hear heartbreaking stories from people who believe they
> were neglected, overlooked, or simply a burden to be dealt with
> by health care workers surrounding their child.
>
> As for my particular situation, I can only praise the care our
> critically ill daughter received and we, her parents, received as
> well. . . Each facility we encountered was not only extremely
> competent in the care of our child but also very sensitive to the
> needs of our entire family.
>
> I could recount many episodes where workers went above
> and beyond the "call of duty" to keep us feeling a part of what
> was going on. Our daughter died from complications following
> her second surgery. Although there is certainly no "easy" way to
> lose a child, I am so fortunate that our daughter's caregivers
> understood and responded to our pain and anguish.

Eye contact with bereaved parents; time alone with parents to answer their questions, to listen as they cry, to listen as they talk about the beloved child whom they have lost; use of the child's name when speaking about the dead child; open expression of one's caring; and gentle touch all contribute to the process of healing.

> ...Don't hold back if you want to put your hand on a parent's arm or your arm around a parent's shoulder, or if you want to say, "I'm sorry."
>
> Don't "hit and run." If you break the sad news, try not to rush away immediately.
>
> At the time of informing parents that their child has died, tell them what steps to take next. They are in shock, disbelief and will be confused and need direction and guidance. There is no such thing as an "expected" death. . .
>
> Understand that parents do not wish to hear rationalizations about their child's death. Never tell a parent such things as: "Your child would have been a burden to you as he was," or "She just would have suffered if she had lived."
>
> Talking—expressing shock, pain and grief—helps parents adjust to the death of their child. Be available to listen, knowing that it will take years to adjust to what many people consider the worst loss of all. . . (*Suggestions For Medical Personnel. . .When a Child Dies*, The Compassionate Friends, 1986)

After the death of the child, parents need privacy—time alone with their child to say good-bye, to cry, to hug, to gather their strength for the outside world and the tasks ahead. Given the magnitude of each parent's individual pain and sorrow, parents may be unable to comfort one another. Ask the grieving parents if they would like a trusted family friend or relative to be called for additional support (Jost & Haase, 1989; Cordell & Thomas, 1990).

If the child is stillborn or a newborn who has died in the intensive care unit, many parents appreciate the opportunity to see, touch, and hug their baby. Asking parents if they wish to see their child; swaddling the baby to stress his or her normal features; gently describing the color or temperature differences they will see; and preparing parents for this final farewell—offer parents a tender gift. A lock of hair, a picture, or a footprint will confirm the baby's existence and will be a treasured reminder of the love and dreams that once were this child.

Professionals may fail to understand the bonds of love and commitment parents feel for the most premature, sick baby. Months of waiting, anticipating, and planning have made this baby "real" to the parents and family. Attachment grows as the baby moves and asserts itself as "living," as parents accommodate themselves to the developing pregnancy. The death of the child dashes precious hopes and dreams. Comments intended to comfort parents—such as "You're young. You can always have another child"—may actually do the opposite. No future pregnancy, no future child can substitute for the loss of this beloved baby.

Parents experience many conflicting feelings and distressing emotions following the death of a child whose long struggle with a chronic illness and/or disability has come to an end. Guilt may be intensified. Death has brought peace, an end to the child's suffering, and closure; death has also brought emptiness and intense longing. A mother explains:

> Although it's been 10 years since the death of my son Daniel, I occasionally encounter a memento of his life—a crayoned letter drawn on one of his possessions. As I look at it, it seems to me symbolic of Daniel. Of course, all children are special. Some, however, through birth, accident, or illness, are slightly less than perfect. That slight difference makes the death of those children unique. . .
>
> It is the painful struggle with life that makes the death of a disabled child unique. While the parents miss the child, they probably do not miss the disability. Because of this they feel guilty. . .
>
> Adding to the conflicting emotions of loss and relief is anger. The parents feel frustrated and betrayed by the fact that their child's continual struggle was in vain. A friend expressed this feeling for me when she said, "If there were only to be eight years for Daniel, why did they have to be like that?"
>
> [Given] their many problems, handicapped children require an enormous amount of their parents' time and concern. Suddenly, with the death of the child, there is a huge void. Nothing can fill it. Yet, the longer the void remains, the more acutely the parents feel the loss of the child. . .
>
> . . .Because society is not supportive of grieving parents, it is even less understanding of bereaved parents of handicapped children. Well-meaning friends and relatives often assure parents that both they and the child are now better off. Some even suggest that the parents should be happy that the child is in a "better place." This kind of response promotes parents' anger. As the mother of a child with Down syndrome asked, "Does her disability discount her death?" (Marcia Alig, The Death of Disabled Children, *The Compassionate Friends Newsletter*, Vol. 9, No. 4, Fall 1986)

Parents urge professionals to understand the process of mourning. Sensitivity to parents' long-term pain, silent suffering, and brave struggle will have a major impact on parents' well-being. An intervention as straightforward and as thoughtful as a follow-up phone call made several months following the child's death will positively affect the lives of grieving parents (Schreiner, Gresham, & Green, 1979).

As weeks, months, and even years pass, parents repeatedly stress the healing and comforting role of peer group support. In helping others endure, parents find solace and peace within themselves. The value of such organizations as The Compassionate Friends cannot be overemphasized. Professionals can actively encourage this vital form of fellowship and sharing. A mother and psychiatrist writes:

> Since Compassionate Friends and [other such] groups may play such an important role in the healing process, doctors should be well informed about them. We should know the name and number of each group's contact person and, ideally, we should know some specifics about how they work. As we know from other patients, compliance is directly related to how much and in what way information is related.
>
> A weak "I've heard some people find this helpful" is not likely to motivate parents to get out and try these groups. They need to know that the principles and format of the groups will allow them to remain silent if they wish. They need to hear the pragmatic reasons for going, i.e., everyone there has survived this loss and they may learn some things that will help them survive as well. (Chance, 1987, pp. 135-137)

A mother summarizes many of these points in her poem about Molly's death—a tribute to Molly's life:

A PARENT'S PLEA

I brought my child to the hospital today.
    I'm tired and anxious and so afraid.
She's been sick and we've tried to be brave,
    but now I can see her slipping away.

I turn to the nurses and doctors there;
    "Please make her better" is my silent prayer.
So many people involved in her care—
    I don't know to whom to turn, with whom I can share.

My feelings and emotions irrational may seem.
　　You don't understand why I want to scream.
Please don't judge or criticize—
　　The parents are scared; you must realize.

It's easier to ignore or hide than to cope,
　　but parents need your help and your hope.
So please be honest, gentle, and kind,
　　and give us some of your precious time.

The day finally came when we had to say good-bye.
　　The pain was so bad—all we could do was cry.
Don't leave us now; we need you more than ever—
　　even though you couldn't make her "all better."

The love and support you give in the end
　　helps toward making life easier again.
The next time you see me don't just say, "Hi."
　　Talk about Molly because she was my joy and pride.

(Silvia Dunne, foster mom, in loving memory of Molly)

The Caregivers

A child's death and the parents' pain will evoke strong feelings in those caring for the child. No matter how devastating the illness or poor the prognosis, the actual death of the child may leave caregivers with a profound emptiness and sense of failure. A child life intern writing in his journal shares:

> Earlier in the day...a young child within the first year of life died. ..When all is over and I sit back at night and write this log, I cannot escape the numbing effect that the whole scenario of the death has on me. I can still vividly see the crowd outside of the child's room all placed among the several beeping, pulsing machines. The staff exudes worry; they try to keep their best face on, but somehow, one can still sense the concern. Within the blink of an eye. . . it is all over. The machines, the crowds, the child—all are gone. . .
>
> Without a doubt, in terms of raw emotional impact, this has been, for me, the most difficult thing to deal with at the hospital. (journal entry: child life intern/medical student)

Unfortunately the professional's own grief may, at times, interfere with his or her ability to relate to the parents. A mother describes her experiences as her premature baby was dying:

> Some of our doctors were uncaring when we were hurting. I believe that they couldn't handle failure, and our son not getting better was a failure to them. At times we were ignored; at times our son's pain was explained away. . .
>
> I would like young doctors, nurses, and social workers to understand that although getting to know parents and children in pain can make your jobs mentally harder, parents desperately need your concern and presence. Be there for them. You don't have to talk; let them talk and tell you how they feel.

It is important for caregivers to acknowledge and accept their own inner distress—grief, loss, sense of failure—as they reach out to grieving parents. Understanding one's own sadness and fear helps caregivers to remain available to the family at a time of great anguish.

> Doctors who could not save their little patient may think they have failed. They may be worried about lawsuits. They may not know what to say. They may avoid the parents, be brusque with them, or speak medicobabble. They may tell themselves, "The best thing is to leave them alone." They may use euphemisms, ostensibly to protect the parents' feelings, but in reality to maintain their own emotional equilibrium. How hard it is to admit that we are all helpless in an ultimate sense. . . (Chance,1987, pp. 135-137)

The cumulative impact of death and dying is especially intense for young professionals who spend much of their working lives in acute care settings with very sick children (Frader, 1979; Sahler, McAnarney, & Friedman, 1981; Sack, Fritz, Krener, & Sprunger, 1984; Hardison, 1986). Just as parents need to express their grief, caregivers need a safe forum in which they can share their feelings and reactions to the losses that are inherent in their professional lives. Peer support and recognition of the mourning process enable those on the front lines of care to remain open to parents, to remain steady in the face of parental despair (Shanfield, 1981; Berman & Villarreal, 1983).

> Many caregivers have expressed feelings of failure, sadness and frustration when a child they are caring for dies.
>
> Be aware of your feelings and find a safe outlet for them. Your

honesty and genuine expression of emotion will allow you to be more sensitive to those in your care. Acknowledging these feelings may also enhance your emotional well-being. (*Suggestions For Medical Personnel. . .When A Child Dies*, The Compassionate Friends, 1986)

A parent faced with a nurse's pain openly and honestly describes how difficult these issues are for both parents and professionals:

I was at an inservice once that dealt with infant death. I was sitting with my arms crossed, feeling irritated because a young unmarried social worker, rather than a parent, was speaking about what families need, when a nurse stood up and described her difficulty in coping with the death of a baby to whom she had become attached. She talked about how terrible it had been to go into the nursery the next day and see another baby in the crib. She made me see the magnitude of my demand for personal involvement. . . (Ann Oster, *Equals in this Partnership*, National Center for Clinical Infant Programs, 1985, p. 29)

Both parents and professionals need support and avenues for sharing. For professionals who appreciate what their caring and concern bring to grieving parents, the rewards, as well as the challenges, are great.

Our readiness to be human and to abide with [grieving parents] may make the difference between years of illness and silent suffering and years of health and productive living. We have an opportunity to be true healers. . . (Chance, 1987, p. 137)

HANDLING THINGS BETTER

Situations to ponder

MEDICAL TESTING; PLACING TEST RESULTS IN THE CONTEXT OF PARENTS' CONTINUING WORRIES; THE STORY OF A CHILD WITH A RARE ILLNESS

Diagnostic testing must be viewed against the backdrop of parents' concerns and observations; negative results are examined in conjunction with parents' continuing worries. When parents' knowledge about their child clashes with lab data, further exploration is needed. The mother of a child with a rare metabolic disorder describes her struggle to be taken "seriously" despite her baby's initially "good" test results:

Becky

. . .Repeatedly I consulted the GP. I was convinced my daughter was having mild seizures, was functionally blind and deaf, and was losing ground, failing to thrive. Becky had respiratory emergencies, more uncontrolled shrieking behavior, no use of her arms and hands, severe mucousy congestion; at four months she stared blankly into space and tracked nothing and no one with her eyes, showing no interest in toys or movement. Yet at the doctor's office, at the hospital emergency room, anywhere unfamiliar to her, she'd perk up and seem attentive, lively even, making an effort to hold her head up and take things in.

So the doctor, as often as I expressed my deep terror for the life of my daughter, would as often express his impatience with me: "Look. You're 37 and an older first time mother. You're taking parenthood too seriously!"

He sent us to the local hospital for tests: upper GI series X-ray, CBC, laryngoscopy (by this time Becky's feeding was impeded by a noisy stridor), a barium swallow. All tests returned normal—well, low-normal hemoglobin expected, in an infant 4-6 months old. He told me, "Go home, relax some more." To Rich, my husband and Becky's father, he said, "Mimi's imposing her own neurosis on this child. Get her to a shrink, now." Rich's rage flared, but he said nothing. At home, I had moved to trying solid foods (baby food in jars), bottled breast milk, and formula to feed Becky but she wouldn't hold anything down.

Indeed, by age 5 months she was requiring round-the-clock attempts at feeding. I felt as though she'd been crying for weeks on end, anytime she was awake; yet her sleep didn't seem complete either, as she appeared to be stupefied and semi-conscious even when at rest. The startling episodes recurred often each day, yet by the time Becky was 5 months old, she seemed too weak to startle. She lay pallid and unmoving with a low whine for a cry. Yet she revived in the doctor's office.

I had called La Leche for ideas and had learned nothing new. No one had nursed a baby like mine. The specialist who performed the laryngoscopy pronounced Becky's anatomical features as "pink and normal." Perhaps, he suggested, she had a little "laryngomalacia" that she'd outgrow by 18 months. I badgered the GP, trying to compare Becky's unresponsiveness to deep depression. He never heard her cry, or saw her startle. He smarted at me: "You say this baby has urgent need of help, yet her clinical levels are okay and she looks fine to me. You've used the emergency room inappropriately, and your perceptions are clearly wrong!" He refused to see us for our umpteenth consultation or regular time and slotted us for after hours, at a higher fee. Later he spoke privately with Rich and urged that he have me counselled.

I gathered my shattered confidence and took Becky to another town a couple of days later, when she'd refused all attempts to feed her, to an older lady, a nurse practitioner (PNP) with 4 children and extensive pediatric experience. She agreed that Becky was not thriving and ran further tests at another hospital. The blood technician and the x-ray technician expressed their fears for Becky to this PNP; she noted that the hemoglobin had dropped further and that Becky's signs were even poorer than the first exam had revealed a day before. She and her MDs sent us to the first hospital for further tests including a CAT Scan. Finally the team of MDs at the first hospital paid attention. Becky's blood showed a severe megaloblastic anemia; her CAT Scan showed diffuse cortical atrophy. Now, even at the hospital Becky ate poorly; I struggled to nurse her, but continued with solids and formula.

The hematology and neurology specialists shrugged and said after 2 weeks of tests, "We don't know what's wrong. Go home and we'll call you in 2 more weeks." Rich and I were devastated. No one was saying much, yet our baby was dying. Psychologists came to us: "It's not your fault," they said, "just bad luck."

Two days after discharge I panicked and called the pediatrician who had attended Becky for the latter admission. I told her "Doctor, I am losing my daughter. She'll die today unless someone can do something!" Indeed, Becky was gasping for breath and vomiting everything. The pediatrician said bluntly, "I've called all the specialists I know. Wisdom is not to be had here. Can you pack your things immediately and come here? We're preparing reports for you all to be referred to [a tertiary care center] tomorrow, first thing. Do you know how to get to Children's Hospital?" It's 160 miles to the south, but we did.

At 5 1/2 months Becky was admitted to [Children's Hospital] after we'd struggled for 3 1/2 months to have local people share our concerns. Within hours, we found medical people who asked us dozens of questions, solicited our ideas, explained new terminology, and showed fascination with Becky. The young resident attending the neurology ward where we stayed said to us, "This isn't a nerve problem or a blood problem per se. This is a metabolic error so rare that we'll need some very specialized researchers to say just what she needs. But I think we can help your daughter."

Perspectives

COMMUNICATING WITH "DIFFICULT PARENTS:" THE VALUE OF PEER SUPPORT; HOW "SENIOR PARENTS" CAN HELP

In the following section, parents present ways of understanding and better communicating with "difficult parents." Peer support and the help of "senior" parents offer professionals crucial resources in reaching out to parents who are defensive, who are struggling with new and painful realities.

A mother who has given a great deal of thought to how she coped with her baby's serious illness presents her feelings concerning the needs of parents under stress, professional reactions, and at times the painful clash between the two. She tells movingly of her own "defenses"—guilt, anger, denial—to which she desperately clung during a time of unendurable pain and anguish.

These defenses were protective in nature. And yet, they also separated her from the emotional support she so very much needed and hoped would be available to her. She shares her complex feelings:

> I have spent a lot of time since Nick was born examining how I felt and functioned as a mother when he was ill, turning over in my mind relationships with professionals and my family and other parents. The most destructive factor during that period was my own difficulty in accepting my emotional reactions.
>
> Viewed more objectively, the mechanisms that defend us from despair are logical. Guilt implies a comforting measure of control over a situation with no rational explanation. Anger defends us against blame. Emotional detachment numbs the fear of loss. Denial gives us time to learn new ways of coping and the energy and humor to fight the facts in ways that sometimes generate new services and better futures for our children.
>
> Those mechanisms were logical and necessary, but at the same time they insulated me from the people that I loved as well as from the painful fact of Nicky's illness. I wondered what was wrong with me, and I was too vulnerable to the judgments of the

> professionals who cared for Nick to ask for their help directly. I
> pretended to be more competent than I felt and missed opportu-
> nities for help. I was defensive and demanding. . . (Ann Oster,
> *Equals in this Partnership*, NCCIP, 1985, p. 28-29)

This mother suggests an effective way of reaching out to lonely parents in
crisis, of alleviating gripping isolation and terror. Peer support is the
powerful therapeutic "tool" that enabled her to rebuild her battered self-
esteem and to move forward.

> The most realistic way to decrease families' isolation is by pro-
> viding them with access to their peers: the other families for
> whom this contact is part of their own healing. . .
>   I will never forget the incredibly intense feeling of recognition
> and kinship that I experienced during that hour-long talk in a
> hospital cafeteria. And later, as our parent group flourished, I
> saw so many other mothers and fathers experiencing the remark-
> able sense of connection that had kept a group of strangers
> talking in a hospital parking lot until midnight after our first
> meeting. (Ann Oster, *Equals in this Partnership*, NCCIP, 1985, p.
> 32)

A first step in helping parents struggling with complicated feelings is to
"see beyond" their anger and demandingness; to understand their intense
vulnerability and confusion—pain barely hidden beneath a "difficult"
exterior.
    "Senior" parents help professionals to "see beyond" the parents' rage
or denial and to appreciate the parent's anguish. "Senior" parents are often
able to communicate with parents struggling to stay afloat and can serve
as bridges between difficult parents and those caring for children in need.
Patrick's mother, a nurse and veteran parent, discusses her role with
parents of newly diagnosed children:

> When parents become defensive as they hear painful informa-
> tion and professionals become mechanical as they convey pain-
> ful information, a senior parent should step in to reach out to
> parents and to help caregivers understand the parents' grief.
> Caregivers who appreciate the role of senior parents offer a
> genuine gift to parents and children under their care.

Carl's mother emphasizes:

Many times a distraught parent has trouble communicating with professionals who appear remote. Defensive, vulnerable parents will often reveal their deepest fears and worries to another trusted parent. Parents, desperate and overwhelmed, find it easier to cry and to be comforted in the presence of a parent who has experienced great anguish and *has* endured. It is crucial for veteran parents, who have their own situation well in hand, to be on the care team.

Visions:
Present and Future

In one situation the medical student helped with the necessary therapy for a seven-year-old with cystic fibrosis. As he was tucking him into bed and listening to his nightly prayers, the child included the following, ". . . and bless Mommy and Daddy and help Jack [the medical student] with his test tomorrow." The medical problems were forgotten; and this made a real impact on the student. (Widrick, Whaley, DiVenere, Vecchione, Swartz, & Stiffler, 1991, p. 97)

Summary: A Journey with Families

In the past chapters, professionals have accompanied parents and children as they find their way through complex, ever-unfolding paths—the unexpected peaks and valleys of life with a serious chronic illness and/or disability. Parents at various points along this journey of change and hope have discussed their fears, joys, sorrows, needs, and triumphs. Throughout the child's experience, professionals will be called upon to travel with parents; to join parents in creating mutual goals; to offer support; to alleviate isolation; and to remove roadblocks to good care. The mother of Michael, a little boy whose first 80 days of life were spent in the NICU, speaks to both caregivers and parents:

> We need you [health care professionals] on our side. In these days of mass production medicine, people often feel alone and helpless. It is exhausting, heartrending work to be the parent of a child with cerebral palsy, or mental retardation, or genetic abnormalities, or asthma, or any type of chronic medical problem.
>
> But we parents must also recognize that it is not easy to be in your shoes; it is hard to be a health professional who works with such children and their families. It is difficult to remain human in sometimes inhuman circumstances. But please, don't distance yourselves from the bodily and psychic pain suffered by babies

and their parents. Honesty, patience, humility, and kindness on both sides will help move us from anguish to healing action. (Ronnie Londner, IVH Parents, 1991)

How can professionals be of greatest assistance to parents? How can professionals help parents as they chart new territory in the care of their children and navigate complex health systems? Although the road from diagnosis through ongoing care is unique for each child and family and is constantly changing, the common landmarks of good care emerge:

- the importance of values in caring for children who are not perfect
- respect for each family's unique needs and strengths
- the healing power of *listening* to parents
- equality in the decision-making process
- partnership.

Parents as Resources for Student Professionals

Parents are sharing their insights and hard-won expertise as consultants to state agencies, as members of hospital boards, and as parent consultants/ advocates on hospital wards and in clinics (Damrosch, Lenz, & Perry, 1985; Pitel, Pitel, Richards, Benson, Prince, & Forman, 1985; Diffine & Stanton, 1989). In order to reap the full benefits of a growing awareness of the pivotal role of the family in the comprehensive care of children, students need parents to participate in their earliest clinical training and professional experiences. Writing in the *Physician Education Forum Report*, a physician describes the power of the parent consultant role in changing perspectives—broadening his awareness and, thus, the awareness of his students:

> One day our parent consultant stopped a physician in the hall to tell him that a family had been waiting awhile to see him; I might as well tell you that the physician was me. It was in the middle of clinic, and I was teaching a resident; we were reviewing a chart.
>
> I told the parent consultant that, although I understood that the family had been waiting, we were a teaching hospital and that there were many benefits to patients and families from being in a teaching hospital. I said I would go to the family as quickly as I could, but that it was my responsibility to teach the resident. You can imagine the spiel that I made.
>
> The next day, the parent consultant came to see me. She asked me, "What is it that you are teaching these students? You are

teaching them that people can wait."

That was not what I wanted to be teaching them. I decided no more of this! We teach after people go home. I tell our students and residents to shadow me. If I can teach them a few points, that's one thing, but people do not wait. I want them to learn that in our clinic. [This] experience provided an insight that turned our program around. (Edwin Forman, 1990, pp. 28-29)

It is hoped that "model programs," burgeoning opportunities for students and parents, will encourage a new educational agenda: the integration and full participation of parents in clinical teaching (Guralnick, Richardson, & Heiser, 1982; Shonkoff, 1983; Desguin, 1986; Healy & Lewis-Beck, 1987; Poyadue, 1988; Sharp & Lorch, 1988; Physician Education Forum Report, 1990; Widrick, Whaley, DiVenere, Vecchione, Swartz, & Stiffler, 1991). A mother speaks of her role in the continuing education of occupational therapists:

I was a bit intimidated by the term "parent faculty." Although I had worked with professionals in a variety of settings, now I was being asked to actually "teach" occupational therapists about being a parent of a child with special needs. . .

In attending many multi-disciplinary meetings, I have observed that parents often group together, perhaps seeking strength, reassurance, and comfort. At the project's "trial run" weekend. . . we were separated in small groups so that each parent had the opportunity to interact with several O.T.'s. As the weekend progressed, I found that my input was asked for and listened to, even though my experience with occupational therapy (OT) was very limited. I had a unique perspective that the others in my group did not have—I had lived for 18 years with a child who has special needs. . . (Betsy Trombino, member of the new AOTA training program for occupational therapists working with infants and toddlers, *ACCH Network*, Vol. 7, No. 1, Winter, 1989)

Parents stress that from the moment of birth they are accumulating experiences, learning from their children, and developing new ways of understanding family life. The road traveled by parents of children with special needs is long and complex; change and accommodation are constant features of parents' journeys. For example, newly-informed parents appreciate the support of meeting veteran parents but may not fully believe they will ever achieve the equilibrium they see the experienced parents displaying.

Young professionals will work with parents at various places along the path. Of crucial importance is respect for each parent's experience and perspective. Laura's mother explains:

> Experiences with our children may be "felt" differently (a) when they occur, (b) a little later, and then (c) much later—"in retrospect." Students gain from seeing parents at all stages along the journey. . .

Although the following comments and suggestions address the needs of medical students and young physicians, they also apply to health care professionals of many disciplines A mother offers *A Few Words to Young Professionals* (Sherelyn Campbell):

• **Invite experienced parents to speak to medical students both in classroom and informal settings.** A personal encounter with a family living with hemophilia or cystic fibrosis gives perspective and depth to textbook/lecture learning and will enhance clinical experience.

• **Include parents as discussion leaders, panelists, and guest speakers when planning seminars for health professionals.** They are an untapped resource, and most would welcome the opportunity to share their hard-earned wisdom.

• **Allow medical students ample opportunities for role-playing.** Possible assignments could include: negotiating a dispute between parents and house staff over a particular procedure; giving bad news to a family waiting near the operating room; talking with a distraught mother who is transferring her anxieties to her sick child, etc. Role-playing can involve experienced parents playing "devil's advocate" or doctors exchanging roles with parents.

• **Encourage "home residencies" for medical students, interns and/or residents.** A week spent with a family coping with a chronic illness or disability gives doctors a realistic look at the therapies, medication schedules, and activity limitations they will be prescribing. It also gives the doctor a chance to view the impact an illness has on the rest of the family.

• **Let young professionals help to staff respite care facilities as part of their training.** The term "on call" takes on a whole new meaning when you have 24 hour a day/ 7 day a week responsibility for someone.

When Families and Students Share Experiences

Initial steps in creating such learning situations—sharing a meal with a family; spending an afternoon in the home of a family—may deeply affect student attitudes and perspectives. A medical student describes his reactions to such an experience—his coming to know Paul, a 25-year-old man with Down syndrome, and Paul's family:

> To interview a family with a son who has a mental handicap was challenging for me, not only because of my lack of knowledge, but also because I would have to go into a home and interview a family I did not know. It was my first real contact with someone who might be a patient. Compounding these two anxieties was my apprehension of having contact with an individual with a mental handicap. My past experience with people with a mental handicap was very limited. Questions came to my mind: "How will I react?" "Will I be comfortable?" "What will he look like?" "Will I be able to talk to him?" "Will he talk to me?" "Can he talk?" I was totally unaware of what I was getting into. I did not know enough to have an opinion but, as in most unknown situations, I was afraid to face it. . .
>
> Paul's mother, Jane, is a warm person, and she made me very comfortable. I felt progressively more comfortable asking her questions about most aspects of her family life, but when it came to asking questions about Paul, I couldn't. The words would not come out of my mouth. She kept reassuring me that any questions I asked she surely had heard before. The fact that Paul was present right beside me made it even harder. I didn't want to say anything to upset or downgrade him.
>
> Paul's father was quieter. . .but from his remarks I learned that as much as possible, he treated Paul as he treated his other son. . .
>
> I was dismayed by the attitudes toward Paul taken by aunts and uncles, friends, professionals and his community. Upon learning that Paul indeed had a mental handicap, all of the family no longer felt it essential to visit. Paul was no longer the cute baby he once was, but rather an oddball who should be ignored. . .Paul and his family were completely shut off emotionally from the rest of the family.
>
> This situation repeated itself with most of their friends. Even people whom the family had known for long periods of time

would no longer visit. Within the first few minutes, the family always knew who would accept him and who wouldn't. . .

. . .There is no doubt that Paul's development relied on his mother's push to get things done. Because of the lack of support available, it took special parents to raise Paul.

The most staggering information gained from the interview was the attitude taken by the medical profession. They were shocking. There was often a coldness towards the family. The family learned over the telephone that their son had Down Syndrome. The family needs to be comforted and the doctor should be available to help. The doctor's opinion was categorical. He believed that people with a mental handicap are unfit to make decisions and should be treated as children.

Paul was to have an operation when he was old enough to sign the consent form but the doctor asked his mother to sign. She would not sign it and forced the doctor to let Paul sign.

Neglect was also a major problem, as shown by both his dentist and doctor. After having his wisdom teeth out, Paul had an adverse reaction and regurgitated all over himself. Although she was told he would be cleaned up, his mother found nothing had been done when she came back the next day. . .

The trouble a family must go through to get proper care for their son or daughter is excessive. There is no reason why one individual should be treated better than another. Of course, these attitudes are not held by all professionals and may be due to an uneasiness, anxiety and inadequate training in medical schools . . .

When asked by Paul's mother what I had learned from the interview, I replied, "Everything." Of course, my new knowledge was far from everything, but I had learned so much. Attitudes held by many are due to ignorance, and this leads to improper treatment of people with a mental handicap. . .

The knowledge and understanding about people with a mental handicap that I have gained from this experience will remain with me for the rest of my life. It has given me the opportunity to challenge my attitudes about mental handicaps. Finally, my promise to the family was to make my colleagues aware that individuals with a mental handicap are people too and should be treated as such.

In relating my experience to my classmates, I was not surprised to find that they were as ignorant as I had been. The group discussions centred around the immediate family strengths, the abandonment of the extended family and friends, as well as our attitudes as physicians. It was pointed out to me that my discussion centred mainly around Paul's mother. I believed that my lack of interaction with Paul was related to my inexperience but also to my self-consciousness and fear of offending him. I also understood that in this way I was not treating him like an adult.

The group was appalled at the treatment given to people with a mental handicap and couldn't believe something like this was actually happening in Canada. Everyone agreed they learned a great deal and that their minds opened up to a totally unfamiliar aspect of medicine. They learned enough that they hoped their treatment of people with a mental handicap would be far better than that given to Paul. (Yves Talbot and Richard Shaul, 1987, pp. 7-9)

How will this new vision and enhanced point of view be reinforced, even rewarded, as students begin to provide care for patients and families? Will such positive goals fade under the pressures and constraints of demanding training programs that emphasize technical knowledge at the expense of "care"?

Creating a Healing Environment

The care of children with chronic illnesses and/or handicaps presents health care professionals with a constant series, barrage, of professional and personal challenges. High levels of job-related stress and chronic exposure to pain and loss lead to intense vulnerability (Werner & Korsch, 1976; Hardison, 1986; Jellinek, 1986). How will young professionals learn to respond to these "occupational hazards"? (Gorlin & Zucker, 1983)

Some professionals will react by choosing extreme positions—the highly driven (if resentful) professional who spends more time at the hospital than at home with his or her family; the professional, bruised and burdened by ever-increasing bureaucratic and patient demands, who leaves practice entirely.

Most health care professionals will strive for balance and integration in both their professional and private lives—reaching toward ways of respectfully caring for patients or clients while creating fulfilling personal lives. A partnership with parents furthers these goals. A partnership with parents helps caregivers to set priorities that enhance professional satisfaction and self-esteem; to counteract stress and despair.

The impact of emotionally wrenching experiences on caregivers' ongoing professional lives is all too often unacknowledged by training programs. Despite such "silence," young professionals continue to struggle with painful responses (Werner & Korsch, 1976). They seek support and guidance: What does it mean for me to care for children who may never be totally well? How can I best manage the powerful feelings my work evokes within me? When such help in defining one's professional role is not forthcoming, young caregivers may withdraw from beleaguered children and parents in an attempt "to protect" themselves. Ultimately, both aloofness and emotional "over involvement" prove unsatisfactory; professional self-esteem and good care suffer.

A sense of being a part of a team—whether in a tertiary-care hospital, a private practice, or a service agency—contributes to professional renewal. Communicating with colleagues and reaching out across professional boundaries alleviate isolation and deepen one's own contribution to the care of children in need. Discussion of difficult situations in a safe, nonjudgmental forum is the crux of a healing milieu. The caregivers—as well as those cared for— can find support vital.

Professionals work toward steadiness and stability. Parents depend upon such equilibrium. Boundaries between personal and professional spheres are necessary; professional objectivity is required. A surgeon would not be expected to operate on his or her own child. A physical therapist would not be asked to direct his or her own child's rehabilitation program. However, objectivity in the practice of one's professional skills is not synonymous with distancing from parents; objectivity is not to be confused with coldness and aloofness. Bill's mother, a veteran parent, candidly shares:

> I feel, especially for young professionals, it is crucial not to "hide behind" the supposed knowledge that has been absorbed. It is worth absolutely nothing if it cannot be applied to the situation at hand, and to do that requires communicating—a very risky business—with the persons you want to help. Being a professional should not be armor against the threat of vulnerability; it should be an extra chance to share, and communicate, with others.

Openness to partnership with parents helps caregivers to develop a perspective which clarifies one's professional mission. Although a child's chronic illness cannot be cured or "taken away," professional support can add strength to the process of family adjustment. Although one may be unable to add years to a child's shortened life, he and his family can be helped to live as fully as possible within the span of time they do share. Although a child cannot regain use of her legs, she can be helped to see that her most important qualities remain.

Understanding one's limits as a professional while fully appreciating what can be accomplished is the ongoing challenge for those who care for children with chronic conditions. Good care embraces the truly possible; the truly possible, even under the most devastating circumstances, includes open communication with parents, conscientious "listening" to their concerns, and respect for their struggles and triumphs. The mother of a child with severe cerebral palsy writes with deep gratitude:

> We have great regard for those health care providers who look at our child for who he is—our son whom we dearly intended to have, to hold, and to love regardless of the challenges.

Given the current climate of clinical training and practice, young professionals may feel trapped between "caring" for the child and parents and satisfying institutional requirements that devalue warm, human responses to families in need. Must such a dichotomy continue to exist? A father and family practitioner illustrates this dilemma and calls for change—change that respects both the family's needs and the young professional's healing identity:

> My son was in the hospital for a prolonged and complicated illness. One afternoon, a few days after his surgery, I finally succeeded in getting him comfortable enough to sleep. As I began to doze as well, a medical student walked in and prepared to listen to his lungs. My son had already been rounded on that morning by seven subspecialty services, each with a student, a resident or two, an attending, and a fellow.
>
> I reached over and grabbed the stethoscope as it neared my son's chest. "What are you doing?" I asked the student.
>
> "I need to examine your son."
>
> "You are not going to wake him up. . .I just got him to sleep."
>
> "I need to examine him," he repeated. "It's necessary for his care that I do so."
>
> At that point I again firmly stated, "You are not going to examine my son."
>
> The student paused, looked confused, then nearly broke down, "What will I do? We are going to be having rounds in 20 minutes, and if I can't tell them how his lungs sound, they will think I am a bad student, and then I'll get a bad grade. I want to go into Surgery and if I don't do well on this rotation, I might not get into a good residency."
>
> The student was lost. He didn't know what to do. To him, his entire career depended on disturbing my sleeping son.
>
> We need to make an environment in which the student could

confidently say on rounds, "I didn't examine the child because he had just fallen asleep and his father said it wasn't the right time." We need to have role models around who will say, "Good choice, you did well." (Bill Schwab, 1990, p. 5)

A reorientation of training will require that change begin at the top, that the trainers of young professionals embrace the new context of care, the concept of family-centered practice, that they incorporate its principles in graduate school programs and clinical practice and make it a reality.

In summary, the development of this book has been the expression of a sense of mission, both professional and personal: to narrow the gaps of experience; to give voice to needs; to guide those who would build bridges; to encourage the creation of healing environments for children, parents, and professionals; to invite all who read it to join in a caring partnership.

References

Abramson, E. (1990). Helping children prepare for a hospital stay or visit. . .What parents have done. *AboutFace,* 4: 5, 4.

Adams, D. & Deveau, E. (1987). When a brother or sister is dying of cancer: The vulnerability of the adolescent sibling. *Death Studies,* 11, 279-295.

Alexander, R. & Tompkins-McGill, P. (1987). Notes to the experts from the parent of a handicapped child. *Social Work,* 32, 361-362.

Alig, M. (1986). The death of disabled children. *The Compasssionate Friends Newsletter,* 9, 1 & 6.

Arango, P. *When Parents and Professionals Communicate. . .Tips for Professionals,* New Mexico Parents Reaching Out - (PRO).

Barbera, M., Cheesman, M., Fay, S., Hankins, L., Lambert, J., Newman, B., Olsen, D., Pirtle, R., Shuster, S., Smith, E., Snow, M., Stacy, D., Stacy, K., Sullivan, C., & Toth, B. (1988). *Family needs: Perspectives of parents and professionals.* A report to the Indiana Department of Education, Division of Special Education, The Family Needs Task Force.

Beckett, J. (1985). Comprehensive care for medically vulnerable infants and toddlers: A parent's perspective. In *Equals in this Partnership* (pp. 6-13). Washington, D.C.: National Center for Clinical Infant Programs.

Bergman, A.B. (1988). Resident stress. *Pediatrics,* 82, 260-263.

Berman, S. & Villarreal, S. (1983). Use of a seminar as an aid in helping interns care for dying children and their families. *Pediatrics,* 22, 175-179.

Boyce, B. & Boyce C. (1990). From the heart. *Families and Disability Newsletter,* Beach Center on Families and Disability, University of Kansas, 2: 1, 8.

Brotman, M. (1988). New ears for Derek. *Let's Face It*, 2: 1, 1.

Brown, J. & Ritchie, J. (1990). Nurses' perceptions of parent and nurse roles in caring for hospitalized children. *Children's Health Care*, 19, 28-36.

Brunnquell, D. & Hall, M.D. (1982). Issues in the psychological care of pediatric oncology patients. *American Journal of Orthopsychiatry*, 52, 32-44.

Calman, K. C. (1988). Memories: A neglected concept in care. *The Lancet*, 2, 1184-1185.

Chan, J. & Leff, P. (1992). Delivery of family-centered care: Challenges for health care professionals. *World Pediatrics and Child Care: Journal of the International Academy of Pediatric Transdisciplinary Eduction* (in press).

Chance, S. (1987). Doctors and bereaved parents. *Resident and Staff Physician*, 33, 135-137.

Chesler, M. (1986). editorial. *Candlelighters Childhood Cancer Foundation Quarterly Newsletter*, 10: 2/3, Spring/Summer, 1986, 2.

Chesler, M. & Barbarin, O. (1987). *Childhood cancer and the family: Meeting the challenge of stress and support.* New York: Brunner/Mazel.

Clyman, R.I., Sniderman, S.H., Ballard, R.A., & Roth, R.S. (1979). What pediatricians say to mothers of sick newborns: An indirect evaluation of the counseling process. *Pediatrics*, 63, 719-723.

Comegys, A. (1988). Family perspectives. *Massachusetts Department of Mental Retardation Family Support Newsletter*, May, 1988, 4-7.

Conniff, J. C. G. (1985). About Men: Manchild Coming of Age. *The New York Times Magazine*, August 18, 1985, p. 62.

Constance, V. (1990). From the heart. *Families and Disability Newsletter*, Beach Center on Families and Disability, University of Kansas, 2: 2, 8.

Constantino, M. (1990). Helping children prepare for a hospital stay or visit. . .What parents have done. *AboutFace*, 4: 5, 4.

Cordell, A. & Thomas, N. (1990). Fathers and grieving: Coping with infant death. *Journal of Perinatology*, 10, 75-80.

Cornell, D. (1989). Being the father of a disabled child. *Family Support Project, Focus Report, Fathers of Special Children*. Oklahoma State Department of Health, MCH/Pediatric Division, Fall, 1989.

Crater, J. (1987). Just be there. *Down Syndrome News*, September, 1987, 96.

Crutcher, D. (990). From the heart. *Families and Disability Newsletter*, Beach Center on Families and Disability, University of Kansas, 2: 1, 8.

Damrosch, S., Lenz, E., & Perry, L. (1985). Use of parental advisors in the development of a parental coping scale. *Maternal-Child Nursing Journal*, 14, 103-109.

Darling, R.D. (1983). Parent-professional interaction: The roots of misunderstanding. In M. Seligman (Ed.), *The Family with a handicapped child* (pp. 95-121). New York: Grune & Stratton.

Daubenspeck-Ulrich, B. (1990). Sibling group. *Family Support Project, Focus Report, Siblings of Special Children*, Oklahoma State Department of Health, MCH/Pediatric Division, Winter 1990

Davis, P. (1990). Excerpts from remarks made by fathers of children with special needs. *ACCH Network, Family-Centered Care for Children with Special Health Needs*, 8: 2, 8.

Deatherage-Newsom, M. (1988). Have you seen your medical records? *The Bridge*, Winter 1988, 16-17.

Deatherage-Newsom, M. (1988). From the mailbag. . .Tales of Torey. *The Bridge*, Fall 1988, 4-5.

DeGraw, C., Edell, D., Ellers, B., Hillemeier, M., Liebman, J., Perry, C., & Palfrey, J. (1988). Public Law 99-457: New opportunities to serve young children with special needs. *The Journal of Pediatrics*, 113, 971-974.

Desguin, B. (1986). Chronic illness in children: An educational program for a primary-care pediatric residency. *American Journal of Diseases of Children*, 140, 1246-1249.

Diehl, S.F., Moffitt, K.A., & Wade, S.M. (1991). Focus group interview with parents of children with medically complex needs: An intimate look at their perceptions and feelings. *Children's Health Care, 20,* 170-179.

Diffine, L. & Stanton, M. (1989). *Parent advisory council activities that promote parent-professional collaboration,* Phoenix Children's Hospital, Phoenix, Arizona.

Doernberg, N.L. (1982). Issues in communication between pediatricians and parents of young mentally retarded children. *Pediatric Annals* 11, 438-444.

Duffy, S. (1984). Surviving the first three years: One parent's perspective In S. Duffy, K. McGlynn, J. Mariska, & J. Murphy (Eds.) *Acceptance is only the first battle* (pp. 31-36). Missoula, Montana: Montana University Affiliated Program.

Duffy, S. (1984). Parents, professionals, and conflict. In S. Duffy, K McGlynn, J. Mariska, & J. Murphy (Eds.) *Acceptance is only the first battle* (pp. 37-43). Missoula, Montana: Montana University Affiliated Program.

Duffy, S. (1984). Plaudits for professionals. In S. Duffy, K. McGlynn, J Mariska, & J. Murphy, (Eds.) *Acceptance is only the first battle* (pp. 28-30). Missoula, Montana: Montana University Affiliated Program

Duffy, S., McGlynn, K., Mariska, J., & Murphy, J. (1984). Things some professionals did that drove us nuts and made us crazy: parents speak to professionals. In S. Duffy, K. McGlynn, J. Mariska, & J Murphy, (Eds.) *Acceptance is only the first battle* (pp. 25-27). Missoula, Montana: Montana University Affiliated Program.

Dunst, C., Trivette, C., & Deal, A. (1988). *Enabling and empowering families Principles and guidelines for practice.* Cambridge, MA: Brookline Books.

Farrell, P. & Fost, N. (1989). Long-term mechanical ventilation in in pediatrics respiratory failure: Medical and ethical considerations *American Review of Respiratory Diseases,* 140, 536-40.

Forman, E. (1990). Possible solutions: Exemplary programs and models. In *Physician Education Forum Report* (pp. 25-34). Bethesda: Association for the Care of Children's Health.

Fox, A. M. (1988). How to be an assertive parent on the treatment team. *Participating Families*, 1: 2, 2-5.

Frader, J.E. (1979). Difficulties in providing intensive care. *Pediatrics*, 64, 10-16.

Frey, K., Fewell, R., Vadasy, P., & Greenberg, M. (1989). Parental adjustment and changes in child outcome among families with young handicapped children. *Topics in Early Childhood Special Education*, 8, 38-57.

Frey, K., Greenberg, M., & Fewell, R. (1989). Stress and coping among parents of exceptional children: A multidimensional approach. *American Journal on Mental Retardation*, 94, 240-249.

Fussichen, K. (1988). One man's view. *The Advocate*, 3: 1, 9.

Gabriele, M. (1990). A mother writes. . . *AboutFace*, 4: 2, 1.

Gorlin, R. & Zucker, H. (1983). Physicians' reactions to patients: A key to teaching humanistic medicine. *New England Journal of Medicine*, 308, 1059-1063.

Gould, P. & Moses, L. (1985). Mild developmental delays from a parent's perspective. In *Equals in this Partnership* (pp. 14-17). Washington, D.C.: National Center for Clinical Infant Programs.

Green, M. (1979). Parent care in the intensive care unit. *American Journal of Diseases of Children*, 133, 1119-1120.

Groves, J. (1978). Taking care of the hateful patient. *New England Journal of Medicine*, 298, 883-887.

Guralnick, M.J., Richardson, Jr., H.B., & Heiser, K.E. (1982). A curriculum in handicapping conditions for pediatric residents. *Exceptional Children*, 48, 338-346.

Hammon, S. (1990). Excerpts from remarks made by fathers of children with special needs. *ACCH Network, Family-Centered Care for Children with Special Health Needs*, 8: 2, 8.

Hardison, J.E. (1986). The house officer's changing world. *New England Journal of Medicine*, 314, 1713-1715.

Healy, A. & Lewis-Beck, J. A. (1987). *The Iowa health care guidelines project: Improving health care for children with chronic conditions.* Division of Developmental Disabilities, University Hospital School, Iowa City, Iowa 52242.

Hett, J. (1988). From the Mailbag. . .Tales of Torey. *The Bridge,* Autumn, 1988, 4-5.

Holmes, K. (1980). My child is in the hospital. *Parents Magazine,* 42-50.

Hoyt, D. (1990). Grief. *ACCH Network, Family-Centered Care for Children with Special Health Needs,* 8: 2, 5 & 10.

Iris, M. (1988). The parent/professional relationship: Complex connections, intricate bonds. *Participating Families,* 1: 6, 4-6.

Jacobs, R. (1987). A son's disability , through his mother's eyes. *The New York Times,* Sunday, November 8, 1987, 33.

Jeffery, L. (1988). Slice of life. . . *Participating Families,* 1: 6, 1.

Jeffery, L. & Jeffery, B. (1988). From our readers. . . *Participating Families,* 1: 2, 9.

Jellinek, M.S. (1986). Recognition and management of discord within house staff teams. *Journal of the American Medical Association,* 256, 754-755.

Jost, K. & Haase, J. (1989). At the time of death: Help for the child's parents. *Children's Health Care,* 18,146-152.

Kolata, G. (1991). Parents of tiny infants find care choices are not theirs. *The New York Times National,* Monday, September 30, 1991, pp. 1 &14.

Koocher, G. & Berman, S. (1983). Life-threatening and terminal illness in childhood. In M. Levine (Ed.), *Developmental-behavioral pediatrics* (pp. 488-500). Philadelphia: Saunders.

Kunzman, L. (1972). Some factors influencing a young child's mastery of hospitalization. *Nursing Clinics of North America,* 7, 13-26.

Lau, C. (1988). Dear friends. . . *Facial Expressions Newsletter,* November 1988, 1-3.

Lawson, C. *Prescription for participation.* Fort Dodge, Iowa: Iowa Pilot Parents, Inc.

Leff, P. T. (1987). Here I am, ma: The emotional impact of pregnancy loss on parents. *Family Systems Medicine,* 5,105-113.

Leff, P. T. (1989). A piece of my mind: So much more to say. *Journal of the American Medical Association (J.A.M.A.),* 262, 402.

Leff, P. T., Chan, J. M., & Walizer, E. H. (1989). Talking to parents: Enhancing parent-professional relationships. *Children's Hospital Quarterly,* 1, 171-174.

Leff, P. T., Chan, J. M., & Walizer, E. H. (1991). Self-understanding and reaching out to sick children and their families: An ongoing professional challenge. *Children's Health Care,* 20, 230-239.

Lipp, M. (1986). *Respectful treatment: A practical handbook of patient care.* New York: Elsevier.

Londner, R. (1991). *Address Delivered to the North Central Neonatology Issues Confab,* Koehler, Wisconsin.

Mariska, J. (1984). Finding and founding support groups. In S. Duffy, K. McGlynn, J. Mariska, & J. Murphy (Eds.) *Acceptance is only the first battle* (pp. 10-13). Missoula, Montana: Montana University Affiliated Program.

May, J. (1991). *Fathers of children with special needs: New horizon.* Bethesda: Association for the Care of Children's Health.

May, J. (1990). What about fathers? *ACCH Network, Family-Centered Care for Children with Special Health Needs,* 8: 1, 1-2.

May, J. (1987). Images of fathers. *Focus on Fathers: A Newsletter about Programs and Services for Fathers of Children with Special Needs,* 1, 1-2.

McCollum, A. (1981). *The chronically ill child: A guide for parents and professionals.* New Haven: Yale University Press.

McGlynn, K. (1984). Plaudits for professionals. In S. Duffy, K. McGlynn, J. Mariska, & J. Murphy (Eds.) *Acceptance is only the first battle* (pp. 28-30). Missoula, Montana: Montana University Affiliated Program.

Mentzer, S. (1986). Advocating for your child: A parental perspective. *The Candlelighters Childhood Cancer Foundation Quarterly Newsletter*, 10: 2/3, Spring/Summer, 1986, 5.

Meyer, D., Vadasy, P., Fewell, R., & Schell, G. (1985). *A handbook for the fathers program: How to organize a program for fathers and their handicapped children*. Seattle: University of Washington Press.

Meyer, D., Vadasy, P., & Fewell, R. (1985). *Living with a brother or sister with special needs: A book for sibs*. Seattle: University of Washington Press.

Moore, C. (1990). *A reader's guide for parents of children with mental, physical, or emotional disabilities*. Rockville, MD: Woodbine house.

Moosereiner, D. (1990). From the heart. *Families and Disability Newsletter*, Beach Center on Families and Disability, University of Kansas, 2: 1, 8.

Moses, K. (1983). The impact of initial diagnosis: Mobilizing family resources. In J. A. Mulick & S. M. Pueschel (Eds.), *Parent-professional partnerships in developmental disability services* (pp. 11-34). Cambridge: Academic Guild Publishers.

Murphy, J. (1984). Plaudits for professionals. In S. Duffy, K. McGlynn, J. Mariska, & J. Murphy (Eds.) *Acceptance is only the first battle* (pp. 28-30). Missoula, Montana: Montana University Affiliated Program.

Myers, G. J. (1984). Myelomeningocele: The medical aspects. *Pediatric Clinics of North America*, 31, 165-175.

Nathanson, M. (1982). Family roles in medical decisions. *The Candlelighters Childhood Cancer Foundation Quarterly Newsletter*, 6: 1, 1 & 3.

Novick, B. (1985). Parent volunteers: Breaking down barriers. *UCLA Cancer Center Bulletin*, Fall, 1985.

Oberhart, D. (1990). From the heart. *Families and Disability Newsletter*, Beach Center on Families and Disability, University of Kansas, 2 2, 8.

Odle, K. (1988). Parents are saying. . . *ACCH Network, Family-Centered Care for Children with Special Health Needs*, 6: 4, 4.

Olson, J., Edwards, M., & Hunter, J. A. (1987). The physician's role in delivering sensitive information to families with handicapped infants. *Clinical Pediatrics*, 26, 231-234.

Oster, A. (1985). Keynote address. In *Equals in this Partnership* (pp. 26-32). Washington, D.C.: National Center for Clinical Infant Programs.

Park, C. (1985). Book review. *Journal of Autism and Developmental Disorders*, 15, 113-119.

Patterson, J. & Geber, G. (1991). Preventing mental health problems in children with chronic illness or disability. *Children's Health Care*, 20, 150-162.

Pendleton, E. (1980). *Too old to cry, too young to die.* Nashville: Thomas Nelson.

Physician education forum report, National Center for Family-Centered Care (1990). Bethesda: Association for the Care of Children's Health.

Pitel, A., Pitel, P., Richards, H., Benson, J., Prince, J., & Forman, E. (1985). Parent consultants in pediatric oncology. *Children's Health Care*, 14, 46-51.

Pizzo, P. (1983). *Parent to parent: Working together for ourselves and our children.* Boston: Beacon Press.

Powell, T. A. & Ogle, P. A. (1985). *Bothers and sisters - A special part of exceptional families.* Baltimore: Paul H. Brookes Publishing, Co.

Poyadue, F. S. (1988). Parents as teachers of health care professionals. *Children's Health Care*, 17, 82-84.

Richardson, J. (1990). Lauren's story. . . *AboutFace*, 4: 6, 1-2.

Robinson, C.A. (1987). Roadblocks to family-centered care when a chronically ill child is hospitalized. *Maternal-Child Nursing Journal*, 16, 181-193.

Rosenthal, R. (1991). As more tiny infants live, choices and burden grow. *The New York Times National*, Sunday, September 29, 1991, pp. 1 & 26.

Sack, W.H., Fritz, G., Krener, P.G., & Sprunger, L. (1984). Death and the pediatric house officer revisited. *Pediatrics, 73,* 676-681.

Sahler, O.J., McAnarney, E.R., & Friedman, S.B. (1981). Factors influencing pediatric interns' relationships with dying children and their parents. *Pediatrics, 67,* 207-216.

Saphier, M. K. (1984). When being challenged, know your role as a parent. *The Candlelighters Childhood Cancer Foundation Progress Reports,* 4: 4, 13-15.

Sassaman, E. A. (1983). The parent-physician decision-making team. In J. A. Mulick & S. M. Pueschel (Eds.), *Parent-professional partnerships in developmental disability services* (pp. 43-52). Cambridge: Academic Guild Publishers.

Saunders, J. (1988). Letters to *Let's Face It. Let's Face It,* 2: 1, 3.

Scheck, A. (1989). Residents-in-disguise: Find that being patient for a day is lonely, uncomfortable, humbling. *Resident Reporters,* 6, 3-4.

Schreiner, R. L., Gresham, E. L., & Green, M. (1979). Physician's responsibility to parents after death of an infant. *American Journal of Diseases of Children,* 133, 723-726.

Schwab, W. (1990). Introduction and overview. In *Physician Education Forum Report* (pp.1-8). Bethesda: Association for the Care of Children's Health.

Shanfield, S. (1981). The mourning of the health care professional: An important element in education about death and loss. *Death Education,* 4, 385-395.

Sharp, M. C. & Lorch, S. C. (1988). A community outreach training program for pediatric residents and medical students. *Journal of Medical Education,* 63, 316-322.

Shelton, T., Jeppson, E., & Johnson, B. (1987). *Family-centered care for children with special health needs.* Washington, D.C.: Association for the Care of Children's Health.

Shonkoff, J. P. (1983). A perspective on pediatric training. In J. A. Mulick & S. M. Pueschel (Eds.), *Parent-professional partnerships in developmental disability services.* Cambridge: Academic Guild Publishers.

Simon, R. (1987). *After the tears: Parents talk about raising a child with a disability.* San Diego: HBJ.

Steele, K. (1987). Caring for parents of critically ill neonates during hospitalization: Stragegies for health care professionals. *Maternal-Child Nursing Journal, 16,* 13-27.

Stevens, D., Stagg, R., & McKay, I. (1977). What happens when hospitalized patients see their own record. *Annals of Internal Medicine, 86,* 474- 477.

Stone, D. (1989). A parent speaks: Professional perceptions of parental adaptation to a child with special needs. *Children's Health Care, 18,* 174-177.

Talbot, Y. & Shaul, R. (1987). Medical students learn about attitudes and handicaps. *entourage: A magazine promoting community living for persons with mental handicaps, 2,* 6-9.

Tarran, E. (1981). Parents' views of medical and social-work services for families with young cerebral-palsied children. *Developmental Medicine & Child Neurology, 23,* 173-182.

Trombino, B. (1989). Training program adopts a collaborative model. *ACCH Network, Family-Centered Care for Children with Special Health Needs, 7:* 1, 2.

Troy, J. (1988). *Facial Expressions Newsletter,* August, 1988, 6-8.

Turnbull, H. & Turnbull, A. (1987). *Parents speak out: Then and now.* Columbus, Ohio: Charles E. Merrill.

van Eys, J. (1985). Caring toward cure. *Children's Health Care, 13,* 160-166.

Vincent, L. (1985). Family relationships. In *Equals in this Partnership* (pp. 33-41). Washington, D.C.: National Center for Clinical Infant Programs.

Vining, E. & Freeman, J. (1985). Discussion and explanation of seizures to the parents and child. *Pediatric Annals, 14,* 737-739.

Wachendorf, D. (1988). Indianapolis comes face to face with people who care. *Let's Face it, 2:* 1, 5.

Walker, K. (1990). *Heart-to-Heart Newsletter,* April, 1990, p. 3.

Waller, D.A., Todres, D., Cassem, N.H., & Anderten, A. (1979). Coping with poor prognosis in the pediatric intensive care unit. *American Journal of Diseases of Children,* 133, 1121-1125.

Werner, E.R. & Korsch, B.M. (1976). The vulnerability of the medical student: Posthumous presentation of L.L. Stephen's ideas. *Pediatrics,* 57, 321- 328.

Widrick, G., Whaley, C., DiVenere, N., Vecchione, E., Swartz, D., & Stiffler, D. (1991). The medical education project: An example of collaboration between parents and professionals. *Children's Health Care,* 20, 93-100.

Wikler, L., Wasow, M. & Hatfield, E. (1981). Chronic sorrow revisited: Parent vs professional depiction of the adjustment of parents of mentally retarded children. *American Journal of Orthopsychiatry,* 51, 63-70.

Wikler, L., Wasow, M. & Hatfield, E. (1983). Seeking strengths in families of developmentally disabled children. *Social Work,* 28, 313-315.

Wolfensberger, W. (1967). Counseling parents of the retarded. In A. A. Baumeister (Ed.), *Mental retardation: Appraisal, education, & rehabilitation.* Chicago: Aldine.

Wolraich, M. (1982). Communication between physicians and parents of handicapped children. *Exceptional Children,* 48, 324-329.

Wolraich, M. (1987). Pediatricians' perceptions of mentally retarded individuals. *Pediatrics,* 80, 643-649.

Wurzbach, L. (1985). The coping process. In *Ed/Med Training Modules, Instructor Guide.* Developed by M. Hudler, C. Cranston, G. Ulrey, M. Bass, & S. Johnson, California State Department of Education, Special Education Division, University of California Davis School of Medicine, Department of Pediatrics and The Special Education Resource Network.

Wynn, E. (1989). Adult with cleft lip and palate seeks information from LFI members. *Let's Face It,* 2: 2, 5.

Zisook, S. & Gammon, E. (1981). Medical non-compliance. *Psychiatry in Medicine,* 10, 291-303.

Resources: Parent Literature and Organizations

AboutFace Newsletter; We All Have Different Faces AboutFace, 99 Crowns Lane, 3rd Floor, Toronto, Ontario, Canada M5R 3P4

ACCH Network: Family-Centered Care for Children with Special Health Needs, Association for the Care of Children's Health, 7910 Woodmont Ave., Bethesda, Maryland 20814.

ACL, Association for Community Living in Colorado, Inc., Colorado Club Building, 4155 East Jewell Ave., Suite 916, Denver, Colorado, 80222.

The Advocate, 502 Mount Dora Lane, Indianapolis, Indiana 46229.

The Bridge, published quarterly by Parent Resources on Disabilities, P. O. Box 1439, Portland, Oregon, 97214.

The Candlelighters Childhood Cancer Foundation Quarterly Newsletter and Progress Reports, The Candlelighters Childhood Cancer Foundation, 1312 18th Street, N.W., Suite 200, Washington, D.C. 20036.

Children in Hospitals, Inc., 31 Wilshire Park, Needham, Mass. 02192.

The Compassionate Friends Newsletter; Suggestions for Medical Personnel... When a Child Dies, The Compassionate Friends, Inc., National Office, P.O. Box 3696, Oak Brook, Ill. 60522-3696.

The Compassionate Friends, Central Jersey Chapter, Twelve Hobart Street, Marlboro, N. J. 07746-1521

Connecticut Parent Advocacy Center, 5 Church Lane, Box 579, East Lyme, Connecticut, 06333.

Cues for Special Parents, c/o Parent to Parent of Florida, Inc., 3500 East Fletcher Ave., Suite 225, Tampa, Florida 33612.

D.A.D.S., c/o David Cornell, 302 N. Kimberly, Shawnee, Oklahoma 74801.

Down Syndrome News: The Newsletter of the National Down Syndrome Congress, 1800 Dempster St., Park Ridge, Illinois 60068.

Duffy, S., McGlynn, K., Mariska, J., & Murphy, J. (1984). *Acceptance is only the first battle: How some parents of young handicapped children have coped with common problems.* Montana University Affiliated Program, Missoula, Montana 59812.

entourage: A magazine promoting community living for people with a mental handicap. The G. Allan Roeher Institute, Kinsmen Building, 470C Keele Street, York University, Downsview, Ontario, Canada M3 1P3.

Equals in this Partnership: Parents of disabled and at-risk infants and toddlers speak to professionals (1985). The National Center for Clinical Infant Programs, 2000 14th Street North, Suite 380, Arlington, Virginia 22201-2500. *Equals in this Partnership* is available free of charge from: The National Maternal and Child Health Clearinghouse 38th and R Streets, N. W. Washington, D. C. 20057

Families and Disability Newsletter, The University of Kansas, Beach Center on Families and Disability, c/o Institute for Life Span Studies, 3111 Haworth Hall, Lawrence, Kansas, 66045.

Heart-to-Heart Newsletter, Heart-to-Heart, P.O. Box 832203, Richardson, Texas 75083-2203.

Institute on Community Integration, A University Affiliated Program on Developmental Disabilities, University of Minnesota, Pattee Hall 150 Pillsbury Dr, S.E., Minneapolis, Minnesota, 55455.

Iowa Pilot Parents, Inc., 33 North 12th St., Box 1151, Fort Dodge, Iowa 50501.

IVH Parents Newsletter, IVH Parents, P.O. Box 56-1111, Miami, FL 33156

Let's Face It published by Let's Face It—A network for people with facial disfigurement, Box 711, Concord, Mass. 01742.

National Fathers' Network, c/o James May, The Merrywood School, 16120 Northeast Eighth Street, Bellevue, Washington, 98008.

National Society for Children and Adults with Autism, 1234 Massachusetts Ave., N.W., Suite 1017, Washington, D.C. 20005

New Mexico Parents Reaching Out - PRO, 1127 University N.E., Albuquerque, New Mexico 87102.

Parents Helping Parents, 535 Race Street, Suite 220, San Jose, Calif. 95126.

Participating Families, c/o Ontario Federation for Cerebral Palsy: Participating Families Program, 1020 Lawrence Ave. W., Suite 303, Toronto, Ontario, Canada M6A 1C8.

Pilot Parents of Minnesota, 201 Ordean Building, Duluth, Minnesota, 55802.

Reflex Sympathetic Dystrophy Syndrome Association, 322 Haddon Ave., Suite C, Westmont, N.J. 08108

TASH, The Association for Persons with Severe Handicaps, 7010 Roosevelt Way N. E., Seattle, Washington 98115.

Washington P.A.V.E., 6316 South 12th, Tacoma, Washingtion, 98465.

Suggested Readings

Bernstein, Jane *Loving Rachel: A Family's Journey from Grief* Boston: Little, Brown, 1989

Bombeck, Erma *I want to grow hair, I want to grow up, I want to go to Boise* NY: Harper & Row, 1989

Coshan, Margaret & Ioannou, Miria *The Family Book: A resource for parents who have learned their child has a mental handicap* Downsview, Ontario: G. Allan Roeher Institute, York University, 1986

Dan, Bruce B. & Young, Roxanne K., eds. *A Piece of My Mind: America's doctors share their most dramatic, inspiring, and moving experiences* NY: Random House, 1988

Deford, Frank *Alex: The life of a child* NY: New American Library, 1986

compiled by Dougan, Terrell; Isbell, Lyn; and Vyas, Patrical *We Have Been There: A Guidebook for Families of People with Mental Retardation* Nashville: Abingdon Press, 1983

Featherstone, Helen *A Difference in the Family: Life with a disabled child* NY: Viking, 1986

Glasser, Ronald J., MD *365 Days* NY: Geo. Braziller, Inc., 1971; 1980 and *Ward 402* NY: Braziller, 1973

Gutkind, Lee *One Children's Place: A profile of pediatric medicine* NY: Grove Weidenfeld, 1990 and *Many Sleepless Nights: The world of organ transplantation* NY Norton, 1988

Hart, Charles *Without Reason: A Family Copes with Two Generations of Autism* NY: Harper Row, 1989

Hosford, Bowen *Making Your Medical Decisions: Your Rights and Harsh Choices Today* NY: Frederick Ungar Publishing Co., 1982

Killilea, Marie Lyons *Karen* NY: Prentice-Hall, 1952 and *From Karen, with Love* Englewood Cliffs, NJ: Prentice-Hall, 1964

Klass, Perri *A Not Entirely Benign Experience* NY: New American Library, Signet NY NAL Penguin NY, 1987

Klitzman, Robert, MD *A Year-long Night: Tales of a Medical Internship* NY Viking, 1989

Konner, Melvin, MD, PhD *Becoming A Doctor: A journey of initiation in medical school* NY: Viking, 1987

Kubler-Ross, Elisabeth, MD *On Children and Death* NY: MacMillan Publishing Co., 1983

Kupfer, Fern *Before and After Zachariah: A Family Story about a Different Kind of Courage* NY: Delacorte Press, 1982

LeBaron, Charles *Gentle Vengeance: An Account of the First Year at Harvard Medical School* NY: R. Marek, 1981

Lipp, Martin R., MD *The Bitter Pill: Doctors, Patients, and Failed Expectations* NY: Harper & Row, 1980

Mantle, Margaret *Some Just Clap Their Hands: Raising a handicapped child* NY: Adana Books, 1985

Massie, Robert and Suzanne *Journey* NY: Alfred Knopf, 1975

Miller, Robyn *Robyn's Book: A True Diary* NY: Scholastic Books, 1986 (Robyn died of cystic fibrosis a month before the book came out.)

Neeld, Elizabeth Harper, PhD *Seven Choices: Taking the Steps to New Life After Losing Someone You Love* NY: Clarkson N. Potter, Inc., 1990

Park, Clara Claiborne *The Siege: The first 8 years of an autistic child, with an epilogue, fifteen years later* Boston: Little, Brown, 1982 and Park, with Shapiro, Leon N. *You Are Not Alone: Understanding and dealing with mental illness: A guide for patients, families, doctors, and other professionals* Boston: Little, Brown, 1976

Payer, Lynn *Medicine & Culture* NY: Henry Holt & Co., 1988

Pray, Lawrence M., with Evans III, Richard, MD *Journey of a Diabetic* NY: Simon & Schuster, 1983

Schiff, Harriet Sarnoff *The Bereaved Parent* NY: Crown Publishers, 1977 and *Living Through Mourning: Finding comfort and hope when a loved one has died* NY: Viking, 1986

Severo, Richard *Lisa H., The True Story of an Extraordinary and Courageous Woman* NY: Viking Penguin, Inc., 1985

Shorter, Edward, PhD *Bedside Manners* NY: Simon and Schuster, 1985

Turnbull, Ann, ed. *Parents Speak Out: Views from the Other Side of the Two-way Mirror* Columbus, OH: Charles E. Merrill, 1978

Woodson, Meg (pseud. for Elsie Baker) *Turn It Into Glory* Minneapolis, MN: Bethany House, 1991, also *If I Die at Thirty*; Grand Rapids: Zondervan, 1975; *Following Joey Home*; Grand Rapids: Zondervan, 1978; *The Time of Her Life*; Grand Rapids: Zondervan, 1982; *I'll Get To Heaven Before You Do*; Nashville: Abingdon Press, 1985

Glossary

ALL - acute lymphocytic leukemia

ACCH - Association for the Care of Children's Health

BPD - bronchopulmonary dysplasia

CCU - coronary care unit

CIC - clean intermittent catheterization

CP - cerebral palsy

DS - Down syndrome

EEG - electroencephalogram

EKG - electrocardiogram

ER - emergency room

g. t. - gastrostomy tube

IV - intravenously; intravenous solution

IVH - intraventricular hemorrhage

IVP - intravenous pyelogram

NCCIP - National Center for Clinical Infant Programs

NG - nasogastric

NICU - neonatal intensive care unit

OR - operating room

OT - occupational therapy

PDA - patent ductus arteriosus

PICU - pediatric intensive care unit

PT - physical therapy

TS - Turner syndrome

About the Authors

Patty Leff is a child psychiatrist. For the past several years, she has practiced in a city hospital clinic and school-based mental health program. She has also worked in a hospital clinic serving children with developmental disabilities. A graduate of Vassar College, Patty began her career as a teacher-therapist in a pioneering day treatment program for children with severe cognitive and emotional problems. Prior to graduating from the State University of New York, Health Science Center at Brooklyn, Patty earned a masters degree in special education from Teachers College, Columbia University. Patty has held an abiding interest in the care of children with chronic illnesses and disabilities and their families; she completed a pediatric internship and a fellowship in consultation-liaison child psychiatry. Married to John, an internist, Patty is the mother of two boys, Mike and Phil. She spends her Saturday mornings with flowers, pencil, and watercolor at the Brooklyn Botanic Garden.

Elaine Hilburn Walizer, a native of Georgia, holds a B.S.Ed. in mental retardation and elementary education from Georgia State College, and an M.Ed. in learning disabilities and behavior disorders from The University of Cincinnati. She was a special education teacher from 1969 until 1980, when her first child was born with severe medical problems. Since that time, Ms. Walizer has focused efforts on support networks, writing for parent newsletters, and contributing to the development of better styles of caregiving. She and her husband Donald, a psychologist, live in Northeastern Ohio with their two children, Laura and Nathaniel.

Index

Abramson, E.R., 151

Adams, D., & Deveau, E., 229

adoptive and foster care families, 11

Alexander, R., & Tompkins-McGill, p., 105, 237, 251

Alig, M., 258

anecdotal histories

Allen, 117; Becky, 183, 263; Carl, 107; Connie, 62, 179; Danny, 235; Dave, 106; Eddie, 59; Janet, 234; Janie, 60; Jimmy, 64; Joshua, 171; Keough, 65, 180; Laura, 180, 200; Linda, 61, 175; Livia, 63; Maria, 174; Marilyn, 113; Michael, 182; Neil, 109, 172; Nicholas, 171; Penny, 111; Rochelle, 115; Rosa, 113; Ryan, 112; Sandy, 108; Sarah, 57; Stuart, 107; Thomas, 101; Timmy, 199; Tony, 66

Arango, p., 162

attitudes and values, 36

congenital and facial defects, 62

how professionals define their work, 55

when professionals clash, 65

autism, diagnosis of, 110

bad news, bearers of, 85

caregiver stress, 85, 113

choosing words carefully, 115

guidelines, 87

Barbera, M., 95

Beach Center on Families with Disabilities, 16, 23, 237

Beckett, J. , 2, 3, 34, 81, 132, 214

Bergman, A.B., 24, 28

Berman, S., & Villarreal, S., 261

bestowing credit, 229, 231

beyond call of duty, 231

bonds, building for long term, 197, 198

Boyce, B., & Boyce, C., 213

Braker, K., 8

Brown, J., & Ritchie, J., 169

Brunnquell, D., & Hall, M.D., 193

building bridges, 54, 99

Calman, K.C., 5

Campbell, S., 29, 33, 38, 159, 193, 202, 219, 230, 243, 272

Chan, J., 17

Chan, J., & Leff, P., 152

Chance, S., 259, 261, 262

Chesler, M., 103

Chesler, M., & Barbarin, 0., 37, 38

child life specialist, 16

Children in Hospitals, Inc., 149

child's world, entering, 202

Clyman, R.I., Sniderman, S.H., & Ballard, R.A., 84

Clyman, R.I., Sniderman, S.H., Ballard, R.A., & Roth, R.S., 74, 89

Comegys, A., 136, 213, 214, 215

comments, suggestions to young health care professionals, 272

communication, poor, among staff members, 84

Compassionate Friends, 99, 164, 256, 257, 259

self-help group, 99

value of mutual support, 99

compliance with treatment program, 250

parent-professional relationship, 250

conflicts, 166

between parents and professionals, 166, 169

Constance, V., 150

context of care, new, 1

changing focus, 1

community-based care, 2

Cordell, A., & Thomas, N., 257

Cornell, D., 209, 225

Costantino, M., 152

Crater, J., 71

Crouzon Syndrome, 101

Damrosch, S., Lenz, E., & Perry, L., 270

Darling, R.D., 29, 123

Davis, P., 88

Deatherage-Newsom, M., 163, 241, 252

death of a child, 253
  caregivers, 260
  communication with parents, 253, 255
  cumulative impact, 261
  siblings, needs of, 255
DeGraw, C., Edell, D., Ellers, B., Hillemeier,
    M., Liebman, J., Perry, C., & Palfrey,
    J., 211
Desguin, B., 20, 271
diagnosis, 69
  emotions and reactions of grief, 71
  fear, 70
  impact of, 70
  isolation, 71
  loss of control, 72
  pessimism, 73
  placing guilt and blame, 73
  shock, disbelief, anger, 72
  sleeplessness, 73
diagnosis, seeing beyond, 195
diagnosis, timing of, 73
  after previous troubling diagnoses, 78
  after trouble-free beginning, 78
  dawning recognition, 76
  neonatal period, 74
diagnostic testing, 242 test results, waiting
    periods, 243
Diehl, S.F., Moffitt, K.A., & Wade, S.M., 20
difficult parents, 245
  communicating with, 265
  peer support, value of, 265, 266
  senior parents, help of, 265, 266
Diffine, L., & Stanton, M., 270
divorce, separation, and single parenthood,
    10, 234
Doernberg, N.L., 85, 89
Down syndrome, 108
Duffy, S., 30, 40, 43, 97, 136, 138, 199, 215, 219,
    241
Dunne, S., 260
Dunst, C., Trivette, C., & Deal, A., 39

Egly, P., 9
emotions and reactions of grief, 71
empowering parents, 158, 219, 220
Exceptional Parents, 16

family life, importance of, 2
  children with special needs, 2
Farrell, P., & Fost, N., 75, 76
fathers' special needs, 222, 234

critical role of, 222
deep involvement of, 224
divorced fathers, 234
importance of, 223
peer support, 225
focusing on solutions to problems, 246
Forman, E., 271
Fox, A.M., 35
Frader, J.E., 24, 261
Frey, K., Fewell, R., Vadasy, P., & Green
    berg, M., 222
Frey, K., Greenberg, M., & Fewell, R., 222
Fussichen, K., 33

Gabriele, M., 120
genetic counseling, 172, 173
Gorlin, R., & Zucker, H., 275
Gould, P.T., & Moses, L., 165, 166
Green, M., 168
grief, coping and renewal, 119
  differences between men and women,
    224
grief, model of, 124
  caveats, 125
  misuse of, 133
  need for flexibility, 124
grief work, 120, 126
  coming to terms with process of, 130
  parental anger, 127
  parent-professional dialogue, 123
Groves, J., 245
guiding parents, 96
guilt, 137 Guralnick, M.J., Richardson, H.B.
    Jr., & Heiser, K.E., 271

Hammon, 5., ACCH Network, 20
Hardison, J.E., 24, 261, 275
Health Care Professionals and Parents
  context for the relationship, 20
  relationship under stress, 19
Healy, A., & Lewis-Beck, J.A., 16, 271
Heart-to-Heart, 222
Hett, J., 251
Holmes, K., 21
honesty, 163, 180, 182
  clarity of language, 163
  mutual trust, 163
  sharing concerns, 169
  sharing medical information, 163
  when mistakes occur, 180, 182
hope

meaning of, 103
    power of, 105
Hoyt, D., 133

integration, dawning of renewal, 130
    common threads, 130
Iris, M. , 22, 31

Jeffery, L., & Jeffery, L., 121, 227
Jellinek, M.S., 275
Jost, K., & Haase, J., 257

Kingsley, E., 131
Kolata, G., 76
Koocher, G., & Berman, S., 186
Kunzman, L., 186, 187

landmarks of good care, 270
language, people first, 45
    positive terminology, 45
language, use of to describe child, 203
Lau, C., 32, 218
Lawson, C., 35, 73, 94, 144, 241
Leff, P.T., 27, 144, 153, 208, 236, 250
Leff, P.T., Chan, J.M., & Walizer, E.H., 2, 6, 7,
    24, 28, 69, 70, 74, 80, 82, 83, 86, 87, 89,
    91, 94, 95, 100, 144, 148, 150, 167, 169,
    170, 185, 186, 187, 191, 193
Lipp, M., 37
listening to parents, 4, 56
Loftis, D., 8
Londner, R., 11, 75, 89, 125, 193, 247, 270

Mariska, J., 44, 90, 91, 99, 103
May, J., 102, 139, 222, 223
McCollum, A., 80 McGlynn, K., 142
McGuire, A., 98
medical and diagnostic testing, 242
medical records, access to, 239
    discouraged by some professionals, 240
Mentzer, S., 153
Meyer, D., Vadasy, p., & Fewell, R., 229
Meyer, D., Vadasy, P., Fewell, R., & Schell,
    G., 102, 224, 230
model of care, reframing, 36, 38, 39
Montana University Affiliated Program
    (MUAP) , 23, 156, 147
Moore, C., 16
Moosreiner, D., 41
Moses, K., 69, 83, 94, 122, 123, 245
mother-child dyad, 8

Murphy, J., 141
Myers, G.J., 37

Nathanson, M., 90, 100, 57, 163
needs of changing families, 8
neonatal period, care during, 106

Oberhart, D., 232
Odle, K., 39
Olson, J., Edwards, M., & Hunter, J.A., 70, 85,
    95
Ongoing care, 135, 185, 209, 237
    preparing child for painful procedures,
        192
    respecting family unit, 209
    respecting parents, 135
    special concerns, 237
    understanding child's perspective, 185
    understanding child's priorities, 191
Oster, A., 22, 98, 171, 220, 231, 262, 266

paperwork, 244
parental concerns, 136
    guilt, 137
    isolation, 138, 139
    vulnerability, 136, 139
parental narratives, 11
    negative, 12
    positive, 11
parental worry, accepting and honoring, 164,
    183
parent-child relationship, 81
parent consultant role, power of, 270
parent-professional communication, 6, 19,
    160, 168, 180, 233, 250, 252, 255, 256
    guidelines, 252
    professional attitude, 256
    when a child dies, 255
parent-professional partnership, 2, 5, 6, 23,
    30, 33, 50, 54, 55, 58, 67, 69
    differences of opinion, 33
    human-to-human contact, 50
    parents' perspective, 23, 30
parent-professional relationship, eroding of
    trust, 77
Parent Resource Directory, 15
parents and professionals, 37, 39
parents, roles of
    as advocates, 152-155, 177
    as case managers, 156
    as decision makers, 156, 179

as learners, 144, 170, 172
as nurturers, 147, 150, 173
as partners, 156, 220
parents' world, appreciation of, 4
parent-to-parent support, 97, 98, 100, 103, 221
   Congenital Adrenal Hyperplasia Support Association, Inc. (CAHSA), 101
   Crouzon Syndrome, 101
   Parent-to-Parent meeting, 221
Park, C., 40
partnership with parents, 275, 276
partners in care, 3, 4
Patterson, J., & Geber, G., 186, 191
Pendleton, E., 185
Physician Education Forum Report, 271
Pitel, A., Pitel, P., Richards, H., Benson, J., Prince, J., & Forman, E., 270
Pizzo, P., 6
Powell, T.A., & Ogle, P.A., 229
Poyadue, F.S., 70, 80, 87, 120, 271
professionals and parents
   pivotal role of parents, 20
   relationship under stress, 19
professionals as nurturers, 191
professionals, building bridges, 43
   most important asset of: responsible parents, 35
Public Law 99-457, 211

Quraishi, H., 9

recognition of caregivers, 230
respect for children, 188, 194, 196
   understanding their developmental & cognitive abilities, 190, 199
   understanding their fears, 199
   understanding their need for parental support, 188
respect for family unit, 209, 233
   child in the family, 209
   empowerment, 219, 220
   life of the family, 211
   role of family, 211
   stress and grieving, cycles, 217, 233
respect for parents, 135, 140, 170, 241
   as learners and partners, 241
   listening to parents, 140
   physical assistance to, 160
   respectful conduct, 159
Richardson, J., 41, 73

Robinson, C.A., 36
role-playing among nurses, benefits of, 86

Sack, W.H., Fritz, G., Krener, P.G., & Sprunger, L., 261
Sack, W.H., Krener, P.G., & Sprunger, L., 24, 27
Sahler, O.J., McAnarney, E.R., & Friedman, S.B., 24, 261
Saphier, 143
Sassaman, E.A., 32
Saunders, J., 63
Schreiner, R.L., Gresham, E.L., & Green, M., 259
Schwab, B., 278
second opinions, 179
security objects, child's, 189
   value and limitations of, 189
Shanfield, S., 24, 261
sharing experiences, families and students, 273
sharing humanity, 50
Sharp, M.C., & Lorch, S.C., 271
Shaul, R., & Talbot, Y., 275
Shelton, T., Jeppson, E., & Johnson, B., 2, 39, 84
Shonkoff, J.P., 85, 271
siblings, 226
   support groups for, 229
Simon, R., 40, 69, 80, 123
special concerns, 237
   evaluations, 237
   "blitz" evaluations, 238
Steele, K., 81
stereotypes in health care of disabled, 20
   cultural, 55
Stevens, & McKay, 240
Stone, D., 128
stress and grieving, cycles, 217
stresses on caregivers, 173
stressors
   for parents, dependency, 21
   for student caregivers, 24, 56
   identification of, 55
Sweet, G., 9

Tarran, E., 69
terminology, people first, 45
test results, waiting periods, 243
tips for professionals, 162
Trombino, B., 271

Troy, J., 79, 119
Turnbull, H., & Turnbull, A., 12, 21, 69, 123
two-income families, 9

van Eys, J., 37
"veteran parents" program, 101
victories, sharing, 229
Vincent, L., 36
Vining, E., & Freeman, J., 95, 250
visions, present and future, 269
    journey with families, 269
    landmarks of good care, 270
visiting by parents, importance of, 105

Wachendorf, D., 101
Walker, K., 222

Waller, D.A., Todres, D., Cassem, N.H., &
    Anderten, A., 168
Werner, E.R., & Korsch, B.M., 24, 275, 276
Widrick, G., Whaley, C., DiVenere, N., Vec-
    chione, E., Swartz, D., & Stiffler, D.,
    20, 269, 271
Wikler, L., Wasow, M., & Hatfield, E., 84, 128
Wolfensberger, W., 128
Wolraich, M., 69, 85
world views in conflict, 31
    exploration of, 55
Wurzbach, L., 123
Wynn, E., 59

Zisook, S., & Gammon, E., 250

SPINNER

High in a corner of the hospital
in a crevice where people seldom look,
there is a hidden world; a spider spins
its web and waits. On a couch below
I wait, bewildered and concerned. Wondering,
watching the clock tick the minutes ever
so slowly, seeming to hold time
longer than anyone could wish.
As I pace and think, I feel the constant
wonder and despair closing in on me, while
my child is prepped for open heart surgery;
what will happen and when?

One place is not enough; I am restless
as if hungry and I'm not hungry at all.
Time is not patient, it keeps on passing
no matter where I am. Quiet corners lend
a space to think, to pray, waiting
as the spider for its prey. Only my mother's embrace
fills the void, comforting the queasiness.
Standing in the hall feeling helpless
I watch the hospital elevator take
my daughter up to another corner where
her life is in many hands. I feel like
an earthquake has trembled, opened the ground, ready
to take my little girl and I want to reach
for her, but know my hands couldn't help.

I jump at the ring of the innocent waiting room phone.
It's my turn to answer, to see if my child came through.
A doctor touches me on the shoulder and says,
"all is well". I catch my breath and realize
the web has taken what it needs today

— Joyce Duggan Autrey